# Women and Work

# Women and Work:
# A Research and Policy Series

The Sage series **Women and Work: A Research and Policy Series** brings together research, critical analysis, and proposals for change in a dynamic and developing field—the world of women and work. Cutting across traditional academic boundaries, the series approaches subjects from a multidisciplinary perspective. Historians, anthropologists, economists, sociologists, managers, psychologists, educators, policy makers, and legal scholars share insights and findings—giving readers access to a scattered literature in single, comprehensive volumes.

**Women and Work** examines differences among women—as well as differences between men and women—related to nationality, ethnicity, social class, and sexual orientation. The series explores demographic and legal trends, international and multinational comparisons, and theoretical and methodological developments.

## SERIES EDITORS

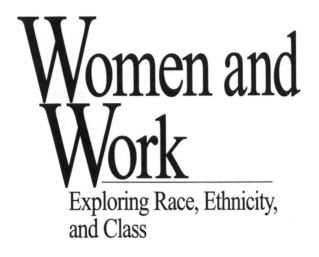

# Women and Work

## Exploring Race, Ethnicity, and Class

editors

## Elizabeth Higginbotham
## Mary Romero

### Volume 6
### Women and Work

**SAGE Publications**
*International Educational and Professional Publisher*
Thousand Oaks   London   New Delhi

*For information:*

SAGE Publications, Inc.
2455 Teller Road
Thousand Oaks, California 91320
E-mail: order@sagepub.com

SAGE Publications Ltd.
6 Bonhill Street
London EC2A 4PU
United Kingdom

SAGE Publications India Pvt. Ltd.
M-32 Market
Greater Kailash I
New Delhi 110 048 India

Printed in the United States of America

*Library of Congress Cataloging-in-Publication Data*

ISBN 0-8039-5058-6 hardcover
ISBN 0-8039-5059-4 paperback
ISSN 0882-0910

This book is printed on acid-free paper.

97  98  99  00  01  02  03  10  9  8  7  6  5  4  3  2  1

| | |
|---|---|
| *Acquiring Editor:* | Marquita Flemming |
| *Editorial Assistant:* | Frances Borghi |
| *Production Editor:* | Astrid Virding |
| *Production Assistant:* | Karen Wiley |
| *Typesetter/Designer:* | Danielle Dillahunt |
| *Indexer:* | Cristina Haley |
| *Cover Designer:* | Lesa Valdez |
| *Print Buyer:* | Anna Chin |

*In memory of*
*Leonard Russell Higginbotham, Senior,*
*who taught me to think seriously*
*about the work that people do*

—EH


*For the working women who shared*
*their experiences and wisdom in*
*shaping my research and writing*

—MR

# Contents

Series Editors' Introduction          ix
    *ANN STROMBERG, BARBARA A. GUTEK,*
    *and LAURIE LARWOOD*

Acknowledgments          xiii

Introduction          xv
    *ELIZABETH HIGGINBOTHAM*

**Part I. Historical and Economic Perspectives**      **1**

1. An Economic Profile of Women in the United States      5
    *BÁRBARA J. ROBLES*

2. Speaking Up: The Politics of
    Black Women's Labor History      28
    *SHARON HARLEY*

**Part II. Manufacturing and Domestic Service**      **53**

3. The Evolution of Alohawear:
    Colonialism, Race, Ethnicity, Class,
    and Gender in Hawaii's Garment Industry      57
    *JOYCE N. CHINEN*

4. Women's Resistance in the Sun Belt:
   Anglos and Hispanas Respond to Managerial Control          76
   *LOUISE LAMPHERE and PATRICIA ZAVELLA*

5. Working "Without Papers" in the United States:
   Toward the Integration of Legal Status in
   Frameworks of Race, Class, and Gender                     101
   *PIERRETTE HONDAGNEU-SOTELO*

**Part III. Health Care, Professions, Managerial Positions,
and Entrepreneurship                                          127**

6. Class Experience and Conflict in a Feminist Workplace:
   A Case Study                                               131
   *SANDRA MORGEN*

7. Black and White Professional-Managerial Women's
   Perceptions of Racism and Sexism in the Workplace          153
   *LYNN WEBER and ELIZABETH HIGGINBOTHAM*

8. Korean Immigrant Wives' Labor Force Participation,
   Marital Power, and Status                                  176
   *PYONG GAP MIN*

**Part IV. Working for a Better Community:
Dilemmas in Building Solidarity                               193**

9. Working-Class Mexican American Women
   and "Voluntarism": "We Have to Do It!"                      197
   *MARY PARDO*

10. The Third Shift: Black Women's Club
    Activities in Denver, 1900-1925                            216
    *LYNDA F. DICKSON*

Epilogue                                                       235
*MARY ROMERO*

Author Index                                                   249

Subject Index                                                  254

About the Contributors                                         265

# Series Editors' Introduction

The **Women and Work** series' inaugural volume announced three purposes for the series. The first was "to spotlight women and work as an important and intriguing social reality and area of research." Although the growth in rates of women's labor force participation in recent decades had been so significant as to constitute a "silent revolution" that increasingly involved women at all stages of the life cycle, social science research on women had tended to neglect the study of their paid and unpaid labor while studies of work and occupations had focused primarily on men. A second goal was to provide a multidisciplinary form in which scholars from different academic disciplines could be engaged in dialogue. We believed that the field of women and work could be best advanced if researchers became aware of findings from a variety of specialties and could engage in discussions of the implications for policies that would benefit women. The third goal was to contribute to the development of this emerging new field of women and work. We wanted to encourage research that would fill in the many gaps in knowledge about women and work—for example, research on women's experiences in all industries and occupations, in self-employment as well as in organizations, in unpaid labor as well as paid work. We saw it as crucial to explore differences among women as well as differences between women and men, and identified nationality, race, ethnicity, social class, and sexual orientation as aspects of identity and experience that we encouraged authors to address.

In the first three volumes, published in 1985, 1987, and 1988, we invited scholars in the emerging field of women and work to prepare original chapters that would inform readers about state-of-the-art research, drawing on experts from anthropology, economics, education, history, law, medicine and public health, political science, psychology, and sociology. Within these volumes we offered symposia of several chapters on explanatory frameworks of earnings differentials (Volume 1), occupational health and statement workers (Volume 2), and international perspectives that widened our horizons by addressing women in the global economy (Volume 3).

By the time we began planning for the fourth volume, research on women and work seemed to be coming together rapidly, and we realized that there was sufficient material to support volumes dedicated to single topics. With that volume we adopted a new strategy, inviting guest editors with expertise in an area to organize collections that would summarize research, present case studies and new thinking, and advance the interdisciplinary discussion of important topics. Our first guest editor, Ellen A. Fagenson, provided an exciting volume on women and management that explored both the growing opportunities and barriers to women in this field. Margaret S. Stockdale edited Volume 5 of the series, addressing a topic of great importance, sexual harassment in the workplace. As did Fagenson, she secured original chapters from leading experts whose contributions have resulted in volumes of lasting value.

It gives us pleasure to introduce the sixth and final volume of the **Women and Work** series, *Women and Work: Exploring Race, Ethnicity, and Class,* edited by Elizabeth Higginbotham and Mary Romero. The volume addresses this crucial problem: while the field of women and work has grown significantly in recent years, the questions asked and the research designed have too often ignored the experience of women of color and issues of social class, culture, and national origin as well. In her thoughtful introductory chapter to the volume, Elizabeth Higginbotham frames key issues and challenges us to consider how we conceptualize race, ethnicity, and social class, and their meaning for women's experience. Drawing broadly on relevant literature, she provides a valuable context for the volume's chapters, written by colleagues from anthropology, Chicana/Chicano studies, economics, history and Afro-American studies, sociology, and women's studies. The contributions are organized around four topics—Historical and Economic Perspectives; Manufacturing and Domestic Service; Health Care, Professions, Managerial Positions, and Entrepreneurship; and Working for a Better Community, which addresses the unpaid work of women in advocacy and community building. Each chapter highlights important issues in the exploration of race, ethnicity, social class, and citizenship status in the lives of working women. Mary Romero's comprehensive and thought-provoking conclusion underscores important themes from the volume, helps us to conceptualize work in new ways, and proposes directions for future research needed on gender, race, ethnicity, culture, class and work. We are confident that this is a volume that will be greatly appreciated as a text by students and an important reference source by scholars. It is also a reminder of the work that remains to be done by all who are concerned with social justice.

We are keenly aware that much is left to accomplish—in research, in education, in social change—regarding women and our productive and reproductive work. At the same time, we are satisfied that the field of women and work, which seemed so young and scattered when we began the series, is now well established and maturing in the questions it explores, its theory and methods, its commitment to be inclusive. As we have seen the literature burgeon, we have concluded that there is no longer a pressing need for the series. The field of women and work has developed and continues to develop in exciting ways, and we hope we have contributed to this success.

The series has been a collaborative effort, and we thank with deep appreciation the colleagues who have served on our editorial board. They have guided our selection of topics and authors, and generously reviewed in the most constructive manner the authors' submissions. They have supported us with good humor and excellent advice. We are also appreciative of the contributions of other outside reviewers who have assisted us and our authors. We are grateful to our guest editors, Ellen A. Fagenson, Margaret S. Stockdale, Elizabeth Higginbotham and Mary Romero, for their expertise, vision, and hard work. It has been a genuine pleasure to work with them. We thank the scholars who have contributed to these volumes with their creativity and to the field of women and work with their research. We especially acknowledge the support of our families and close friends who have supported in this effort spanning a decade and a half, and finally we express our appreciation for those at Sage Publications who have worked with us. Like the field of women and work, Sage has grown in impressive ways since we began this series, and it has been a pleasure to be part of that change.

—*Ann Stromberg*
*Barbara A. Gutek*
*Laurie Larwood*

# Acknowledgments

Many people and several institutions have contributed to the completion of this edited collection, thus we want to make sure to thank them all. We particularly appreciate Ann Stromberg for the invitation to edit a volume that addressed race, ethnicity, and social class for the **Women and Work** series. She helped us conceptualize the project and has provided support and suggestions throughout the long process. The other series editors, Laurie Larwood and Barbara A. Gutek, have also provided us and the contributors with excellent comments along the way. Harry Briggs and his staff at Sage Publications have provided assistance in reaching reviewers and in giving words of encouragement. A special thanks to Marquita Flemming at Sage who was instrumental in helping with the final push to move the manuscript into production.

We do thank the contributors for working with us over the years as we developed a volume that took a unique look at the worlds of work for women. Reviewers played a central role in working with us to help contributors develop their chapters to speak to an interdisciplinary audience. The members of the **Women and Work** Editorial Board and the ad hoc reviewers who worked on this publication are Rose Brewer, Esther Chow, Faye Crosby, Myra Marx Ferree, Alice Kessler Harris,

Louise Lamphere, Patricia Martin, Devon Pena, Pam Roby, Anna Santiago, Stephanie Shaw, Natalie Sokoloff, and Rhonda Williams.

Elizabeth offers special thanks to the University of Memphis for long term support that promoted work on this volume. Many of the small but necessary tasks involved in a contributed book were performed by graduate assistants and support staff at the Center for Research on Women, particularly Andreana Clay, Tonye Smith, Lauren Rausher, Shannon Diamond, and Jo Ann Ammons. Furthermore, her position as Visiting Race/Gender Professor in the Center for Afroamerican and African Studies and Women's Studies at the University of Michigan and a Faculty Development Leave from The University of Memphis gave her an opportunity to complete the manuscript. Patrice Dickerson, in a graduate assistantship supported by Women's Studies at the University of Michigan, helped with gathering census data and reading drafts. Friends have also provided Elizabeth with support as she faced the challenges of writing her own sections and working long distance with all the contributors. She has special praise for Maxine Baca Zinn, Margaret Andersen, Bonnie Thornton Dill, Martha Foschini, and Lynn Weber.

Mary is very grateful to the many authors she worked with and appreciates their patience and good humor in seeing this edited book to completion. She also thanks Shelly Kowalski for her editing assistance which included running down missing and incomplete references and revising references. Special thanks to Michal McCall who was extremely helpful in obtaining institutional support and encouragement during her year as the McKnight Visiting Associate Professor at Macalester College, and Rhonda Levine who was crucial to her continued work on this project during her semester at Colgate University as the A. Lindsay O'Connor Associate Professor of American Institutions. This project has profited from the insight Mary's gained from conversations with Joan Acker, Esther Chow, Evelyn Nakano Glenn, Myra Marx Ferree, Vilma Oritz, Dorothy Smith, and Abby Stewart. In particular, Mary would like to thank Eric Margolis for his critical comments, consistent encouragement, and intellectual support.

# Introduction

## ELIZABETH HIGGINBOTHAM

Perhaps no area of social life has changed so profoundly for women in the United States in the last half of the 20th century as the area of employment. Patterns of employment for women—that is, who is involved in paid employment, how long women work over their lifetimes, and the types of work that women do—have shifted. If one takes a picture of employment for women in 1947, when, after World War II, women were being pushed out of war industries and other factories and back into the home and traditionally female occupations, and compares that with the scene in 1997, one can learn a great deal.

Current patterns of education and employment for women are sharply different from those of the past. In the 1960s and 1970s, women had made substantial progress in closing the education gap that separated them from men (Bianchi 1995). In fact, women in the late baby boom cohort have levels of educational attainment very similar to those of

men in the same group. Gains in educational attainment have opened
new occupations for women and enhanced women's earnings relative to
men's (Bianchi 1995).

In 1948, the labor force participation rate for women 20 years and
older was 31.8%; in 1994, the rate was 59.3% (U.S. Department of
Labor 1995). As a whole, this group spends more years in the labor force
than did the earlier same age cohort. For some women, employment
begins in high school; a recent U.S. Department of Labor (1995) report
indicates that two-fifths of high school seniors have jobs. Furthermore,
even contemporary women who have school-age children and children
under 3 years of age are more likely to be employed than earlier cohorts.
In looking at the enhanced diversity among families in the United
States, Sara McLanahan and Lynne Casper (1995) found that since
1960, married mothers have increased their participation in paid employment. They conclude: "By 1990, currently married mothers were
nearly as likely to be in the labor force (59%) as formerly married single
mothers (64%), and they were more likely to be employed than never-
married mothers (48%)" (pp. 12-13).

In the 1940s and 1950s, most women worked within a narrow range
of occupations. Today, traditional female occupations for women at all
levels of educational attainment are still their major sources of employment, even though thousands more men have entered these work spheres
(Reskin and Roos 1990). Thus women are still subject to sex segregation
in the labor market.

Women's increasing long-term involvement with paid labor has consequences for shifting patterns in other areas of social life, especially
the family. Working outside the home means that women who are
married, have children, or both, face double duty, as they are still primarily responsible for the home and the care of children. These stresses
have implications for all involved. Although we can celebrate increases in consumer goods and services, we are still facing an era
when few new institutions have developed to help with family reproductive labor. Thus it is up to families, often the wives and mothers, to
coordinate, monitor, and oversee the new services and products that are
available.

Women do not receive financial rewards for all the labor they perform
outside their homes. Women in the United States have long been involved in volunteer work that ranges from church activities, social
reform efforts, and the support of civic and cultural institutions to direct

outreach and delivery of social services that improve the lives of members of their communities. Women's volunteer work, while often invisible, has been the topic of recent research that addresses how gender as well as race and class shape the motivations of women volunteers, the types of work these women do, and how such work is received (Daniels 1988; Shaw 1996). Through the century, nonpaid work for women has also changed. The demands of paid employment have led some women to reduce their volunteer work. New social movements have shifted the nature of the nonpaid work that women do. As new populations face various stages of racial oppression, women may continue to feel a critical urgency to work for their communities and families, but these changes may take them into new arenas. Also, as members of disadvantaged communities, women of color and working-class women might feel the need to continue such work along with paid employment, even if it means facing triple duty as they work on the job, in the home, and in the community.

There have clearly been critical changes over the past 50 years in how women work during their lifetimes, in both paid and nonpaid work. In the face of these dramatic changes, critical differences have persisted within the population of employed women. Major inequalities in U.S. society shape where women work, their working conditions, their wages and salaries, their abilities to control their work environments, and how they see themselves and their options in the workplace. Inequalities also shape their sense of urgency to add community work to their other weekly tasks. Thus attention in scholarship on women and work to gender as the sole dimension of analysis is insufficient to address the major sources of inequality among women.

As the editors of this volume, Mary Romero and I decided to explore central issues for working women by focusing on the intersection of race, ethnicity, and social class, because these dimensions need to be looked at with a deeper appreciation of the meaning of the issues they raise and their implications for women's work lives. Race, ethnicity, and social class are key factors that can shed light on the diversity of situations for working women. Along with gender, they are key links to understanding a matrix of domination. As noted by Patricia Hill Collins (1990), a specific configuration of race, social class, and gender relations in society can form an interlocking system of domination, and so it is important to explore all of the links in the matrix. Previous collections in the Sage Publications **Women and Work** series have not fully explored the dimensions of race, ethnicity, and social class. These earlier volumes were pioneers in exploring the central role of work in women's lives, and they made efforts to be inclusive; however, they were not able to provide the space for an in-depth, critical examination of race, ethnicity, and social class along with gender.

In this volume, we want not only to address race and ethnicity, but to investigate the role of nativity and citizenship. Citizenship is a privilege that many native-born U.S. citizens take for granted. Yet inequalities in work options and political resources among native-born citizens and many levels of naturalized citizens and resident aliens have been expressed in several ways in historical and contemporary life. In the 19th century, and earlier in the 20th century, whether or not an immigrant was eligible for citizenship was key in shaping his or her employment options as well as political rights. Chinese, Japanese, and Korean immigrants faced legislation that limited their employment options, taxed them on the work that they could do, and limited where they could live. Because they were denied the right to become citizens, they were limited to the use of the courts and protests by their native governments as the means of challenging discrimination and their disadvantaged status (McClain 1994; Takaki 1990). Although many immigrants faced hard times, the option of citizenship meant that at some point they could enter the political system. Like African Americans, denied the right to vote for decades in the South, Asian immigrants and even second-generation Asian Americans used the courts and general social and economic betterment in their own communities to advance within the system. In the contemporary United States, recent immigration laws have also structured narrow employment options for new immigrants, especially those who are not documented. The rights and access to resources of those legal immigrants who do not become naturalized citizens are also at risk. Thus, increasingly, scholars addressing the issues surrounding women and their employment cannot avoid looking at the varied circumstances of recent immigrants.

When we look at this complex web of rights, privileges, and disadvantages, we learn much about how the matrix of domination works to create or limit employment options and how people are often forced to struggle in and outside work settings to shift the balance of power in society. An exploration of these dimensions of inequality is critical to an understanding of women's situations in paid employment and volunteer work.

## CONCEPTUALIZING RACE,
## ETHNICITY, AND SOCIAL CLASS

Race, ethnicity, and social class shape distinctive circumstances for women throughout the life cycle; given that most women in the United States spend many years in the workforce, this has dramatic implications for their lives. In examining this area, it is central to consider that race, ethnicity, and social class are recognized as critical dimensions of analysis for all women, not just women who lack privileges with regard to these social categories. Thus they are critical for understanding the lives of women who are privileged with regard to race, ethnicity, or both, and those who are members of the upper or middle classes. In the arena of women and work, race, ethnicity, and social class can be critical tools for analysis. The contributors to this volume acknowledge that there are many other dimensions of inequality, such as age, sexual orientation, and family status, as well as residence in urban, rural, or suburban areas, that are also central to shaping choices and chances for women. However, we can learn much about the current levels of inequality in our society by focusing on the interaction of gender with race, ethnicity, and social class.

Traditional approaches to research on employment that address race and ethnicity often assume that the male experience speaks for the group. For example, in *The Declining Significance of Race,* William J. Wilson (1978) used data on the employment patterns of Black men to reach his conclusions about the increasing number of Black people employed in middle-class occupations and thus the enhanced stratification within the Black community. However, looking at the experiences of women from various racial, ethnic, and social class groups can shed needed light on critical dimensions of the experiences of groups exposed to racial and/or ethnic privileges or disadvantages. For example, in the past 20 years, many middle- and working-class families have responded to the decline in male wages, relative to the cost of living, by sending married women into the labor force (Timmer, Eitzen, and Talley 1994). Thus we find large increases in the percentages of married women in the labor market. Looking at both male and female employment patterns is critical to understanding central changes in the U.S. economy and their impacts on workers. We cannot understand how individuals and families have faced deindustrialization and downsizing by looking only at male employment patterns.

Examining women's employment patterns within racial and ethnic groups is also important for understanding how individuals and families respond to shifts in the larger political economy. For example, in conducting comparative research on professional and managerial women in the Memphis, Tennessee, area, Lynn Weber and I found important racial differences among college-educated women in the baby boom cohort. We found that most of the raised working-class and raised middle-class African American women had mothers who were involved with paid employment. Thus, when asked about having working mothers, these respondents did not think it was a big deal. A minority of the raised working-class and raised middle-class White women in the same study had mothers who worked outside the home. Many of the White women reported feeling very different from other children in their neighborhoods because their mothers worked outside the home.

In the 20th century, the percentages of women working outside the home have not been the same for all racial groups. According to 1990 data, it is now very common for mothers to work in the labor market (McLanahan and Casper 1995). However, this trend represents major increases in the proportions of working mothers among White women, but not very significant increases among Black women, because Black women have had a long-established pattern of involvement in work outside the home, even when they are married and have children (Dill 1988; Jones 1985; Shaw 1996). This trend also tells us that a pattern of coping with economic marginality among Black families has expanded to other groups, as the wages of the male breadwinners are insufficient to meet all family needs.

As noted above, the contributors to this volume are seeking not only to highlight how race, ethnicity, and social class as dimensions of inequality are critical for understanding women's lives, but also to help readers develop a deeper appreciation for the meanings of these concepts. Often people think about race and ethnicity as simply categories that one checks on census and other required forms. Further, race and ethnicity are employed as variables in social science research to analyze the presence or absence of discrimination, patterns of association and community, and attitudes of employers. Thus they are often characterized as differences, especially as they deviate from the dominant group. This perception focuses on how those who are not members of the majority group are different, and particularly on factors that might account for their "disadvantaged status" relative to the dominant group. Such a perspective tends to view those who are not part of the majority as victims who can end their victim status by assuming more of the attributes of the dominant group.

This perspective is evident in many of the examinations of employment status among men and women that have focused on human capital variables—that is, job skills, years of educational attainment, and work experience. These factors are seen as shaping employment options and even the attitudes of potential employers. It is assumed that as members of disadvantaged groups—that is, people of color, members of the working class, the working poor, and so forth—take on the characteristics of the majority, their problems in the labor market will disappear. This vision of obstacles to equity in employment does not recognize a power dimension. If we look at race and ethnicity as sources of social stratification in society, we can better understand their central role in a matrix of domination. Working within a social stratification perspective, we can better recognize the relational nature of these categories and how power is a critical part of these social categories.

Ethnicity entails more than simply cultural patterns or characteristics of national origin; it also speaks to persistent ties that connect people to each other and shape how they may interact with people from different ethnic groups. Again, there is a power dimension involved in these relationships. For example, people from the majority group define what is and is not appropriate and limit the terms employed to judge who is allowed to join the majority.

A social stratification model of race and ethnicity has received less attention than class in the social sciences, but it is important for understanding what happens when people come together in a workplace, where they clearly are different in terms of their power in that environment and the overall society. The role of power is plainly evident in institutionalized racism, a dynamic feature of the modern U.S. labor market. Many scholars are familiar with the legacy of colonial labor markets in the 18th and 19th centuries, but in the 20th century job ceilings and other forms of institutionalized discrimination ensured that men of color were barred from industrial work, so that they were available for other work, often agricultural, service, and preindustrial types of labor (Barrera 1979; Takaki 1990; Nee and Nee 1973; Harris 1982). These jobs were lower in pay, more dangerous, and had fewer benefits than the industrial jobs reserved for White males. The ill treatment faced by men of color jeopardized their ability to provide for their families and also pushed women of color into paid employment (Amott and Matthaei 1991; Dill 1988; Jones 1985).

Patterns of institutionalized racism are also found in the experiences of women in U.S. labor markets. Clerical and sales jobs, which are clearly recognized as women's work, would be better classified for most of the 20th century as White women's work, as women of color have gained significant access to white-collar positions only since the 1970s. Evelyn Nakano Glenn (1992) argues that the overrepresentation of women of color in paid reproductive labor, particularly domestic work, is evidence of racial and gender barriers in the labor market. Regional differences are apparent, but race and gender have operated to keep women of color in domestic work as other options have not been available, due to level of industrial development or the fact that other work was reserved for White women. Glenn documents the complex factors that have restricted employment options for women of color: the need to work because male earnings were insufficient to support their families; the limitations they faced in educational opportunities that could lead to other work; and the limitations on legal and civil rights, making it difficult for them to make demands on the system. A legacy of domestic work is found among Mexican American women in the Southwest, African American women in the South, and Japanese men and women in California and Hawaii. Glenn and other scholars who explore the ways that women of color are pushed into the labor market (Amott and Matthaei 1991; Dill 1988; Higginbotham 1983; Jones 1985) have also documented the consequences for their families. However, we need more investigations into the intersection of work and family with an eye to racial, ethnic, and social class differences.

During World War II, women of color found new employment options, especially in industrial work, but—like White women at the time—many were pushed out of these jobs as soldiers returned following the war. Many working-class women and women of color returned to a narrow range of occupations, because employment was still critical for family survival (Marks 1989; Jones 1985). However, as the sociologists Michael Omi and Howard Winant (1994) note, the political gains made during the New Deal and World War II gave people of color new leverage for challenging political economic arrangements and thus the racial hierarchy. People of color made inroads, often the men first, into manufacturing and service industries that offered better pay. Many more men of color were unionized, especially in Congress of Industrial Organizations (CIO) drives. Political and economic gains provided the backdrop for additional challenges to the racial hierarchies of the 1950s, 1960s, and 1970s. These struggles were played out in the workplace, as people strived to improve their individual and groups' positions. There were also struggles within communities around issues of housing, schools, public service accommodations, and others areas, as racial hierarchies were also challenged in these spheres (Massey and Denton 1993; Omi and Winant 1994; Pohlmann 1990).

The years since the end of World War II have witnessed successes in some arenas. The nation's racial/ethnic populations have become more economically diverse, as members have moved into business and professional and managerial occupations. Even during the regressive policies of the Reagan-Bush era in the 1980s and the early 1990s, the communities of color in the United States developed middle-class segments, following patterns of polarization among the general population. Although the majority of middle-class people in this nation continue to be White, there are increasing numbers of people of color in this group. Yet we cannot assume that their entrance into the middle class or even professional and managerial occupations means these groups are like the majority group in terms of their experiences in the world of work and in their communities. We have to explore how race and ethnicity may shape their experiences as they enter the more privileged social classes.

There is also a downside to this increased polarization. In this period of slow economic growth, the economic stability of many middle- and working-class people is threatened; thus we need to know more about how race and ethnicity, as well as gender, will shape the impacts of these trends (Marks 1989; Timmer et al. 1994; Wilson 1978). Central questions revolve around how people cope with structural inequalities in work, the nature of their resistance, and consequences for their families and communities. These questions take on particular significance in an era of shrinking government and civic responsibility for those who face major structural barriers to full participation in U.S. life.

The political era after World War II was a time of loosened immigration restrictions, and eventually the United States passed a new law in 1965 that ended national differences in quotas for entrance. This legislation has meant dramatic increases in Asian immigration, the group most targeted by previous restrictions (Takaki 1990). However, the implementation of quotas in the Western Hemisphere has meant that national groups that had not previously been subjected to quotas, such as persons from Mexico and the nations of the Caribbean, now have quotas lower than the numbers of people who previously immigrated annually. These immigration changes have meant new expressions of privileges and disadvantages that have had impacts on many residents of the United States. As Sylvia Pedraza (1991) notes, we need to look at women's participation in migration and the consequences for them, especially the impact of new work roles on family life.

In the United States we are often comfortable thinking about social classes as status groups that are arranged in some sort of hierarchy. Working within a distributional framework, social classes become defined as job categories, qualities of jobs, or specific levels of income. Such approaches enable people to avoid discussions of power and many of the complexities of modern social life (Lucal 1994). There is coexisting tradition in which scholars employ a relational model that seeks to explore how social class relates to social relationships. People are not set only in some rankings along a scale, but in relationships with each other.

Increasingly popular is the use of a professional-managerial/working-class dichotomy that builds on the work of Braverman (1974) and Poulantzas (1974). This perspective, notes Reeve Vanneman and Lynn Weber Cannon (1987), is in line with the views of most Americans, who do recognize social class divisions that relate to power: "To be middle class in America is to own productive property, or to have supervisory authority, or to perform mental labor at the expense of manual workers" (p. 61).[1] Throughout this volume, the contributors employ different definitions of social class divisions, depending upon their disciplines. However, several direct attention to the implications of social class membership for interactions across social class lines and how people in working-class jobs survive in the face of exploitation.

Issues of power for women, as they relate to control and supervision, encourage us to ask many new questions. Scholars can move beyond examining how securing a professional occupation enables one to attain a certain middle-class lifestyle and attend to how power dynamics might give women more or less flexibility on the job and how that relates to the integration of work with other roles, especially those of spouse and mother. What are the implications of women's moving into new roles in the workplace? Does a woman's employment in middle-class occupations alter the balance of power within the family? How do coworkers adjust to having women in professional and managerial occupations? Does the reception of women in new roles vary by race, ethnicity, and social class background? Also, social class can shape the inhabitants of jobs, so that middle- and working-class people bring different perspectives to the workplace and to their work in their communities.

As we conceptualize race, ethnicity, social class, and gender in the workplace, we also have to think about how individuals consider these issues in their day-to-day interactions. In particular, race, ethnicity, and social class involve membership in specific communities, with particular legacies and sets of resources for political and social action and webs of family obligations. To explore these issues, I borrow from the key concepts of human recognition, social space, and social time that Joe Feagin, Hernan Vera, and Nikitah Imani (1996) employ in their research on Black students in colleges and universities.

We know that the major ideology with regard to race among White Americans is color blindness—that is, a willingness to ignore the reality of race and just see people as people (Omi and Winant 1994; Frankenberg 1993). Indeed, in our study of professional and managerial women in Memphis, Lynn Weber and I found middle-class White women who claim not to notice race (see Chapter 7, this volume). As a stance, this "color-blind" perspective can be a powerful force for the preservation of the racial status quo. Adoption of this position means that people of color are not seen when they enter new work settings—they are invisible as full human beings as coworkers and supervisors work not to notice their race. Employers, fellow workers, and clients might fail to see them as unique human beings with "distinctive talents, virtues, interests and problems" (Feagin et al. 1996, p. 14). As individuals enter work settings, they can be appreciated for themselves, including the unique perspectives they bring to the work group. Ignoring these qualities or pretending that race does not matter is a way of silencing them as individuals. Further, this is not the path to ending racial discrimination. We can also see this problem with interactions across social class lines, where social class origins might not be very clear. We have to work to address the sources of material differences in people's lives and what that means for the different parties.

As social pressures and legislation have opened many doors for individuals, women of color and members of the working class might enter middle-class work settings and find the atmosphere chilling, which then influences the interactions in those spaces. We have to recognize that as people of color and working-class persons enter spaces that were formerly middle-class and all White, there is a cost for them. These settings might be hostile and alien and, in their physical reality, not welcoming to people who are different. These are also places where interactions can be scripted by race, ethnicity, and social class, with people playing their appropriate roles. Legislation and social movements have meant new occupations for many previously disadvantaged groups, so it is not unusual now for coworkers to come from widely varying groups. However, when people move out of their previous prescribed roles and come together in new ways without their old scripts, there can be tensions and problems. It is important that employers, administrators, and those responsible for justice in the workplace hold supervisors accountable for ensuring that tensions are not translated into new structures of inequality.

In terms of social time, there is a historical memory among "outgroups" that is rarely recognized by members of the majority group, because they are often taught sanitized histories of oppression (Feagin et al. 1996). Stories of biased treatment and exploitation are kept alive in the families and communities of the disadvantaged, where the legacy of oppression is validated by others. For example, as a young Chicana enters domestic work, she may be very clear that this job is the type of work that her mother and perhaps her grandmother did before her (Romero 1992). Thus she might view and interpret her interactions on the job with White employers through that collective history, whereas the White employer may look only to the immediate interaction for clues to what is happening.

We have to keep in mind that as members of any group enter new social settings, those individuals might carry with them and understand their present experiences in terms beyond their personal experiences because they are conscious of familial and communal racial and social class histories. Thus women and men carry more than just visible signs of their race, ethnicity, and possibly social class origins with them into a workplace. They use their communal and personal histories as lenses through which they view the racial, ethnic, and social class privileges and disadvantages they find on the job. Rather than pretending that differences do not exist, we can learn to appreciate the histories and perspectives of individuals who have faced disadvantages in the past. Such insights can help us to revamp work settings to make them welcoming for all.

A key purpose of this volume is to use these more expansive definitions of race, ethnicity, and social class to identify what they mean for women in the workplace and in their work for better communities. By exploring not only women's work situations but their visions of the work and its relationship to other aspects of their lives, we can understand much about gender and work. We can also see whether changing conditions of work mean genuine shifts in social structural arrangements and judge whether additional changes are needed to end major gender inequalities.

## THE PERSISTENCE OF
## GENDER INEQUALITY

Attention to the differences among women should not divert political attention and social science research from exploring the persistence of gender differences. Comparisons of women with men indicate that there are major inequalities. Women's earnings still lag behind men's in the United States. In 1996, women who usually work full-time had median earnings of $415 a week, or 75.2% of the $552 median for men (U.S. Department of Labor 1996b). This earnings gap is indicative of the fact that women still face discrimination in gaining access to employment and also on the job, especially in traditional male occupations across the spectrum, from mining and other industrial work to the professions and corporate boardrooms.

We cannot attribute the earnings gap to lack of educational attainment on the part of women. An analysis of U.S. Census data by the Economic Policy Institute found great similarities in the earnings of college-educated Black and White women who had been in their jobs for 1-5 years: Black women had slightly higher earnings, with an average hourly rate of $11.41, whereas White women's average rate was $11.38 per hour in 1991 (U.S. Department of Labor 1996c). College-educated Black males' rate was slightly lower than those of the women at $11.26 per hour, but White males' average hourly rate was the highest at $12.85.

When this information was reported in the *New York Times* (Roberts 1994), the article's author highlighted the earnings difference between college-educated Black men and Black women and pondered the impact on marital options, even though nothing in the data addressed issues of marriage. However, the real story is the gap between White men and Black men and all women. Although it is a matter of cents that distinguishes the earnings differential between Black women and White women and Black men, the *New York Times* article did not give attention to the $1.44 gap between Black women's earnings and those of White men. We could all appreciate a headline that notes "College-Educated White Males Still Ahead in Hourly Earnings." At least that would expose the way much of the public still takes for granted the higher earnings of White males and shifts the discussion to who among the previously disadvantaged is improving over the others.

Natalie Sokoloff (1992), in a comparative study of occupational segregation among Black and White women in professional occupations, also brings the persistence of White male privilege into view. She notes that the decades from 1960 to 1980 witnessed the creation of many new middle-class jobs. Many of these positions went to women and Black men, but the majority went to White men. Thus it is important to look at the data from various perspectives, and to be critical of mainstream approaches. Biased presentation of statistical data can drive a political wedge between oppressed groups and leave White male privilege unexamined. The quest should be to remove barriers for all people. To do so, we have to look at all groups and their complexities of privileges and disadvantages.

In the 1990s, we find that the range of occupations in which women are employed is more varied than in 1947, although the majority of women are still in sex-segregated occupations. In 1995, 16.9 million women were employed in professional and managerial specialties (U.S. Department of Labor 1996a), but the majority were in traditionally female occupations (Sokoloff 1992): 24.1 million in technical, sales, and administrative support positions, and another 10.2 million in service occupations (U.S. Department of Labor 1996a).

However, women can now be found tending bar, baking bread outside the home, selling real estate, and in positions in banking other than behind tellers' windows. As scholars have explored the trend of women's moving into many traditionally male occupations, they have identified significant patterns. Barbara Reskin and Patricia Roos (1990) have found that women may have gained particular occupational titles, but where they work in formerly predominantly male fields can be different from where the men work. For instance, women might be clustered into certain segments of an occupation, or limited in their areas of specialty or task. It is also common for women to practice their occupations or professions in the public sector rather than the private sector; this is often the case for educated Black women (Reskin and Roos 1990; Higginbotham 1987, 1994).

Reskin and Roos (1990) also found that women are likely to enter fields as men abandon them in response to structural changes and/or earnings decline. Polly Phipps (1990) documents the case of pharmacy, where small, entrepreneurial, independent drugstores are in decline as most prescriptions drugs are dispensed either by large firms (Walmart,

Walgreen, Rite Aid, Osco, and other major stores) or in hospitals. We also see that this field has shifted from 87.9% male in 1970 to 76% male in 1980 and then 68% male in 1988.[2] As men have left pharmacy and the actual demand for pharmacists has grown, women have attended pharmacy schools and taken an increasing percentage of the positions in the field.

The changes in where women work, although they challenge the dominant pattern of sex segregation of the workplace, have not given us genuine integration of workplaces that benefits all women. As women enter new fields, they rarely close the wage gap. However, they have increasingly entered jobs that pay better than many traditionally female occupations. Yet the general national decline in wages means that women's benefits are limited. Also, the payoff for women of additional training and higher education may be minimal rather than the major rewards they expect as they enter professions and other formerly predominantly male occupations. What is critical here is the way that gender bias is still evident in the decline of wages in these fields.

Public action and advocacy against gender inequality are necessary to redress women's blocked access to jobs and mobility within traditionally male occupations and professions, and to promote equal pay for comparable work, higher wages for traditionally female professions, and other efforts that seek to address important differences in employment prospects for men and women. Yet, to further these efforts, particularly as they involve building coalitions among women, it is equally important to address the varied circumstances among women. Our aim as editors of this volume is to contribute to discussions that may build such coalitions across lines of gender, race, ethnicity, and social class.

The volume is organized into four parts: "Historical and Economic Perspectives"; "Manufacturing and Domestic Service"; "Health Care, Professions, Managerial Positions, and Entrepreneurship"; and "Working for a Better Community: Dilemmas in Building Solidarity." All of the chapters that follow highlight key issues in the exploration of race, ethnicity, or social class in the lives of women working for pay and as volunteers in efforts to change their lives.

Much of the research presented in this volume is qualitative, involving field observations and interviews as well as historical content analysis, to help us get at the deeper meanings of race, ethnicity, and social class for shaping aspects of women's work lives. There are also chapters that report on traditional social science quantitative research that addresses key issues for populations of working women.

This volume does not promise to address all women of all races, ethnicities, and social classes in the United States. Instead, the collection brings together a sampling of scholarly work that highlights some central questions that address race, ethnicity, and social class. Primary attention is given to the work situations of women of color and working-class women, groups that are often neglected in other volumes. We hope that these essays are illuminating for others.

## NOTES

1. In *The American Perception of Class*, Vanneman and Weber Cannon (1987) build on class divisions as specified by Nicos Poulantzas (1974) and then use quantitative analysis to explore the validity of these divisions with respect to the U.S. public.

2. I calculated these percentages based on Table 1.6 in Reskin and Roos (1990, pp. 17-18).

## REFERENCES

Amott, Teresa L. and Julie Matthaei. 1991. *Race, Gender and Work: A Multicultural Economic History of Women in the United States.* Boston: South End.

Barrera, Mario. 1979. *Race and Class in the Southwest.* South Bend, IN: University of Notre Dame Press.

Bianchi, Suzanne. 1995. "Changing Economic Roles of Women and Men." Pp. 107-54 in *State of the Union: America in the 1990s, Vol. 1, Economic Trends,* edited by R. Farley. New York: Russell Sage Foundation.

Braverman, Harry. 1974. *Labor and Monopoly Capital.* New York: Monthly Review Press.

Collins, Patricia Hill. 1990. *Black Feminist Thought: Knowledge, Consciousness, and the Politics of Empowerment.* New York: Routledge, Chapman & Hall.

Daniels, Arlene Kaplan. 1988. *Invisible Careers: Women Civic Leaders from the Volunteer World.* Chicago: University of Chicago Press.

Dill, Bonnie Thornton. 1988. "Our Mothers' Grief: Racial Ethnic Women and the Maintenance of Families." *Journal of Family History* 13:415-31.

Feagin, Joe R., Hernan Vera, and Nikitah Imani. 1996. *The Agony of Education.* New York: Routledge.

Frankenberg, Ruth. 1993. *White Women, Race Matters: The Social Construction of Whiteness.* Minneapolis: University of Minnesota Press.

Glenn, Evelyn Nakano. 1992. "From Servitude to Service Work: Historical Continuities in the Racial Division of Paid Reproductive Labor." *Signs: Journal of Women in Culture and Society* 18:1-43.

Harris, William. 1982. *The Harder We Run: Black Workers since the Civil War.* New York: Oxford University Press.

Higginbotham, Elizabeth. 1983. "Laid Bare by the System: Work and Survival for Black and Hispanic Women." Pp. 200-215 in *Class, Race and Sex: The Dynamics of Control,* edited by A. Swerdlow and H. Lessinger. Boston: G. K. Hall.

———. 1987. "Employment for Professional Black Women in the Twentieth Century." Pp. 73-91 in *Ingredients for Women's Employment Policy,* edited by C. Bose and G. Spitze. Albany: State University of New York Press.

———. 1994. "Black Professional Women: Job Ceiling and Employment Sectors." Pp. 113-31 in *Women of Color in U.S. Society,* edited by M. Baca Zinn and B. T. Dill. Philadelphia: Temple University Press.

Jones, Jacqueline. 1985. *Labor of Love, Labor of Sorrow: Black Women, Work, and Family from Slavery to the Present.* New York: Basic Books.

Lucal, Betsy. 1994. "Class Stratification in Introductory Textbooks: Relational or Distributional Models?" *Teaching Sociology* 22:139-50.

Marks, Carole C. 1989. *Farewell—We're Good and Gone: The Black Labor Migration.* Bloomington: Indiana University Press.

Massey, Douglas S. and Nancy A. Denton. 1993. *American Apartheid: Segregation and the Making of the Underclass.* Cambridge, MA: Harvard University Press.

McClain, Charles J. 1994. *In Search of Equality: The Chinese Struggle against Discrimination in Nineteenth-Century America.* Berkeley: University of California Press.

McLanahan, Sara and Lynne Casper. 1995. "Growing Diversity and Inequality in the American Family." Pp. 1-45 in *State of the Union: America in the 1990s, Vol. 2, Social Trends,* edited by R. Farley. New York: Russell Sage Foundation.

Nee, Victor and Brett DeBary Nee. 1973. *Longtime Californ': A Documentary Study of an American Chinatown.* Boston: Houghton Mifflin.

Omi, Michael and Howard Winant. 1994. *Racial Formation in the United States: 1960-1990,* 2nd ed. New York: Routledge.

Pedraza, Sylvia. 1991. "Women and Migration: The Social Consequences of Gender." Pp. 303-25 in *Annual Review of Sociology,* Vol. 17, edited by W. R. Scott and J. Blake. Palo Alto, CA: Annual Reviews.

Phipps, Polly A. 1990. "Industrial and Occupational Change in Pharmacy: Prescription for Feminization." Pp. 111-27 in *Job Queues, Gender Queues: Explaining Women's Inroads into Male Occupations,* edited by B. F. Reskin and P. A. Roos. Philadelphia: Temple University Press.

Pohlmann, Marcus D. 1990. *Black Politics in Conservative America.* New York: Longman.

Poulantzas, Nicos. 1974. *Classes in Contemporary Capitalism.* London: New Left.

Reskin, Barbara F. and Patricia A. Roos, eds. 1990. *Job Queues, Gender Queues: Explaining Women's Inroads into Male Occupations.* Philadelphia: Temple University Press.

Roberts, Sam. 1994. "Black Women Graduates Outpace Male Counterparts." *New York Times,* October 31, pp. A8, A12.

Romero, Mary. 1992. *Maid in the U.S.A.* New York: Routledge.

Shaw, Stephanie J. 1996. *What a Woman Ought to Be and to Do: Black Professional Women Workers during the Jim Crow Era.* Chicago: University of Chicago Press.

Sokoloff, Natalie. 1992. *Black Women and White Women in the Professions.* New York: Routledge.

Takaki, Ronald. 1990. *Strangers from a Different Shore: A History of Asian Americans.* Boston: Little, Brown.

Timmer, Doug, D. Stanley Eitzen, and Kathryn D. Talley. 1994. *Paths to Homelessness: Extreme Poverty and the Urban Housing Crisis.* Boulder, CO: Westview.

U.S. Department of Labor. 1995. *Report on the American Workforce.* Washington, DC: Government Printing Office.

U.S. Department of Labor. 1996a. *20 Facts on Women Workers* (Women's Bureau Fact Sheet No. 96-2, September). Washington, DC: Government Printing Office.

U.S. Department of Labor. 1996b. *Usual Weekly Earnings of Wage and Salary Workers, Third Quarter of 1996* (Bureau of Labor Statistics release, October 24). Washington, DC: Government Printing Office.

U.S. Department of Labor. 1996c. *Black Women in the Labor Force* (Women's Bureau Fact Sheet No. 96-4, November). Washington, DC: Government Printing Office.

Vanneman, Reeve and Lynn Weber Cannon. 1987. *The American Perception of Class.* Philadelphia: Temple University Press.

Wilson, William J. 1978. *The Declining Significance of Race: Blacks and Changing American Institutions.* Chicago: University of Chicago Press.

# PART I

# Historical and Economic Perspectives

The two essays in this section offer important perspectives as well as present socioeconomic data on women in the United States and on the historical experience of African American women. The background information in these two chapters provides a framework for looking at race, ethnicity, and social class as they affect women's labor force participation and community work. Both chapters summarize issues in their respective fields, economics and women's history, as well as present new empirical data. This historical and economic information is key to setting the stage for the chapters that follow.

In Chapter 1, Bárbara Robles, an economist, provides an overview of demographic information essential to an understanding of the varied circumstances of women across race and ethnicity. Her essay provides readers with demographic data on the status of women in the U.S. population in general as well as in the labor force. Robles provides a rigorous examination of the available U.S. Census data on White American, African American, Asian American and Hispanic women. Her analysis of census data is critical for the exploration of the socioeconomic issues that are central to women's participation in the world of work.

Robles's presentation helps readers understand that the wide variations in age, fertility, and family composition, as well as educational attainment and occupational distribution, among U.S. women are central to an analysis of the dynamics behind major inequalities in income and poverty. All households are not the same. There is no level playing field from which to launch women into employment. Through her analysis of socioeconomic data, Robles reveals the depths of the structural inequalities among women in the United States. She helps to develop a macro picture of the structures in a matrix of domination. Working around major limitations in the collection of data, she provides a framework and launches this book with clear attention to the sets of obstacles and supports that exist for women in the United States.

Furthermore, Robles raises some central questions about the benchmarks used to develop popular statistics and what they say about the circumstances of women in the United States. Using different benchmarks, she helps us see the larger pictures of specific populations in a new light. Often the structural biases for inequalities are not captured in those numerical pictures of different populations. The collection of data assumes that we are comparing similar populations, yet racial and ethnic groups vary in age composition, family arrangements, educational attainment, and other attributes that set the stage for different socioeconomic statuses that are often just attributed to the racial or ethnic groups themselves, rather than to the specific demographic characteristics of the groups.

Robles also helps us appreciate the micro struggles that are to follow in many of the chapters, where we see the people behind the numbers. Empirical studies can help us see what it means for women to cope with poverty, the challenges of work for recent immigrants, and how women with high levels of educational attainment fare in the workplace.

As noted in the introduction to this volume, historically race, ethnicity, and social class have shaped important work options and circumstances for women in the United States. Although the field of U.S. women's history initially explored primarily the past of native-born White women, over the years research on European immigrant women and women of color has increased. And over the same time period, more attention has been paid to the experiences of working-class women, as labor historians have ended their almost exclusive focus on men. This new scholarship has much to contribute to the interdisciplinary study of women and work. Yet, in the arena of women's history, gender has been given privileged status in analysis, whereas the interdisciplinary fields of race and ethnic studies have attended to race and ethnicity. Sharon Harley, a noted historian of African American women, addresses these issues in Chapter 2 as she identifies major themes found in investigations of the work histories of African American women by herself and other scholars. She also notes how the three themes of the work/family nexus, worker identity, and resistance have a prominent role in the new scholarship on other women of color, primarily Latina and Asian American women.

Given that the legacy of disadvantage has meant that many women of color have been pushed into the labor market, Harley notes that the work and family connection is central to an understanding of the experiences of women who have always had a high level of labor force participation. Early in the contemporary feminist movement, many White feminists viewed the high employment rates of Black women as evidence that these women were already liberated. Their unwillingness to look at the history of work from an African American perspective meant that they were unable to grasp the cost of work for Black women and their families. Yet, as increasing numbers of women in U.S. society work and raise families, we can learn from Harley's presentation of the research on African American women, which highlights some key issues and tensions that laboring for pay has created for women and family relations.

Many women of color have long labored in traditionally female and service occupations, and we can ask how they have come to terms with their circumstances. Since the publication of Patricia Hill Collins's (1990) *Black Feminist Thought,* more scholars are cognizant that African American women have a perspective on their experiences that differs from the dominant culture's vision of their lives. Harley explores the work identity and consciousness of African American women by looking at their involvement with organized activities and the legacy they have left. We cannot let employers speak for these women, especially when we have scholarship that provides evidence of their different views in their own voices.

Finally, Harley discusses new scholarship that documents the legacy of resistance that has been neglected by many. The means Black women have employed to challenge working conditions are evident in new histories of labor union activities as well as in the networks that Black women developed in clubs, mutual aid groups, and church organizations. Opening the quest for the exploration of resistance to new spheres helps us to understand the struggles of other women of color, who were often neglected by trade unions, which, early in the century, actively discriminated against women and people of color. Identifying a range of tactics and strategies, Harley reminds us that this scholarship can help us to expand what we define as resistance and to appreciate the actions that workers in struggle take in their own behalf.

Just as Robles helps us move to the micro with an eye on macro issues, Harley helps us move into contemporary studies with an eye on key historical issues. The integration of work and family, women's visions of their own work and consciousness as employees, and women's resistances to exploitative and limiting work are themes addressed in other chapters. Thus both of the essays in Part I prepare the stage for an examination of what is shared and what is unique as we look at chapters on specific women whose experiences vary with regard to race, ethnicity, and social class.

## REFERENCE

Collins, Patricia Hill. 1990. *Black Feminist Thought: Knowledge, Consciousness, and the Politics of Empowerment.* New York: Routledge, Chapman & Hall.

# 1

# An Economic Profile of Women in the United States

## BÁRBARA J. ROBLES

The changing demographic makeup of the United States is causing a growing awareness of cultural, ethnic, and racial diversity within the body politic. Before policy debates can be understood in historical, current, and future contexts, an assessment of the socioeconomic profiles of the differing racial and ethnic groups is required. This chapter investigates socioeconomic issues such as population and fertility statistics, educational attainment rates, occupational and wage status, and, finally, income and poverty distributions employing U.S. Census data for White American, African American, Asian American and Hispanic females. Consequently, this chapter reports on the current economic reality of females; it does not pursue an explanation of why such an economic actuality has arisen. Instead, it describes the existing economic reality of "average" or "typical" females belonging to specific populations. Clearly, much information is forfeited when one employs quantitative data to portray basic socioeconomic conditions for any population. Each individual story or "voice" is lost. What is gained, however, is an overall understanding of the economic status of women in the United States today.

Recent policy debates over dismantling entitlement programs, curtailing welfare enrollments, limiting the growth of long-standing health

5

care programs, and reducing spending outlays on programs designed to encourage market participation by groups that have historically been excluded from particular economic opportunities have increased the interest in and awareness of current changing demographic factors in the United States. The 1990 U.S. Census reports that non-Hispanic White Americans constitute 75.6% of the total U.S. resident population; non-Hispanic African Americans constitute 11.8%; Hispanics, 9%; non-Hispanic Asian Americans, 2.9%; and non-Hispanic Native Americans, 0.7%. The Census Bureau projects that by 2030, the demographics of the United States will have changed sufficiently to alter the population distribution of racial and ethnic group members. The projections indicate that non-Hispanic White Americans will constitute 60.1% of the resident population in the United States; non-Hispanic African Americans, 13.4%; Hispanics, 17.9%; non-Hispanic Asian Americans, 7.7%; and non-Hispanic Native Americans, 0.8% (U.S. Bureau of the Census 1994e).

These projected demographic changes signify that the socioeconomic status of the groups that are growing as a percentage of total population will have an equally increasing impact on the overall health of the U.S. economy as well as on the sociological characteristics of U.S. culture. With these changes in mind, my intent in this chapter is to report and profile the socioeconomic characteristics of average female members of the African American, Asian American, Hispanic (Mexican American, Puerto Rican, and Cuban American), and non-Hispanic White American populations.[1]

This chapter is organized by socioeconomic topics. The first section addresses the overall population numbers and relative characteristics of the groups discussed. The second section is devoted to marital status, household information, and fertility statistics of the groups. The third section contains descriptions of the educational attainment characteristics of females in these groups and their correlation with labor occupational status and labor force participation. The final section reports income and poverty statistics for female heads of households compared with family units (as defined by the U.S. Census) for each group.

## POPULATION CHARACTERISTICS

The U.S. Census survey of 1990 found 248 million people residing in the United States. More recent estimates report the total U.S. population at 263 million (U.S. Bureau of the Census 1994e). Before I proceed with a discussion of the racial and ethnic composition of the population, it is important that I address the manner in which the Census Bureau defines and categorizes members of the racial and ethnic groups that reside within the United States. The five "racial" categories the U.S. Census Bureau employs are as follows: White; Black; Asian and Pacific Islander; Native American, Aleut, and Eskimo; and Other. The category of "Hispanic origin" is treated as an "ethnic" category, because White, Black, Asian, and Native Americans can also claim "Hispanic" ethnicity.[2] The Asian and Native American categories do not account for a large presence in the Hispanic ethnic component, but the Black racial category continues to be an important component of the Hispanic community. The White category claims the bulk of the Hispanic-origin racial classification. This category is a misnomer, given that there is no choice of mestizo among the racial codes listed on the census survey. For my purposes, I will assume White to exclude Hispanic-origin White unless otherwise noted on the tables and in the text in discussion of population characteristics. The same holds for African Americans.

Census Bureau estimates for 1995 indicate the following percentage breakdowns for racial/ethnic categories: The White population constitutes 73.6% of the total U.S. population; African Americans, 12%; Hispanics, 10.2%; Asian Americans, 3.5%; and Native Americans, 0.7%. For comparison, allowing the racial categories to include those of Hispanic origin yields a somewhat different story: White, 82.9%; Black, 12.6%; Asian and Pacific Islander, 3.7%; and Native American, 0.8%. Clearly, this indicates that 9.3% of the White population is Hispanic, that 0.6% of the African American community is Hispanic, that 0.2% of Asian Americans self-identify as Hispanic, and finally, that a minute 0.1% of the Native American population signals Hispanic origin.

Allowing individuals to self-identify concerning country/ethnicity of origin in census surveys has revealed an interesting pattern concerning maintenance of cultural identity. Ethnic self-identity is a widespread phenomenon among all Americans. For example, in the 1990 census survey of ancestry of the U.S. population, German ancestry was identified by 45.5 million Americans, Polish ancestry was reported by 6.5 million, and those simply identifying as U.S./Americans amounted to 13 million. The list of countries/ethnicities of origin is substantial (for details, see note 2).

**TABLE 1.1** Population Statistics, United States, 1995

|  | Median Age | Total Population | Percentage Population |
|---|---|---|---|
| Total United States | 34.0 | 263,434,000 | 100 |
| White | 36.2 | 193,900,000 | 73.6 |
| African American | 29.0 | 31,648,000 | 12.0 |
| Hispanic origin | 26.5 | 26,798,000 | 10.2 |
| Native American | 27.1 | 1,927,000 | 0.7 |
| Asian American | 30.4 | 9,161,000 | 3.5 |
| Females in United States | 35.2 | 134,749,000 | 51.2 |
| White | 37.4 | 99,184,000 | 73.6 |
| African American | 30.5 | 16,689,000 | 12.4 |
| Hispanic origin | 27.0 | 13,188,000 | 9.8 |
| Native American | 28.1 | 979,000 | 0.7 |
| Asian American | 31.4 | 4,708,000 | 3.5 |

SOURCES: U.S. Bureau of the Census (1993b, 1994e).

The Census Bureau (1994b) released a special report on the Hispanic population that indicates the following distribution among the five components tracked under the Hispanic-origin category: Mexican, 64.3%; Puerto Rican, 10.6%; Cuban, 4.7%; Central and South American, 13.4%; and "other Hispanic," 7.0%. "Other Hispanic" comprises those people identifying themselves as "from Spain or people identifying themselves as Hispanic, Spanish, Spanish-American, Hispano, Latino and so on."

Table 1.1 reports the 1995 census categories for total U.S. population, non-Hispanic White, non-Hispanic African American, Hispanic, non-Hispanic Asian American, and non-Hispanic Native American. The striking characteristic that stands out from the table is the changing composition of the U.S. population in terms of median age by cultural/racial/ethnic identification. This age distribution has a substantial impact on the growth rates of segments of the population. The older the median age of a particular group, the more the presence of fertility and growth factors decline and the more stable the population becomes in terms of dynamic catalysts. The median ages of females reported for the different groups constitute one of the major explanations for the changing demographic components of total U.S. population. For example, the youngest female median age of 24.6 years belongs to the largest component of the Hispanic population, Mexican Americans. Puerto Ricans report 26.9, Cubans 43.6, Central and South Americans 28.6, and "other Hispanics" report 32.5 as the median age for their communities. For the U.S. total population, the female median age is 34.2 years, whereas for the White American population the median age is 37.4. The census has found a median age for African American females of 30.5 years, for Native American females of 28.1, and for Asian American females of 31.4. Clearly, these statistics will have consequences for which segments of overall population will continue to grow rapidly.

The Bureau of the Census projects that between 1990 and 2030, the average annual growth for the Asian American community will be 3.59%, making it the fastest-growing group. Hispanics follow with an annual average growth of 2.7%; African Americans are third, with 1.37%; Native Americans are fourth, with growth of 1.25%; and growth among the White American population is projected to be .31% annually.

## MARITAL, FERTILITY,
## AND HOUSEHOLD STATISTICS

The decade of the 1990s has seen a critical reassessment of the socioeconomic changes of the 20th century. Of concern for women of color has been the political debate over familial arrangements for those populations that have not benefited from economic and market growth. Having provided statistical evidence of the changing demographics in the United States and the inherent dynamism of the changes in distribution of racial and ethnic populations due to differences in median ages among the components of the resident population, I now address the task of placing these changes within the framework of "household" characteristics. The Census Bureau reports information on fertility rates, marital status, and living arrangements for women of various age cohorts and racial/ethnic populations. Table 1.2 reports the marital status of both males and females by percentage breakdowns and fertility rates for all five groups by varying age cohorts for the female population 15 years of age and older.

The marital status data indicate that White Americans (male and female) have the lowest percentage of never-married persons, followed in order by Asian Americans, Hispanics, and African Americans. In the married category, White Americans lead with the highest percentage reported. However, White Americans have the second-highest divorce

**TABLE 1.2** Marital Status and Fertility Statistics, United States

| Cohort Group | White American | African American[a] | Hispanic | Asian American[a] | Native American |
|---|---|---|---|---|---|
| **Male and female** | | | | | |
| **marital status** | | | | | |
| 15 years + | 151,710,000 | 21,914,00 | 16,022,000 | 5,247,000 | NA |
| % never married | 23.4 | 39.9 | 32.8 | 31.1 | |
| % married | 60.9 | 42.5 | 56.3 | 56.4 | |
| % widowed | 7.2 | 7.9 | 4.1 | 3.4 | |
| % divorced | 8.5 | 9.8 | 6.8 | 4.0 | |
| **Females** | | | | | |
| **(age groups)** | | | | | |
| 10-14 | 0.5 | 5.0 | 2.3 | 0.7 | 2.0 |
| 15-19 | 42.5 | 115.1 | 99.6 | 28.6 | 104.7 |
| 20-24 | 99.2 | 160.2 | 180.5 | 93.3 | 190.0 |
| 25-29 | 113.4 | 111.2 | 149.8 | 161.6 | 140.1 |
| 30-34 | 78.3 | 66.6 | 95.8 | 136.9 | 75.5 |
| 35-39 | 29.7 | 27.5 | 43.1 | 62.5 | 32.7 |
| 40-44 | 4.7 | 5.2 | 9.2 | 12.9 | 6.9 |
| 45-49 | 0.2 | 0.3 | 0.6 | 1.3 | 0.3 |

SOURCES: For Whites, Hispanics, and Native Americans, U.S. Bureau of the Census (1993d, 1994c); for African Americans, U.S. Bureau of the Census (1991, 1993c); for Asian Americans, U.S. Bureau of the Census (1992).
NOTE: Fertility rates represent live births per 1,000 women in age group indicated. NA = not available.
a. Includes Hispanic origin.

percentage. Asian Americans have the lowest percentage of divorces, and African Americans have the highest. Note that these percentages are benchmarked and calculated on the basis of individual populations.

The youngest female cohort (10 to 14 years of age) with the highest fertility rate is found in the African American population, with the Hispanic and Native American communities following in order of magnitude. The second cohort, ages 15 to 19, has the same communities displaying high fertility rates relative to the White and Asian American populations. The third cohort, ages 20-24, indicates that Native American women have the highest fertility rates, followed by Hispanics, African Americans, and White and Asian Americans. The fourth cohort, ages 25-29, reverses the fertility trend for Asian American women. The fertility rates displayed by Asian American females for this cohort and the following cohort, ages 30-34, indicate delayed reproduction decisions compensated with high rates of differences between other groups' fertility rates in this age bracket. For example, there exists a 58.6 live birth spread per 1,000 women between the Asian and White American female cohort, ages 30-34. This trend is in keeping with the population projections for the Asian American group, which is projected to have the most dynamic increases within the next 30 years.

Before turning to household and family characteristics as reported in Table 1.3, I should point out that statistical information presented by the U.S. Census follows an established methodology that focuses on individual populations. An example of this procedure is the calculation of the percentage of one-parent family groups maintained by mothers for the total population (25.9%), for African Americans (58.4%), and for White Americans (20.2%). The comparison generally evokes concern and leads to troubling interpretations for both African Americans and Whites: Why do these populations differ substantially in their proportions of female-headed families? Is the disparity really so substantial?

Perhaps we should pause and question such reporting methods. The reservation I hold concerning such calculations is in part based on the lack of clarity found in the reporting of the percentages and the underlying notion of "population" within the United States. If the goal is to report on *all* female-headed families, then the proportion of one-parent families maintained by mothers among African American women is 33.6%; the proportion is 63.2% for White American females. How did I get to these figures? I employed the number of one-parent groups maintained by *all* mothers as the basis for comparing White and African American females (see Tables 1.3 and 1.4). This method, of course, is not the procedure used by the Census Bureau for reporting these statistics. Instead, each group's "total family" is used as its own benchmark; thus when the total numbers are small (African Americans) relative to a larger total base (White Americans), they invariably appear skewed. The real question we should be asking is: How should we as a heterogeneous population be reporting our socioeconomic characteristics? As separate enclaves? Or as contributing communities to the total population?

We need to know what is being compared and what benchmarks are employed when we interpret reports on how well or how poorly Americans are faring. Note how different the two portraits of one-parent groups maintained by mothers appear when different reporting procedures are used. Initially, we are told that almost 60% of all African American families are headed by mothers—and this is fact, based on surveys. What is lost in such reporting, however, is any reminder that African Americans constitute only 12% of the *total* population of the

**TABLE 1.3** Family and Household Characteristics

| | Total United States[a] | White American | African American[a] | Hispanic | Asian American[a] | Mexican American | Puerto Rican | Cuban American |
|---|---|---|---|---|---|---|---|---|
| **Families[b]** | 68,144 | 52,855 | 7,470 | 5,318 | 1,536 | 3,210 | 653 | 309 |
| Married couple (%) | 78.0 | 83.5 | 50.2 | 69.1 | 80.1 | 72.3 | 53.4 | 76.1 |
| Female head, spouse not present (%) | 17.5 | 12.7 | 43.8 | 23.3 | 12.7 | 19.4 | 40.5 | 18.2 |
| Male head, spouse not present (%) | 4.4 | 3.8 | 6.0 | 7.7 | 7.3 | 8.4 | 6.2 | 5.7 |
| **Family size (%)** | | | | | | | | |
| 2 persons | 42.0 | 45.2 | 34.5 | 26.2 | 41.6 | 22.8 | 31.7 | 40.3 |
| 3 persons | 23.6 | 23.1 | 26.1 | 23.5 | 23.1 | 21.8 | 26.8 | 29.0 |
| 4 persons | 21.0 | 20.7 | 19.8 | 23.1 | 21.3 | 22.2 | 25.5 | 20.0 |
| 5 persons | 8.9 | 8.0 | 11.0 | 14.5 | 9.0 | 16.1 | 11.0 | 7.6 |
| 6 persons | 3.0 | 2.2 | 5.0 | 6.8 | 3.1 | 8.5 | 3.3 | 2.1 |
| 7 persons + | 1.6 | 0.9 | 3.7 | 5.9 | 1.9 | 8.6 | 1.7 | 1.1 |
| **Mean number of persons** | 3.16 | 3.02 | — | 3.78 | — | 4.01 | 3.33 | 3.06 |
| **Households[b]** | 96,391 | 75,735 | 10,486 | 6,626 | 1,958 | 3,869 | 841 | 405 |
| Family (%) | 70.7 | 69.6 | 71.2 | 80.3 | 78.4 | 83.0 | 77.6 | 76.2 |
| Nonfamily (%) | 29.3 | 30.4 | 28.7 | 19.7 | 29.7 | 17.0 | 22.4 | 23.8 |
| Married couple (%) | 55.2 | 58.1 | 35.8 | 55.4 | 62.8 | 60.0 | 41.4 | 57.9 |

SOURCES: For total United States, Whites, Hispanics, Mexican Americans, Puerto Ricans, and Cuban Americans, U.S. Bureau of the Census (1993d, 1994c); for African Americans, U.S. Bureau of the Census (1991, 1993c); for Asian Americans, U.S. Bureau of the Census (1992).
a. Includes Hispanic origin.
b. In thousands.

**TABLE 1.4** Family and Household Characteristics over Time, 1970-1993

| | 1993 No.[a] | 1993 % | 1990 No. | 1990 % | 1980 No. | 1980 % | 1970 No. | 1970 % | Average Annual % Change 1990-93 | 1980-90 | 1970-80 |
|---|---|---|---|---|---|---|---|---|---|---|---|
| **Total** | | | | | | | | | | | |
| Families with children | 36,058 | 100.0 | 34,670 | 100.0 | 32,150 | 100.0 | 29,631 | 100.0 | 1.3 | 0.8 | 0.6 |
| 2-parent families | 25,157 | 69.8 | 24,921 | 71.9 | 25,231 | 78.5 | 25,823 | 87.1 | 0.3 | -0.1 | -0.2 |
| 1-parent families | 10,901 | 30.2 | 9,749 | 28.1 | 6,920 | 21.5 | 3,808 | 12.9 | 3.7 | 3.4 | 6.0 |
| Mother head | 9,339 | 35.9 | 8,398 | 24.2 | 6,230 | 19.4 | 3,415 | 11.5 | 3.5 | 3.0 | 6.0 |
| Father head | 1,562 | 4.3 | 1,351 | 3.9 | 690 | 2.1 | 393 | 1.3 | 4.8 | 6.7 | 5.6 |
| **White American** | | | | | | | | | | | |
| Families with children | 29,225 | 100.0 | 28,294 | 100.0 | 27,294 | 100.0 | 26,115 | 100.0 | 1.1 | 0.4 | 0.4 |
| 2-parent families | 22,058 | 75.5 | 21,905 | 77.4 | 22,628 | 82.9 | 23,477 | 89.9 | 0.2 | -0.3 | -0.4 |
| 1-parent families | 7,167 | 24.5 | 6,389 | 22.6 | 4,664 | 17.1 | 2,638 | 10.1 | 3.8 | 3.1 | 5.7 |
| Mother head | 5,901 | 20.2 | 5,310 | 18.8 | 4,122 | 15.1 | 2,330 | 8.9 | 3.5 | 2.5 | 5.7 |
| Father head | 1,265 | 4.3 | 1,079 | 3.8 | 542 | 2.0 | 307 | 1.2 | 5.3 | 6.9 | 5.7 |
| **African American** | | | | | | | | | | | |
| Families with children | 5,364 | 100.0 | 5,087 | 100.0 | 4,074 | 100.0 | 3,219 | 100.0 | 1.8 | 2.2 | 2.4 |
| 2-parent families | 1,987 | 37.0 | 2,006 | 29.4 | 1,961 | 48.1 | 2,071 | 64.3 | -0.3 | 0.2 | -0.5 |
| 1-parent families | 3,377 | 63.0 | 3,081 | 60.6 | 2,114 | 51.9 | 1,148 | 35.7 | 3.1 | 3.8 | 6.1 |
| Mother head | 3,135 | 58.4 | 2,860 | 56.2 | 1,984 | 48.7 | 1,063 | 33.0 | 3.1 | 3.7 | 6.2 |
| Father head | 242 | 4.5 | 224 | 4.3 | 129 | 3.2 | 85 | 2.6 | 3.0 | 5.4 | 4.2 |
| **Hispanic** | | | | | | | | | | | |
| Families with children | 3,831 | 100.0 | 3,429 | 100.0 | 2,194 | 100.0 | NA | NA | 3.8 | 4.5 | NA |
| 2-parent families | 2,494 | 65.0 | 2,289 | 66.8 | 1,626 | 74.1 | NA | NA | 2.9 | 3.4 | NA |
| 1-parent families | 1,344 | 35.0 | 1,140 | 33.2 | 568 | 25.9 | NA | NA | 5.5 | 7.0 | NA |
| Mother head | 1,157 | 30.1 | 1,003 | 29.3 | 526 | 24.0 | NA | NA | 4.8 | 6.5 | NA |
| Father head | 187 | 4.9 | 138 | 4.0 | 42 | 1.9 | NA | NA | 10.1 | 11.9 | NA |

SOURCES: U.S. Bureau of the Census (1994c, 1994d).
NOTE: NA = not available.
a. All numbers are in thousands.

United States. Clearly, we need to know what the raw numbers tell us; we cannot rely only upon percentages, because we are rarely informed about how percentages are constructed and what benchmarks are used and why. Further, we need to reassess our approach to assigning economic "well-being" to particular cultural characteristics and preferences, because economic prosperity and cultural diversity are neither equal nor mutually exclusive.

Tables 1.3 and 1.4 give some indication of the changing nature of families and households in the United States today and over time. The Census Bureau notes that familial arrangements have been changing over time and that no "one" definition of family is "normal" or "typical." It does, however, make distinctions between households and families as it tracks data. A *household* consists of the people who occupy a particular housing unit; each household is categorized as family or nonfamily. Family households are broadly categorized into (a) married heterosexual couple families, (b) other families with female householders (no husband present), and (c) other families with male householders (no wife present). In the nonfamily household category are single male and female householders. In the family household category there are married couples with and without own children and female and male heads of households with and without children.

The surprising features of Table 1.3 are the similarities among most communities in family size. At the two extreme ends, we have White Americans (non-Hispanic) with 45.2% two-person families and only 0.9% families of seven persons and more, and Mexican Americans with the lowest proportion of two-person families (22.8%) and the highest proportion of families with seven or more persons (8.6%). Also, note that in the formation of households, among Mexican Americans 83% of households consist of family members, compared with 70.7% for White Americans. This finding reveals, in quantitative terms, different cultural preferences: White Americans are oriented toward the nuclear family model, whereas Mexican Americans retain an orientation toward the extended family model. Between these two models, the rest of the racial ethnic communities appear to be evenly distributed among three- and four-person families. The distribution of family size arrangements appears to be primarily among two-, three-, and four-person families.

The diversity of familial arrangements is reflected in the changing numbers and the growth over time of single-parent family groups (see Table 1.4). The statistics on the growing number of male and female one-parent family groups reveal much about the changing nature of U.S. society's attitude toward the institution of marriage. In order not to presume that sociobehavioral preferences and choices also reveal economic advantages, we need also to ask what attributes these families display: Are they disproportionately represented below the poverty level or are they above the poverty level? What are the median earnings for the male and female household heads? What are the occupational and educational opportunities of these families? The following sections address these questions.

## EDUCATION AND LABOR STATISTICS

The direct correlation between educational attainment and labor outcomes (returns to education) has been established and thoroughly researched in the economics and interdisciplinary literatures.[3] The problem with investigating educational and occupational gains for women of color resides in the lack of availability of longitudinal data. The U.S. Census, although reliable in many contexts, has undergone several measurement and reporting changes that have led to discontinuities in the tracking of information on female employment status. For these and other data-availability reasons, the bulk of economic studies has tended to focus on educational attainment rates for male members of the various populations. The paucity of information simply means that summary statistics for female populations are of extreme value, given there are few data employed to generate modeling results.

The data for high school completion among females 25 years of age and over in our populations of interest (see Table 1.5) indicate that there exists a large pool of female talent untrained and unrealized as the decade of the 1990s closes. Both the African American and Hispanic female populations have an overall low high school completion rate compared with White and Asian American females. It is important to contextualize this result with the reminder that we are dealing not with one single female generation, but rather with a host of cohorts. Further time-series analysis is required before we can draw comprehensive conclusions from these numbers. One could speculate that obtaining a high school diploma was not an educational opportunity that older African American and Hispanic women could readily avail themselves

**TABLE 1.5** Educational Attainment, United States, 1993

| | All Races | White American | African American[a] | Hispanic | Asian American[a] | Native American |
|---|---|---|---|---|---|---|
| **Males and females** | | | | | | |
| Total 25 years + | 162,826,000 | 127,601,000 | 16,751,000 | 12,100,000 | 4,158,000 | NA |
| **Percentage completed** | | | | | | |
| < fifth grade | 2.1 | 0.8 | 5.1 | 11.8 | 5.3 | NA |
| High school + | 80.2 | 84.1 | 66.2 | 53.1 | 81.8 | NA |
| Bachelor's degree | 21.9 | 23.8 | 11.3 | 9.0 | 39.0 | NA |
| **Females[a]** | | | | | | |
| Total 25 years + | 85,442,000 | 72,222,000 | 9,280,000 | 6,097,000 | 2,227,000 | NA |
| **Percentage completed** | | | | | | |
| < fifth grade | 1.96 | 1.68 | 4.2 | 12.1 | 6.2 | NA |
| High school + | 80.0 | 81.3 | 66.5 | 53.2 | 80.0 | NA |
| Bachelor's degree | 19.2 | 19.7 | 10.8 | 8.5 | 11.8 | NA |
| **Raw numbers** | | | | | | |
| Master's degree | 3,942,000 | 3,477,000 | 271,000 | 92,000 | NA | NA |
| Professional degree | 584,000 | 505,000 | 29,000 | 22,000 | NA | NA |
| Doctorate degree | 366,000 | 310,000 | 26,000 | 11,000 | NA | NA |

SOURCES: For all races, Whites, and Native Americans, U.S. Bureau of the Census (1993d, 1994a, 1994c); for African Americans, U.S. Bureau of the Census (1991, 1993c); for Asian Americans, U.S. Bureau of the Census (1992).
NOTE: NA = not available.
a. Includes Hispanic origin.

16

of, due to segregation for the former group and possible language barriers for the latter. Nonetheless, the numbers appear discouraging. Comparisons among the communities with respect to graduate degrees again serve to emphasize the use of baselines or benchmarks for analyzing the proportions of given populations holding advanced degrees. For example, 5% of White American females hold master's degrees, and 3% of African American females hold master's degrees. These percentages are derived from the total female White American and African American populations age 25 years and older. If we use the base numbers for both males and females, the numbers look alarmingly dismal. Again, without time-series data, these numbers do not convey the status of female educational attainment. More research is needed in this area in order to reveal whether educational attainment gains or reversals are occurring for females in all census groups.

Table 1.6 reports labor force participation and occupational and earning information for females in all census groups. The highest proportions of females 15 years and older active in the labor force are found in the Asian and African American populations. The largest proportions of females in managerial/professional occupations are found among White Americans (30.9%) and Asian Americans (27.9%); the lowest representation is displayed by Mexican Americans (13.6%). The highest representation in the service occupation category is found in African American females (27%), with the second highest proportion (24.9%) reported for Mexican American females.[4] The highest representation in the laborer category is displayed by Mexican American females (15.2%). The occupation category that dominates all other categories for females is that of technical, sales, and administrative support. This finding is not surprising, given that the clustering of women in these occupations is well documented in the research on women's employment patterns (Bergman 1986).

The earnings categories were not comparable for all groups, and so differing ranges are presented. African American and Mexican American females have higher proportions (54.0% and 49.6%, respectively) than do other female groups in the less than $10,000 earnings range. Cuban American women have a higher percentage than do White American women in the $25,000 to $49,999 earnings range, and 4.0% of Asian American women earn $50,000 or more, compared with 3.3% of White American women. Median earnings and male-to-female earnings ratios are discussed in the next section.

**TABLE 1.6** Occupational and Labor Participation, United States

| Characteristic | Total United States | White American | African American[a] | Asian American[a] | Hispanic | Mexican American | Puerto Rican | Cuban American |
|---|---|---|---|---|---|---|---|---|
| **Total females 16+** | 100,654 | 77,270 | 11,684 | 2,550 | 7,842 | 4,726 | 883 | 480 |
| In civilian labor force[b] | 57,558 | 44,682 | 6,803 | 1,502 | 4,072 | 2,348 | 408 | 232 |
| % in civilian labor force | 57.2 | 57.8 | 58.2 | 58.9 | 51.9 | 51.6 | 46.2 | 48.4 |
| Employed females | 53,997 | 42,456 | 6,119 | 1,439 | 3,617 | 2,168 | 363 | 216 |
| % unemployed | 6.2 | 5.0 | 10.0 | 4.2 | 11.1 | 11.1 | 11.0 | 7.3 |
| **Occupation (%)** | | | | | | | | |
| Managerial/professional | 28.8 | 30.9 | 18.8 | 27.9 | 15.4 | 13.6 | 18.5 | 18.4 |
| Technical/sales/ administrative support | 42.8 | 43.9 | 39.7 | 43.3 | 40.9 | 40.7 | 48.4 | 49.0 |
| Service | 18.0 | 16.0 | 27.0 | 15.7 | 24.6 | 24.9 | 19.9 | 20.1 |
| Farming/forestry/fishing | 0.8 | 0.9 | 0.3 | 0.2 | 1.8 | 2.8 | — | — |
| Precision production/ craft/repair | 1.9 | 1.7 | 2.3 | 3.0 | 2.5 | 2.8 | 2.4 | 2.0 |
| Operators/fabricators/laborers | 7.7 | 6.6 | 12.0 | 10.0 | 14.8 | 15.2 | 10.8 | 10.6 |
| **Females with earnings** | 62,050 | 48,613 | 10,944 | 1,606 | 4,240 | 2,542 | 424 | 251 |
| Less than $10,000 | 37.9 | 37.0 | 54.0 | 36.0 | 32.7 | 49.6 | 35.9 | 33.3 |
| $10,000-19,999 | — | — | 24.1 | 29.3 | — | — | — | — |
| $10,000-24,999 | 37.9 | 37.7 | — | — | 38.1 | 36.7 | 42.3 | 42.0 |
| $20,000-29,999 | — | — | 11.6 | 17.2 | — | — | — | — |
| $25,000-49,999 | 21.1 | 22.0 | — | — | 14.5 | 12.7 | 20.8 | 23.7 |
| $30,000-39,999 | — | — | — | 8.7 | — | — | — | — |
| $30,000 or more | — | — | 7.3 | — | — | — | — | — |
| $40,000-49,999 | — | — | — | 4.8 | — | — | — | — |
| $50,000 or more | 3.1 | 3.3 | — | 4.0 | 1.4 | 1.0 | 1.0 | 0.9 |
| Median earnings ($) | 13,675 | 14,241 | 9,623 | 14,122 | 10,813 | 10,098 | 14,200 | 14,117 |
| Mean earnings ($) | 16,745 | 17,141 | — | — | 13,587 | 12,588 | 15,656 | 16,456 |

SOURCES: For total United States, Whites, Hispanics, Mexican Americans, Puerto Ricans, and Cuban Americans, U.S. Bureau of the Census (1993d, 1994c); for African Americans, U.S. Bureau of the Census (1991, 1993c); for Asian Americans, U.S. Bureau of the Census (1992).
a. Includes Hispanic origin.
b. All numbers are in thousands.

## INCOME AND POVERTY STATISTICS

Females from all census groups are represented in the labor force, in all occupations, and in smaller numbers in educational attainment percentages. Not surprisingly, females are also a presence in poverty and aid/benefits statistics. We see in Table 1.7 that the female earnings distribution is skewed toward the lower end of the income distribution range. We can see that this is clearly related to the higher representation of female workers in clerical/technical occupations, which tend to have depressed salaries. Median earnings for females reported in Tables 1.6 and 1.7 are different due to the inclusion of non-full-time, non-year-round (seasonal) workers in the former and only full-time, year-round workers in the latter. Nevertheless, these numbers yield a coherent profile of the economic reality of females in terms of income ranges and in terms of how females in all census groups fare compared with their male counterparts.

Table 1.7 reports the median earnings for male and female year-round, full-time workers over several time periods. The female-to-male median earnings ratios indicate the disparity that still exists between male wages and female wages, although improvement is evident. No reporting of the female-to-male earnings ratios of the various populations was undertaken because the raw numbers allow cross-comparison among the varying groups. For example, one can compare African American females to White American or Asian American females, or one can compare Hispanic females to Hispanic males or White American males. The point is that we lose information by focusing only on ratios as opposed to allowing the numbers to speak for themselves. For example, the female-to-male earnings ratio for Mexican American women compared with White American males is .529, which is not very heartening when the female-to-male earnings ratio for the total population is reported at .706, or 71 cents to the male dollar (in median terms).

Asian American females earn more than White American females and Hispanic males but less than Asian American males, African American males, and White American males. For African American females working full-time, year-round, we see increasing gains in median earnings over time. There is a $10,000 disparity between the median earnings reported for all African American females 15 years and older active in the labor force ($9,623) and full-time, year-round workers ($19,819). All females have made gains throughout this period, but the unavailability of complete time series for Asian American and Hispanic females

**TABLE 1.7** Income Statistics, United States, 1992 (Median US$)

| | Males | | | | Females | | | |
|---|---|---|---|---|---|---|---|---|
| | 1992 | 1987 | 1982 | 1977 | 1992 | 1987 | 1982 | 1977 |
| All races | 30,358 | 32,044 | 30,932 | 32,469 | 21,440 | 20,886 | 19,099 | 19,131 |
| White | 31,012 | 32,764 | 31,703 | 33,432 | 21,659 | 21,088 | 19,313 | 19,251 |
| African American | 22,369 | 23,618 | 22,752 | 23,187 | 19,819 | 19,453 | 17,805 | 17,975 |
| Hispanic | 20,049 | 21,532 | 22,574 | 23,951 | 17,138 | 17,939 | 16,308 | 16,685 |
| Asian American[a] | 27,741 | 29,892 | — | — | 21,691 | 22,137 | — | — |
| Mexican American | 18,422 | — | — | — | 16,399 | — | — | — |
| Puerto Rican | 23,749 | — | — | — | 20,178 | — | — | — |
| Cuban American | 23,437 | — | — | — | 19,687 | — | — | — |
| **Female-to-male median earnings ratios,** | | | | | | | | |
| all races | .706 | .652 | .617 | .589 | | | | |

SOURCES: For all races, Whites, Hispanics, Mexican Americans, Puerto Ricans, and Cuban Americans, U.S. Bureau of the Census (1993d, 1994c); for African Americans, U.S. Bureau of the Census (1991, 1993c); for Asian Americans, U.S. Bureau of the Census (1992).
a. Includes Hispanic origin.

should be noted, as well as the erratic movement of the median earnings for female Hispanic full-time, year-round workers. Apparently, African American and White American female median earnings were not affected by the 1982 recession.

Poverty statistics are reported in Tables 1.8 and 1.9 with the intent of capturing trends concerning the presence of racial/ethnic populations below the poverty level. Table 1.8 describes the differences between "persons" and "families" below the poverty level of the various years reported. This table also gives the changes for the periods 1991-1992 and 1989-1992. A word of caution about assessing the changes occurring during this time: A recession was under way, and these numbers, although the latest available, reflect the underlying economic situation of that time. In spite of this, poverty rates for Asian American families fell 1% between 1991 and 1992 and 0.3% for Hispanic families. African American families had an increase of families living below the poverty level of 0.5%, but note the decrease in percentage change between 1989 and 1991 for African American families of 2.6%. This implies a slowing of the previous percentage increases in poverty among African American families. Among White Americans, 0.1% more families were below the poverty level in 1992 than in 1991.

Table 1.9 reports poverty statistics for female heads of households. The numbers do not add up to the total because the individual population numbers are taken from varying U.S. Census publications. The proportions are somewhat dismaying at first glance, with 46.5% of African American, 48.8% of Hispanic, and 60.3% of Puerto Rican female-headed households falling below the poverty level. However, each percentage is reported for the individual population in isolation. This implies that each percentage uses the benchmark of total female heads of households by individual population. If we were to use simply the *total* U.S. female head of household number as a benchmark, we would have the following proportions of female heads of households below the poverty level: White Americans, 39.5%; African Americans, 36.5%; Asian Americans, 1%; and Hispanics, 14.5% (Mexican Americans, 6%; Puerto Ricans, 4%; Cubans, 0.2%; and other Hispanics contributing).

## CONCLUSION

A prudent analysis of census data on the female African American, Hispanic, Asian American, and White American populations reveals

**TABLE 1.8** Poverty Statistics, 1989-1992

| | 1992 | | Below Poverty 1991 | | 1989 | | 1991-1992 Difference | | 1989-1992 Difference | |
|---|---|---|---|---|---|---|---|---|---|---|
| | No. | Rate | No. | Rate | No. | Rate | No. | Rate | No. | Rate |
| **Persons** | | | | | | | | | | |
| Total[a] | 36,880 | 14.5 | 35,708 | 14.2 | 31,528 | 12.8 | 1,172* | 0.3 | 5,352* | 1.7 |
| White | 24,523 | 11.6 | 23,747 | 11.3 | 20,785 | 10.0 | 776 | 0.3 | 3,738* | 1.6 |
| Non-Hispanic White | 18,308 | 9.6 | 17,741 | 9.4 | 15,599 | 8.3 | 567 | 0.2 | 2,709* | 1.3 |
| African American | 10,613 | 33.3 | 10,242 | 32.7 | 9,302 | 30.7 | 371 | 0.6 | 1,311* | 2.6 |
| Hispanic origin[b] | 6,655 | 29.3 | 6,339 | 28.7 | 5,430 | 26.2 | 316* | 0.6 | 1,225* | 3.1 |
| Asian American | 912 | 12.5 | 996 | 13.8 | 939 | 14.1 | (84) | -1.3 | (27) | -1.6 |
| Other races | 1,744 | 17.0 | 1,719 | 17.6 | 1,441 | 16.4 | 25 | 0.6 | 303* | 0.6 |
| **Families** | | | | | | | | | | |
| Total | 7,960 | 11.7 | 7,712 | 11.5 | 6,784 | 10.3 | 248 | 0.2 | 1,176* | 1.4 |
| White | 5,160 | 8.9 | 5,022 | 8.8 | 4,409 | 7.8 | 138 | 0.1 | 751* | 1.1 |
| Non-Hispanic White | 3,860 | 7.3 | 3,719 | 7.1 | 3,325 | 6.4 | 141 | 0.2 | 535* | 0.9 |
| African American | 2,435 | 30.9 | 2,343 | 30.4 | 2,077 | 27.8 | 92 | 0.5 | 358* | 3.1 |
| Hispanic origin[b] | 1,395 | 26.2 | 1,372 | 26.5 | 1,133 | 23.4 | 23 | -0.3 | 262* | 2.8 |
| Asian American | 199 | 12.0 | 210 | 13.0 | 182 | 11.9 | (11) | -1.0 | 17 | 0.1 |
| Other races | 365 | 15.2 | 347 | 15.5 | 298 | 14.7 | 18 | -0.3 | 67* | 0.5 |

SOURCE: U.S. Bureau of the Census (1993e).
a. All numbers are in thousands.
b. Persons of Hispanic origin may be of any race.
*Statistically significant at the 90% confidence level.

**TABLE 1.9** Female Heads of Households, Poverty Statistics, United States

| | United States | Total American | White American[a] | African American[a] | Asian Hispanic | Mexican American | Puerto Rican | Cuban American |
|---|---|---|---|---|---|---|---|---|
| **Below poverty level** | | | | | | | | |
| Female head of household, no spouse present[b] | 4,171 | 1,646 | 1,524 | 43 | 604 | 286 | 160 | 11 |
| Percentage female head of household, no spouse present | 34.9 | 24.6 | 46.5 | 22.3 | 48.8 | 46.0 | 60.3 | NA |
| **Families irrespective of poverty level** | | | | | | | | |
| Total female heads of households | 11,925 | 6,713 | 3,275 | 195 | 1,239 | 622 | 264 | 56 |
| All families | 68,144 | 52,855 | 7,470 | 1,536 | 5,318 | 3,210 | 653 | 309 |

SOURCES: For total United States, Whites, Hispanics, Mexican Americans, Puerto Ricans, and Cuban Americans, U.S. Bureau of the Census (1993d, 1994c); for African Americans, U.S. Bureau of the Census (1991, 1993c); for Asian Americans, U.S. Bureau of the Census (1992).
NOTE: NA = not available.
a. Includes Hispanic origin.
b. All numbers are in thousands.

that socioeconomic characteristics displayed by these groups can be easily misrepresented. Statistical summaries and reporting require far more care than the news media have employed and researchers (academic and nonacademic) have provided. Ultimately, the questions that are asked guide us to the methodologies we select in reporting quantitative data. The underlying raw numbers need to be presented along with various percentages to provide a comprehensive portrait of the economic conditions of women of color.[5] For each topic addressed in this chapter, I have questioned the baseline or benchmark for the reported official percentages and have presented reformulations employing *total* population benchmarks that allow different pattern of socioeconomic attributes to emerge.

In summarizing a cross-sectional comparison of all female census groups (their similarities as well as disparities), it is essential that no one group be held up as "the model"; rather, the data should be allowed to indicate when groups of females bear striking resemblances across ethnic or racial differences and when the distinctions among them are of unique and notable patterns. Clearly, we find compelling evidence for both similarities as well as disparities in the census numbers. It is important to assess the economic reality of individual group data as well as place the data in a larger, comparative context. Both stories are equally informative.

The data indicate that a strong work ethic exists for all the female groups examined. Recall that Asian American and African American women have the largest percentages of 15-year-olds and older in the workforce by own population. The educational attainment rates of women of color are distressing and disheartening. However, the number of women of color and their representation in professional/managerial occupations indicates that in spite of structural barriers, women no longer represent single-digit percentages in this category. The female-to-male ratios of median earnings of year-round, full-time workers show we are not yet at full parity. The proportion of all females heading households below the poverty level is near 35%. Recall that of total families, 17.5% are female-headed households. This situation is exacerbated by the obvious segmentation in U.S. labor markets by occupation, gender, and race, as is evident in the median earnings data.

The economic profile of Asian American females (and to a lesser degree Cuban American females) resembles the economic profile of White American females insofar as educational attainment rates and median earnings are concerned. However, the dynamic fertility rates among Asian American women in the midrange age cohorts are unique; they are most comparable to the fertility rates of Hispanic women in the younger age groups. Further, Cuban American women display an older median age than all of the groups analyzed (43.6 years) and follow the demographic pattern of White American females (37.4 years). African American and Hispanic (with the exception of Cuban American) females appear to have markedly different educational attainment rates, younger fertility increases, labor participation and occupational representation that has consequences for median earnings, and appear to reside in more family households (71.2 and 80.3, respectively). They also have a higher percentage of female-headed households (as reported in the census) below the poverty level.

The data show that there is much room for improvement, but they do not imply that advances and increased opportunities in educational access and occupational dispersion are not present. What emerges from this profile is that historical conditions creating legacies of institutional inertia cannot be dismissed as significant aspects of the current economic conditions faced by all female communities. From the statistical evidence reported by the U.S. Census Bureau, we cannot claim equality in gender or ethnic/racial economic well-being for women in the United States as we approach the 21st century. It appears we are not yet beyond the need for affirmative and proactive policies for all female communities.

## NOTES

1. The trade-off between timely data and availability by ethnic group is unfortunate but very real. There are particular tables missing data that were not available for African Americans, Asian Americans, and Native Americans and the subgroups of Hispanics: Mexican American, Puerto Rican, and Cuban American.

2. *Hispanic origin* is an aggregate term for the following ethnic codes listed in the U.S. Census survey: Mexican, Chicano, Mexican American, Puerto Rican, Cuban, Central or South American, and other Spanish. Other ethnic origin categories available for respondents' self-identification include German, Italian, Irish, French, Polish, Russian, English, Scottish, Afro-American (Black, Negro), Dutch, Swedish, and Hungarian. Other possible responses are "another group not listed" and "don't know."

3. This particular topic has been debated and is still being debated within the economics profession. The question of paramount interest is *who* reaps the benefit (i.e., the larger returns) of investment in education. The consensus within the profession is that this particular theoretical result is in actuality an empirical question. Unfortunately, most empirical economic studies have focused mainly on the schooling of males, and thus provide little insight into returns to education for minority females.

4. The Census Bureau includes the following in the service occupation category: private household occupations (domestics, child-care workers, cooks, servants), protective service occupations (supervisors of and employees in the police, firefighting, detective, and guard occupations), food preparation and service occupations (supervisors of and employees in food serving, bartenders, cooks, assistants of waiters and waitresses, and so on), health service occupations (dental assistants, health aides except nursing, nursing aides/orderlies and attendants), cleaning and building service occupations (supervisors of and maids, janitors, cleaners, elevator operators, and pest control occupations), and personal service occupations (supervisors of and barbers, hairdressers, cosmetologists, guides, ushers, public transportation attendants, baggage porters and bellhops, welfare service aides, family child-care providers, and early childhood teacher's assistants). Comprehensive studies of domestic workers can be found in Mary Romero's *Maid in the U.S.A.* (1992) and in Elizabeth Clark-Lewis's *Living In, Living Out* (1994).

5. Native American women were included as data were accessible and in comparable format for comparison purposes with the other female groups analyzed, but glaring gaps remain. Clearly, more information on Native American women would have contributed to a more comprehensive economic profile of their community. This research remains to be done.

## REFERENCES

Bergman, Barbara. 1986. *The Economic Emergence of Women.* New York: Basic Books.

Clark-Lewis, Elizabeth. 1994. *Living In, Living Out: African American Domestics in Washington, D.C., 1910-1940.* Washington, DC: Smithsonian Institution Press.

Romero, Mary. 1992. *Maid in the U.S.A.* New York: Routledge.

U.S. Bureau of the Census. 1991. *The Black Population in the United States: March 1990 and 1989.* Current Population Reports, Series P-20, No. 448. Washington, DC: Government Printing Office.

———. 1992. *The Asian and Pacific Islander Population in the United States: March 1991 and 1990.* Current Population Reports, Series P-20, No. 459. Washington, DC: Government Printing Office.

———. 1993a. *Money Income of Households, Families, and Persons in the United States: March 1992.* Current Population Reports, Series P-60, No. 184. Washington, DC: Government Printing Office.

———. 1993b. *1990 Census Population, Ancestry of the Population of the United States.* Washington, DC: Government Printing Office.

———. 1993c. *1990 Census Population, Characteristics of the Black Population.* Washington, DC: Government Printing Office.

———. 1993d. *1990 Census Population, Persons of Hispanic Origin in the United States.* Washington, DC: Government Printing Office.

———. 1993e. *Poverty in the United States: 1992.* Current Population Reports, Series P-60, No. 185. Washington, DC: Government Printing Office.

———. 1994a. *Educational Attainment in the United States: March 1993 and 1992.* Current Population Reports, Series P-20, No. 476. Washington, DC: Government Printing Office.

————. 1994b. *The Hispanic Population in the United States: March 1993.* Current Population Reports, Series P-20, No. 475. Washington, DC: Government Printing Office.

————. 1994c. *Household and Family Characteristics: March 1993.* Current Population Reports, Series P-20, No. 477. Washington, DC: Government Printing Office.

————. 1994d. *Marital Status and Living Arrangements: March 1993.* Current Population Reports, Series P-20, No. 478. Washington, DC: Government Printing Office.

————. 1994e. *Population Projections of the United States by Age, Sex, Race, and Hispanic Origin: 1993 to 2050.* Current Population Reports, Series P-25, No. 1104. Washington, DC: Government Printing Office.

# 2

# Speaking Up: The Politics of Black Women's Labor History

## SHARON HARLEY

Focusing on the work/family nexus, work identity and consciousness, and Black female resistance, this essay illuminates the issues and spaces contested by African American women as they seek to survive and even to empower themselves and members of their families and communities in the face of exploitation. Foregrounding of the work experience and working-class consciousness of Black women reveals multiple instances in which their "speaking up" transforms their work sites and conditions. These instances also pose a challenge to labor historians and feminist scholars to engage in their own acts of resistance through a critique of unattenuated assumptions and biases in studies of working women, especially those of darker hue.

The lives and voices of African American, Native American, Asian American, and Latina American women workers seldom reached the shorelines despite the great waves of labor, African American, and women's histories washing against academic beachheads during the late 1960s and the 1970s. Black female workers are often marginalized in histories of the working class, despite the historical and contemporary appropriation of Black female bodies and identities as workers. The low status of their work and unexamined assumptions about the absence of a "working-class consciousness" made women, particularly poorer women and women of color, appear largely "unworthy" of sustained examination in the minds of far too many historians and other scholars. Consequently, the realities of their waged and unwaged work remained lost to all but members of the stable Black working class and a small cohort of scholars for whom marginalizing Black women's labor would be a rejection of themselves and the working grandmothers, mothers, aunts, and working men in their families and communities.

In this essay I seek to explore the labor history of African American women in the United States, focusing on the politics and meaning of their racialized gender and class identities in recent historical scholarship. Through an examination of what I consider to be three of the most critical themes in Black women's labor scholarship, I will reveal the impact of multiple sites of difference (race, gender, sexuality, and class) on Black working women's historical realities.[1] In this essay, I will cut across various historical periods and disciplinary boundaries to examine thematic issues that form the core of Black women's lives and inform contemporary intellectual and policy discourse. Although specific acts of oppression and resistance may vary over time, there is remarkable consistency in how Black women's work experiences are framed by intersecting sexual, gender, racial, and class identities. As more scholars study working women of other racial and ethnic groups, it will be possible to explore simultaneously these and other critical themes in the work lives of other women of color and to engage in more comparative analyses.

Although the focus of this essay is African American women, I will make reference to research findings about other working women of color. Indeed, this research has helped to affirm many of my own conclusions as well as raised questions about African American wage-earning women that the more traditional White/Black binary would not have made possible.

## THEMATIC APPROACH

Three major themes emerge from recently published scholarship in the field of Black women's labor history: (a) the work/family nexus, (b) work identity and consciousness, and (c) the related theme of Black female resistance. Although these are addressed separately in this essay, clearly there is considerable overlap among them as Black working women negotiate the daily courses of their lives. The importance of understanding the interconnectedness of these themes cannot be over-estimated. As Evelyn Nakano Glenn (1985) argues, it is important to consider simultaneously "women's relation to the family, the labor market and the larger political economy in which both family and employment are embedded" (p. 94).

Within the body of historical literature on Black women's work, these themes should not be construed as representative of either the entirety of Black women's work lives or even of the body of scholarship in Black women's labor history. For instance, I do not present a separate discussion of Black female entrepreneurship or of the structural discrimination that Black women workers and other women of color, in particular, face in the labor market. Too often in the past, a separate focus on employment discrimination has led scholars and policy makers to separate oppression from the humanity of people's lives. Moreover, the story of the racial/ethnic domination and oppression of people of color is so interwoven into the daily fabric of their lives that I have chosen not to disconnect the two, even for research purposes. In an effort to combat the often hidden human dimension of racial oppression, Camille Guerin-Gonzales (1994) points out, contemporary Latino and Latina labor historians have made a concerted effort to portray working-class Mexican Americans and Mexican immigrants as "complex, fully-formed, and fully-functional human beings" (p. 548).

Each theme in this essay, then, is applied to reveal how African American women negotiate their daily work and family lives in the face of (and, more important, despite) the exploitation they encounter. I seek to illuminate the issues and spaces contested by African American women as they have sought to survive and even to empower themselves, family members, and coworkers.

## THE WORK/FAMILY NEXUS

Nowhere has the politics of exclusion and misrepresentation been more apparent in the work about African American women's labor than around issues associated with the Black female wage/family nexus. Sociologist Carole Marks (1993) attributes this phenomenon, in part, to Black women's low work status and wages, which serve to impoverish and "to mask the pivotal role they play in the maintenance of themselves and their families" (p. 149). The work/family debate as formulated in contemporary policy arenas outside African American communities frequently fails to address the traditionally low wages and enormously harsh working conditions under which Black women labor on behalf of their families and in clear opposition to the "welfare queen" stereotype. Within the past two decades, however, as more feminist historians have joined feminist sociologists, economists, psychologists, anthropologists, and policy analysts in studying Black women workers, the female work/family nexus in the African American community has become more centrally located in labor, women's, and African American history.

Unlike in their traditional West African homelands, most African women who were kidnapped and enslaved in the Americas controlled few of the fruits of their productive and reproductive labor. Over time, enslaved women and men from diverse African ethnic groups and their American-born descendants combined age-old agricultural and familial customs and the exigencies of chattel slavery to forge a core set of work and family values that helped to sustain them. With resistance as a central theme within the African American core value system, it should not be surprising that African men, women, and children survived in the face of unrelenting work demands, humiliations, and the threat of and actual sexual assaults of enslaved women and girls that characterized the system of chattel slavery practiced in the United States. Gender- and work-related issues reflected the cultural ethos of mutuality (the belief that one should willingly sacrifice for kin and community) but were not without many of the contradictions inherent in systems of human oppression and survival in a patriarchal, racist society (Steady 1981; Gwaltney 1971; Jones 1985; White 1985, 1990; Franklin 1984; Hunter 1995; Higginbotham 1995; Kelley 1994).

The middle-class gender norms that were the guiding principles of the 19th-century "cult of domesticity" were unattainable for enslaved and most free (and newly freed) African American women and men. Moreover, dominant White middle-class social norms of women's proper roles and power relations often conflicted with both African-based attitudes toward female productive and reproductive labor and the realities of African and African American women's work lives in the United States. Clearly, when it comes to these women, and most non-White women, the social norms and gender expectations of the White middle-class community take second place to economic realities and racial/ethnic cultural traditions.

More significantly, the dichotomous categories of male versus female, subordinate versus dominant were inconsistent with both the lived experiences and the cultural ethos of mutuality of Black people in slavery and in post-emancipation United States. About the enslaved African American woman, Deborah Gray White (1990) writes, "Regardless how hard we try to cast her in a subordinate or submissive role in relation to slave men, we will have difficulty reconciling that role with the plantation realities" (p. 30).

In the refractory lens of some contemporary observers, female self-reliance and, correspondingly, limited male authority within slave quarters produced "matrifocal" Black families. Based upon her research on women and slavery and anthropological studies of southern populations in the United States and of Caribbean and West African societies, White (1990) argues that the " 'matrilocal family' . . . does [not] prevent male-female cooperation, or mutual respect, or traditional romance and courtship. It does, however, help to explain how African American men and women survived chattel slavery" (p. 30).

Sociologist Susan Mann (1990) disputes historians White's (1990) and Jacqueline Jones's (1985) claims of gender equality based upon what she asserts is their erroneous assumption that patriarchy was virtually nonexistent in propertyless slave and sharecropping households. Mann argues that institutional patriarchal domination is an inherent aspect of capitalism, and as such it permeates the lives and perspectives of propertied and propertyless classes. In support of her conclusion that "Black women could only have been in an inherently unequal relation to Black men," Mann notes that landowners recognized the Black male as head of his family in slavery and sharecropping households. She adds that because Black men "controlled" the family's income and held higher-status jobs, they therefore held the "domestic decision-making power" in Black sharecropping communities (p. 157).

I would agree with Mann (as I believe White and Jones do) that all families within a capitalist economy, whether property holders or not, reflect the inherent patriarchal tendencies of this mode of production; however, I am not convinced that Black male "control" of family income, recognition as "head" of household, and position in the job market resulted automatically in inherently unequal power relations between husbands and wives in Black families. Mann cites a few examples of domestic violence, unfulfilling interpersonal relations, and higher frequency of Black male participation in production for exchange (as opposed to production for use), but these do not provide compelling enough evidence to conclude that the majority of African American women and men lived their daily lives in interpersonal relations that disadvantaged women or that the Blacks in slave or sharecropping households perceived women as submissive and men as dominant, or that either acted in such a manner. Finally, the bifurcated perception of human behavior and corresponding status is alien to the traditional communal ethos and worldview of Africans and African Americans.

This is not to suggest there were no differences in the work and familial roles of Black men and women or that men were not recognized as "heads" of households and wives as "helpmates," but that these differences rarely were perceived in terms of either dominance or submissiveness or that they directly mirrored power relations in most White families. In support of her argument about sexual inequality among sharecroppers, Mann (1990) quotes from a conversation between a couple in Zora Neale Hurston's *Jonah's Gourd Vine*. In this fictional account, the husband asks if supper is ready, and the wife responds: "Naw hit ain't. How you speck me tuh work in de field right long side uh you and den have supper ready jiz az soon ez Ah git tuh de house?" (p. 144). This conversation reflects a clear difference in gendered expectations regarding unwaged household labor but does not support the dominant/submissive dynamic Mann postulates, nor does it, in and of itself, reveal that "gender inequalities existed alongside the interdependence of husbands' and wives' work" (pp. 143-44). The question that constantly has to be asked is whether the men and women in these families and in these communities at that time viewed these differences as reflective of gender inequality.

Further disputing the gendered assumptions of historians White and Jones, Mann (1990) proclaims, however, "Though male and female roles may have been complementary under sharecropping, this complementarity was not synonymous with equality" (p. 156). Few would argue with Mann's assertion that complementarity and equality are not synonymous, but she seems unwilling to recognize the extent to which gendered assumptions and roles in Black communities are mediated by issues of racial oppression. In her study of the Black Baptist convention, Evelyn Brooks Higginbotham (1993) reveals how the convention women constantly blurred gender lines "as they positioned themselves simultaneously within racial and gendered social space" (p. 142).

In the controversy surrounding the ratification of the 15th Amendment, giving Black males (but not women, of any race) the right to vote, most Black women favored the amendment. Historically, when forced to choose, African American women often have given higher priority to the lives, work, and racial advancement of Black men than to their own.

As a racist and patriarchal society denies African American males and females status and power, even if it does so unevenly, the commonly held view was that it was better for one segment of the Black community to have the vote rather than no one having it. Besides, in the communal worldview of African Americans, when husbands and fathers vote, the wives, mothers, and children in their families and communities do so as well (Terborg-Penn 1985; Brown 1994).

Emancipation should have meant that African American women and children were freer to determine what, if any, gender conventions would be associated with their work in the labor market, in Black households, and in community organizations and institutions—and it did (some-what). However, the huge demand for exploitable farm labor (largely African American men, women, and children) in the rural South, com-bined with the gradual encroachment of middle-class gender norms through middle-class teachers and missionaries, affected the work- and family-related gender attitudes of Black folk, especially in urban Black communities. For instance, in the post-emancipation plantation South, Black mothers and wives who refused to work, as both a marker of their freedom and their desire to devote more time to performing domestic chores for their own families, faced incredible pressure, on the one hand, from landowners to work and, on the other hand, from middle-class Black people and those with middle-class aspirations not to par-ticipate in the paid labor force.

When the demands of southern planters that Black wives and mothers work went unmet, they attempted to coerce Black men into making their wives work the fields, employing a variety of duplicitous methods to force men, women, and children to work (Jones 1985). Fannie Lou Hamer, the youngest of 20 children, told how her family's employer "tricked" her into joining the rest of her sharecropping family members in the Mississippi cotton fields when she was 6 years old. After she had picked 30 pounds of cotton, the "Bossman" offered her some treats and declared her ready to become a full-time cotton picker (Reagon 1990).

If all else failed, especially during the harvest season, plantation owners and overseers threatened to evict entire families if the women in them refused to work. This response toward African Americans, particularly women, by the postbellum southern plantocracy followed the preemancipation pattern of valuing Black women's work roles over their maternal and reproductive roles. This view toward Black women is a fairly persistent one among White employers toward women who are racially or ethnically different from them (Glenn 1985).

The threats of southern landowners were largely unnecessary because the wages paid to Black men were consistently insufficient for most Black families to survive without mothers, wives, and even young children joining husbands and older children in the cotton and tobacco fields, and, increasingly, in the textile and tobacco factories. For the vast majority of southern Black women, the choice between being a full-time housewife or a farm laborer or a domestic was nonexistent. Consequently, the vast majority of Black women, men, and children never left the fields or kitchens of White families during the transition from slavery to freedom and beyond.

Because the work and income of Black women were as crucial as Black men's to the well-being and survival of Black households and community institutions and organizations, both were valued. In a 1902 speech, African American clubwoman, suffragist, and lecturer Mary Church Terrell publicly acknowledged what most members of Black communities knew all too well: Black families suffered when women did not work for wages. This was true although some husbands expressed pride in having non-wage-earning wives and despite occasional public denunciations of Black wives and mothers who worked for wages, especially outside their homes, rather than "stay[ing] at home . . . [where] they can spend time in the training of their children" (Jackson and Davis [1908] 1971, p. 133).

Mann (1990) attributes the post-emancipation intensification of the sexual division of labor to the decline in female field labor and the corresponding rise in importance of unwaged household labor. Indeed, the "mothering" role assumed greater importance as more middle-class Black women and men spoke out at meetings, in the press, and at church gatherings about the importance of raising children and of maintaining clean and wholesome homes. There was early and clear recognition that freedom from chattel slavery would not exempt Black women from work in the marketplace, nor would it exempt them from laboring for their own families and the growing number of community organizations. If anything, the domestic roles and responsibilities of women expanded and took on added importance. Consequently, working mothers, especially those without spouses or extended family members willing to share in the preparation of meals, child care, and housecleaning, continued to experience firsthand workdays without end.

As employment opportunities for Black women and men extended beyond the rural, agrarian-based economy to an urban, industrial-based economy, tensions around the work/family nexus for Black women grew, despite (or maybe even because of) their higher salaries. Leaving behind a family-based sharecropping system for better-paying factory positions, married women often occupied different job sites from their husbands and had male coworkers who were neither spouses nor kin.

The prospect of women, particularly married women, working in close proximity to either White or Black male strangers raised a number of concerns among post-emancipation African Americans. Sexual harassment and exploitation of factory women by early-20th-century southern White foremen was rampant and, according to historian Dolores Janiewski (1985), such treatment of African American women in Durham, North Carolina, was "tolerated" by employers who believed that Black women did not warrant the same sort of protection as did the more "morally pure" members of the White female workforce. On these grounds, some Black husbands vehemently opposed their wives' working for wages outside the home. Janiewski and others tie this attitude to Black male attempts to dominate Black female sexuality by controlling the women's labor activities. Race and economic status determined the extent to which men could exercise such control. On this point, Janiewski argues:

> Black men's protective instincts were activated by white men's refusal to respect their sexual claims over black women. Operating by the same measures of male prestige and economic status, white men restricted the types of labor performed by their women and zealously defended their sexual honor (while attempting to deny the same prerogatives to black men). (p. 52)

Among those who condemned the presence of married women in the paid labor force, undoubtedly, there were some who feared that it would promote a greater sense of female independence. In actuality, whether married or single, rural or urban, most wage-earning Black women's identities and incomes were tied to their households and families, especially in the pre-World War II United States. Increasingly, however, tensions mounted between young girls and their mothers as the former objected to the enormity of their wage-earning responsibilities coupled with the household and child-care chores awaiting them at the end of their paid workday. Based upon oral interviews with more than 60 individuals employed in Durham, North Carolina, during the period between 1900 and 1950, Janiewski (1985) tells the story of Allie Ennis (a pseudonym), who typifies the work experiences of many southern Black girls:

Ennis who helped her mother "wash for white people" as a young girl, cleaned house, ironed, and cooked while her brothers worked in the garden that fed the eleven members of her family. When her father died, she left school to work full-time at domestic and occasional factory work. (p. 136)

A similar tension existed among pre-World War II Issei immigrants from Japan as they shifted from the traditional "family economy" of southern Japan to the U.S. wage labor system. According to Glenn (1985):

Employment enabled [issei] women to retain their traditional role as active contributors to the family economy. In other ways, however, the strategy contradicted traditional values. Under a wage system, the individual, not the household, was the unit of production, and work and household were separate, rather than integrated spheres. Finally, when women were employed outside the household, husbands no longer exercised direct control over wives' labor. (p. 101)

This loss of direct control by husbands resulted in conflict within the households of Issei women.

The combination of increased moral denunciation of working wives and mothers in the labor market, better wages in urban markets, and the preference among employers for unmarried women resulted in an initial decrease in the percentage of married wage-earning women and a corresponding increase in unmarried women in the labor force in the immediate postemancipation period. However, the rate of employment among both married and single women increased significantly, especially in urban labor markets, as a result of several elements: the passage of the Fair Labor Standards Act of 1938, which severely reduced most household forms of production; the passage of child labor laws, which reduced the number of wage-earning child laborers; the decline in fertility rates; technological advances (e.g., the washing machine); and the Great Depression. In 1940, for instance, 71.8% of the females in the workforce of North Carolina textile industries were married, compared with only 33.6% in 1920. Although a slightly higher percentage of married Black women (52.0%) than married White women (41.0%) worked in the Durham tobacco industry in 1935, the labor force participation rates of the two groups began to resemble each other as the " 'family wage' enabling a male breadwinner to keep his wife out of the labor force" was nonexistent in most Durham households (Janiewski

1985). The absence of a "family wage" among African American male wage earners historically has meant that Black wives and mothers with spouses have been more likely to work for wages, regardless of household arrangements. Nationwide, the labor force participation rate for non-White married women, even those living with their husbands, increased each decade from 1940 to 1970 and in each period was higher than the labor force participation rate for married White women. In their comparative study of the labor force participation of Black and Latina (i.e., Puerto Rican, Mexican, and other Hispanic women) women in 1980, sociologists Marta Tienda and Jennifer Glass (1985) found this pattern to be persistent over time among Black wives and mothers, regardless of household arrangements.

Although most single wage-earning Black women lived in their parents' households, some, especially unmarried female migrants, lived with other kin or hometown folk in the opening decades of the 20th century. Other single women resided in group homes, boardinghouses, and local YWCAs. In these group home settings, unmarried women, particularly those without children, may have had fewer day-to-day domestic responsibilities, but not necessarily fewer financial obligations to kin (real and fictive) nearby or "back home."

Yet, as with married female wage earners, single Black working women were subjected to criticism regarding their presence as unmarried women in the labor market. The work/family nexus was turned on its head as unmarried women were criticized for not having close family ties or husbands (or, worse yet, lacking even potential marriage partners). The inherent restraints associated with living with or in close proximity to parents or other family members were missing among unattached, southern rural Black female and male migrants to urban communities, especially in the North. As single women came to outnumber single men by a wide margin, thereby reducing their chances of getting married, questions arose among middle-class Black residents about the moral character of such unattached women. The issue of the uneven sex ratio so concerned early-20th-century sociologist Kelly Miller that he wrote about it in a chapter titled "Surplus Negro Women" in his 1908 book *Race Adjustments.* According to Miller, "The preponderance of one sex over the other forebodes nothing but evil to society. . . . 'Where women preponderate in large numbers there is a proportionate increase in immorality, because women are cheap' " (p. 170).

Despite the fact that few Black women became prostitutes as a consequence of their working alone in urban settings, suspicions about their moral character, however unfounded, had very real consequences. Fearing the possibility that their residences might be viewed as bawdy houses or houses of ill repute, some female boardinghouse operators outright refused to rent to single women, but not to single men (Harley 1981).

With the rise in the numbers of educated, professional (frequently unmarried) Black women, the work/family nexus in the post-1950s United States has taken an unexpected turn. Central to postwar public debates about wage-earning women, especially educated Black women, has been the invented stereotype of the domineering (i.e., emasculating) Black matriarch. The publication of Daniel P. Moynihan's much-debated 1965 report *The Negro Family: The Case for National Action* opened the floodgates for both external and internal criticisms of Black women in the maintenance (and, too often, the destruction) of African American family life. According to sociologist Andrew Billingsley (1992), as well as other scholars, a major implication of the Moynihan thesis is that "there was . . . more need for changing the internal structure of African American families by putting a man in charge of every house" (p. 78). Once again, the importance of Black women's financial contributions to the very survival of the Black family and institutions in the African American community took a backseat to the raging debate about Black women's roles in destroying African American men and the Black family. Moreover, writing about gender roles among female slaves, White (1990) argues that the post-Moynihan emphasis on Black women's assuming more "traditional" submissive roles resulted in some post-1965 scholars' de-emphasizing resistant acts of self-reliance and self-sufficiency.

Fortunately, despite yet another attempt to marginalize Black women's economic contributions, African American working women, their kin, and most members of the Black community seldom lost sight of Black women's critical financial roles in Black households and community organizations and institutions, even if politicians, policy analysts, and "brothers trying to get over" did. A number of Black scholars and writers joined in condemning Moynihan's report, expressing particular concern about its attempt to blame Black familial instability on Black people without considering the daily "economic, political, and educational deprivations" they encounter (Billingsley 1992).

In the work/family nexus discourse there remains still the largely unrecorded and unacknowledged benefit of African American women's unpaid labor as culture bearers of the family and the race. Historian/

folklorist/singer Bernice Johnson Reagon (1990) writes of this important work within societies of enslaved women of the African diaspora in the Americas. Within the African cultural tradition, Reagon contends that "mothering . . . required a kind of nourishing that would both provide food and stamina for survival . . . and the passing on of traditions that would allow for the development of a community" (p. 178).

The work of women, men, and older siblings in raising children "within an alternate value system" is a critical aspect of the work/family nexus within Black, brown, yellow, and poor White communities. By overlooking women's unpaid work as mothers and community builders, we lose sight of a critical arena of self-determination and resistance within oppressed communities. Black women took their work in the church and the community quite seriously, opposing most efforts to interfere with what they saw as their calling. When her husband asked when she was going to curtail her missionary work to spend more time at home, Black Baptist convention leader Virginia Broughton responded, "I belong to God first, and you next; so you two must settle it" (quoted in Higginbotham 1993, pp. 131-32).

The conflicted nature of work and family lives is addressed in the even smaller but growing body of literature on the work lives of women and men of color. Glenn (1985) remarks:

> In the racial ethnic family, conflict over the division of labor is muted by the fact that institutions outside the family are hostile to it. . . . Women do a great deal of the work of keeping the family together and teaching children survival skills. This work is experienced as a form of resistance to oppression rather than a form of exploitation by men. (p. 103)

When addressed at all, issues of dichotomous power (male versus female) dominate the scholarly discourse around work and family in Black households. Rarely addressed is how labor decisions, including decisions about labor migration, were often family decisions. Marks (1993) indicates that mutuality characterized many of the labor decisions about when and which family members would migrate, and, in turn, who would remain at home working until enough money could be earned to reunite the family. Beyond survival, women also worked for the greater good of the family and the community, including providing for a better education for their own children and other relatives (as well as fictive kin), increasing the prospect of the family's being reunited in the North and of institution building. Despite the best intentions, however, family members often experienced long periods of separation; in some cases, they never reunited.

The wage/family connection on multiple levels resulted in a large proportion of the Black female population in the United States being in the labor force, often under the harshest conditions and in the lowest-paid jobs. However, neither the need (in some cases, the desire) nor the deplorable work conditions and wages prevented African American women, men, and children from contesting the exploitative nature of their work, work conditions, and relationships with their employers.

## WORK IDENTITY/CONSCIOUSNESS

As I have outlined in an earlier essay (Harley 1991), a work identity/consciousness among African American women (and other women of color) is forged within conflicting tensions between the status of Black women's work and White middle-class norms regarding women's proper roles, on the one hand, and Black women's self-definitions and need to work, on the other.

Forging a self-identity based upon "respectability" became part of Black women's resistance to subordination within and outside the workplace. In recounting her upbringing, activist Fannie Lou Hamer recalled: "There weren't many weeks passed that she [her mother] wouldn't tell me . . . you respect yourself as a Black child, and when you get grown, if I'm dead and gone, you respect yourself as a Black woman, and other people will respect you" (quoted in Giddings 1984, p. 288). Higginbotham (1993) notes, "By claiming respectability through their manners and morals, poor Black women boldly asserted the will and agency to define themselves outside the parameters of prevailing racist discourses" (p. 192). "Professionalizing domestic servants," according to Higginbotham, "epitomized the Baptist women's politics of respectability, since it constituted an effort to re-define and re-present black women's work identities as skilled workers rather than incompetent menials" (p. 212).

In her boundless efforts to dignify Black women's manual labor, Nannie Helen Burroughs typified the leadership of the Women's Convention of the National Baptist Convention in calling for the economic, political, and social advancement of the working poor. In her report to the 1905 annual session of the Women's Convention, Burroughs appealed to the working poor of the Black Baptist church when she asserted, "It does not require very much character nor brains to scorn labor, but it requires a great deal of both in this day of false pride to earn your bread by sweating for it and holding up your head above public sentiment, feeling in your heart that though you are a servant, yet you are a queen" (quoted in Higginbotham 1993, p. 207).

Their location in non-manufacturing jobs, coupled with unexamined assumptions about female passivity and the race- and gender-exclusionary policies and practices of the labor movement, resulted in the exclusion of Black women and men, and other people of color, historically from most unions and, furthermore, from much of the academic discourse on worker identity and working-class consciousness. Moreover, work-related actions attributed to the working-class identity of male workers are often ignored when exhibited by women, particularly those in low-status occupations. One reason for the failure to attribute a working-class identity to domestic servants, Marks (1993) argues, is that "domestic service is often depicted as merely an extension of the 'natural' female role and its agents judged to be without consciousness" (p. 153). She adds: "Because the job required deference, those who worked at it were considered deferential. Because mistresses often treated their maids as children, maids were thought to be childlike" (p. 154). Yet, whether by traditional markers (labor movement activities) or expanded definitions of working-class consciousness (various nonunionized acts of resistance), Black women, other women of color, and White women have revealed the nature and depth of their working-class consciousness (Romero 1992).

The development of a working-class consciousness outside the trade unionist movement was no less powerful as groups of women began to realize how they were being exploited in the workplace. Tera Hunter (1995) writes of the importance of "neighborhood networks" in organizing some 3,000 supporters for the "massive" washerwomen strike in Atlanta, Georgia, during the summer of 1881. In her analysis of the women involved in this strike and other acts of resistance, Hunter disputes the stereotype of Black domestic workers, laundresses, and maids "as passive victims of racial, sexual, and class oppression." Indeed, she shows how the washerwomen in the Atlanta strike "displayed a profound sense of political consciousness through the organization of this strike" (p. 343).

High unemployment rates, especially among African American and immigrant women during the Depression era, forced legions of Black female domestic workers to congregate on New York City street corners in search of employment. In the tradition of collective networking, often characteristic of the powerless, Black domestic workers joined forces to demand higher wages than their potential White employers wanted to pay (Kessler-Harris 1982).

Networks of working-class women and men gathered and disseminated information and served as organizers for collective and individual acts of resistance for other people of color as well. For example, Patricia Zavella (1987) describes how a critical consciousness developed when Chicana cannery workers learned that they were being assigned certain tasks and discouraged from applying for better jobs through the "work-based networks" they had formed.

From a personal understanding of her own exploitative work experiences, recognizing the conditions of poor Black people in Mississippi, and seeing how hard her mother worked (which brought tears to her eyes and a growing anger), Fannie Lou Hamer grew angrier with each passing year. Her personal campaign for autonomy and resistance of such wrongdoings took the form of "speaking up" about them. On one occasion she openly questioned how Black people could be expected to fight in the U.S. Army when they are so badly treated back home. The "real funny" look on the faces of the plantation owner and other White people who heard her led her to note: "I was rebelling in the only way I knew how to rebel. I just steady hoped for a chance that I could really lash out, and say what I had to say about what was going on in Mississippi" (quoted in Giddings 1984, p. 289). In August 1962, when she registered to vote against the wishes of the plantation owner and, in the process, lost her job as the plantation timekeeper, Hamer "spoke up" in deeds and words. Jones (1985) reports that Hamer "had the last word when her boss told her he did not want her to register to vote." Hamer responded, "But you don't understand. I'm not registerin' for you, I'm registerin' for me!" (quoted in Jones 1985, p. 287).

## WORK AND RESISTANCE

Public acknowledgment of the "hidden history" of Black working-class agency by literary and labor scholars, combined with expanded definitions of working-class consciousness, has contributed greatly to the growing theme of "resistance" in recent historical studies that document the space working African American women, men, and children have created to articulate their demands for decent wages, autonomy, and respect. Historians Deborah Gray White (1990), Tera Hunter (1995), Elizabeth Clark-Lewis (1991), Elsa Barkley Brown (1995), Jacqueline Jones (1985), Robin D. G. Kelley (1994), Rosalyn Terborg-Penn (1985), Melinda Chautevert (1997), Dolores Janiewski (1985), and others have discovered myriad patterns of resistance by Black women to work-related oppression, despite their location at the bottom of the occupational hierarchy and their exclusion historically from most labor unions and labor organizing.

A recurrent theme on the African American historical landscape involves the open and subtle ways in which African American working women and men protested the conditions they encountered. These acts of self-determination and resistance among enslaved women and men ranged from slowing down work to sabotaging equipment, running away, and performing tasks incompetently. With the abolition of chattel slavery, African American women built upon and added new oppositional tactics, including refusing to work, abruptly quitting, "speaking up," and engaging in widely publicized acts of resistance, from boycotts to strikes.

The race- and gender-exclusionary policies of most early-20th-century labor unions and Black women's large presence in traditionally "unorganizable" agricultural and domestic jobs did not discourage Black women from organizing in either unions or unionlike associations. Terborg-Penn, a pioneer in the field of Black women's history, has long embraced a diasporic approach to examining the experiences of Black women in the United States (Terborg-Penn, Harley, and Rushing 1988). In joining a small, but growing, group of scholars who document resistance among Black women workers outside and inside traditional labor union activities, Terborg-Penn emphasizes the African roots of Black Americans' work roles and organizational patterns. Like Terborg-Penn, other key African American women historians, such as Brown, Higginbotham, and Hunter, link Black women's labor associations in the United States to the collective survival strategies and networks that grew out of mutual aid and church associations within African American communities.

Terborg-Penn (1985) has documented the work of Victoria Earle Matthews and the White Rose Industrial Association, a late-19th-century Black women's organization, in easing the burden of Black wage-earning women in New York City. In conjunction with the White Rose Working Girls' Home, the association sought to protect Black female domestics, especially recent migrants from the South, from being either exploited by employment bureaus or forced into prostitution. In 1900, Mary Watson Webster organized the National Sewing Council, a self-help association for Black seamstresses and dressmakers in Washington, D.C.

In 1909, Burroughs, corresponding secretary of the Women's Auxiliary Convention to the National Baptist Convention and founding president of the National Training School for Women and Girls, sought to professionalize domestic service work and to train students in occupations ranging from printmaking and dressmaking to domestic science and clerical work. In an effort to improve the working conditions and wages of all Black wage-earning women, especially domestic servants, in 1920 Burroughs organized the National Association of Women Wage Earners in Washington, D.C. Two of the stated goals of this 1920s association were "to secure a wage that will enable women to live decently" and "to influence just legislation affecting women wage earners." Such goals resembled those of more typical trade unions; other goals focused on improving the efficiency of the worker.

The association, under Burroughs's leadership, differed from most trade unions in its focus on utilizing persuasive tactics to improve the lives of women wage earners. "To [Burroughs]," Barnett (1978) writes, "the interests of the capitalist could be reconciled with those of the worker if both were honest with each other" (p. 102). Despite its failure to critique capitalist exploitation of the working class, the short-lived National Association of Women Wage Earners nonetheless was part of the multifaceted strategy of Black working women to improve their lives as wage earners.

Union organizing along more traditional trade unionist lines did not elude Black working women, despite the many obstacles they encountered. Hunter (1995) demonstrates in her chronicle of the 1881 Atlanta strike by Black washerwomen that other groups of domestic servants and cooks joined the protest over low wages and poor working conditions. In their struggle for living wages and greater autonomy, Black laundresses mobilized members of the community through "door to door recruitment of adherents to their cause" and nightly ward meetings. By striking, Black laundresses "openly proclaimed the usually 'hidden transcript' " of working-class resistance and, in doing so, Hunter argues, revealed why they were the "most outspoken leaders in domestic workers documented in the South" (pp. 351-52). In the end, local institutional forces represented by the city government, the police, and landlords successfully defeated the strikers, but not the spirit that led them, despite the odds, to protest their working conditions in the first place.

The 1881 Atlanta strike, followed by other boycotts and strikes, both reflected the rising political and labor consciousness of Black women and left little doubt about how serious Black women were about improving their wages and work conditions. Thus by 1920, southern Black domestic workers had formed 10 local affiliates of the Hotel and Restaurant Employees' Union of the American Federation of Labor. In 1942, Jean Collier Brown organized the United Domestic Workers Local Industrial Union 1283, an affiliate of the CIO. Continuing this tradition, Carolyn Reed, a former domestic, organized the National Committee on Household Employment in New York City in 1979. Under the auspices of the National Urban League, this committee advocated on behalf of African American and Latina household workers.

Throughout the 20th century, trade union organizing has also been prevalent among other groups of women workers. Yoichi Shimatsu and Patricia Lee (1989) have examined the legacy of organizing among Asian-American women. Following the condemnation in the 1930s of the anti-Asian practices of the Central Labor Council of the Waiters Union by union president Hugo Ernst, Chinese support for the union grew. When the union struck in 1934, the entire Chinese union membership (all 150), including female elevator operators, joined the picket lines. Disparity in the wages and job assignments given to Asian and Latina hotel "room cleaners" in the 1970s prompted them to organize. In their struggle for better jobs and wages, they fought against the discriminatory practices of San Francisco hotels and the old-line labor leadership, "which had failed to keep up with the rapidly changing ethnic composition of the work force" (p. 388).

During a 2-year contract negotiation period from 1978 to 1980, rank-and-file hotel workers received an "unprecedented 44 percent wage increase" and a slight reduction in the workload but decided to strike anyway. Upon returning from a month-long strike for "dignity and respect," Shimatsu and Lee (1989) claim, the striking room cleaners exhibited "an improved sense of worth and self-esteem, and [hoped] that they would never again be discounted by either the management or the union" (p. 389).

Mexican women in Los Angeles are the subjects of Clementina Duron's (1984) research. She reports that "no less than 2,000 Mexican dressmakers" participated in a strike organized by the International Ladies' Garment Workers' Union (p. 156). Duron argues that this effort by

Mexican women directly challenges "the commonly held belief by some labor organizers at the time that Chicanas could not be organized in the workplace," as well as "the present-day notion that they have not played a significant role in Chicano labor history" (p. 145).

Beyond these acts of labor organizing, there are still other largely "hidden histories of resistance" among African American, Asian American, Latina American, and Native American women that have been captured in recent plays, films, scholarly publications, and literary works, as Kelley (1994), Brown (1995), and Baca Zinn and Dill (1994), among others, have noted. Although "hidden" from most employers and until recently from many scholars, Black working women, men, and children employed a variety of tactics to improve their work situations, increase their earnings, and gain respect as human beings. The strategies of resistance utilized by Black wage earners ranged from refusing to perform certain tasks to engaging in work slowdowns, speaking their minds (to a point just short of being fired), abruptly quitting, refusing to "live in," "blacklisting" the most egregious employers, and stealing (i.e., supplementing their low wages by taking more food than employers intended). Acts seemingly engaged in by individual domestics, cooks, laundresses, and factory workers belied the collective nature of African American resistance strategies. Sharing public space on city buses, common washing areas, and in church and mutual aid meetings, working women passed along the names of particularly egregious employers, shared resistance strategies, and formed networks of support (Kelley 1994; Brown 1995; Jones 1985; Hunter 1995).

Before most African American children earned their first wages as southern tobacco field hands or as domestics in private homes, they had been schooled in and often witnessed firsthand various forms of working-class resistance. The communal nature of African American culture was apparent in these resistance strategies. As Kelley (1994) points out, African Americans were part of a community that learned about "veiled protests against the daily indignities" through the songs (mainly religious) they sang collectively (p. 18). Collective support was central to the effective implementation of such strategies. Quitting and blacklisting, for instance, meant that no Black domestic would work for the employer who had been left or whose name had been given to other household workers (Hunter 1995).

In documenting the transformation of domestic service work from largely live-in service to day work, historian Elizabeth Clark-Lewis (1991) reveals how "low-status" working women resisted efforts by employers to control all their time, especially their leisure time, and worked to reduce incidents of sexual harassment. In a recent book, Tera Hunter (1997) offers an engaging analysis of the struggle between wage-earning Black women and their employers (as well as some members of the Black middle class) regarding the time and energy Black domestics expended dancing the night away in Atlanta nightclubs.

The need to exercise greater control over their time and work spaces motivated Black women to engage in an array of income-producing activities, ranging from washing to sewing, in their own homes. In the process, homework became an important site of Black women's resistance strategy. To combat sexual assaults, women factory workers devised a plethora of survival strategies "to resist or mitigate the daily physical and verbal abuse of their bodies, ranging from putting forth a sort of 'asexual' persona, to posturing as a 'crazy' person, to simply quitting" (Kelley 1994, p. 27). Homework could provide a safe harbor from the dirty and unhealthy work spaces reserved for Black factory workers and from the sexual harassment and personal indignities that were daily occurrences for African American women (Janiewski 1985).

## CONCLUSION

The history of African American women's resistance strategies reveals much about their work situations, the dialectic of domination and resistance, the work/family nexus, and the historical shortsightedness of male union leaders and most labor historians. An understanding of the working-class consciousness and work experiences of Black women is one site at which to address the intersection of work, culture, and the politics of oppression within internal Black communities and external communities. This analysis entails more scholars' speaking up and engaging in their own acts of resistance by challenging many of the assumptions within their own communities as well as those of fellow labor historians and feminist scholars. As we transform ourselves in the process, we can appreciate the historical transformation of women's work sites and conditions and have a fuller appreciation of the roles of race, gender, sexuality, and class in the resistance and survival strategies of working women, men, and children (E. B. Higginbotham 1995; E. Higginbotham 1994). The multilayered nature of Black women's oppression and responses begs for analytic frameworks that will attempt to address the totality of their lives and that speak to complexity within the larger racial community as well.

While posing new challenges, recent multicultural histories of women's work have been beneficial in helping historians sort out the complexities of Black women's work and avoid the conundrum of comparing Black and White women's work lives where no comparison truly exists. The recent scholarship on working women of color has served as a liberating force, encouraging a fuller exploration of similarities and differences with less fear of difference being interpreted as deviance from the mythical White female norm.

## NOTE

1. For an excellent analysis of the racial construction of these sites of difference—gender, class, sexuality—and "race as a double-voiced discourse," see Higginbotham (1995).

## REFERENCES

Baca Zinn, Maxine and Bonnie Thornton Dill, eds. 1994. *Women of Color in U.S. Society.* Philadelphia: Temple University Press.

Barnett, Evelyn Brooks (Higginbotham). 1978. "Nannie Helen Burroughs and the Education of Black Women." Pp. 97-108 in *The Afro-American Woman: Struggles and Images,* edited by Sharon Harley and Rosalyn Terborg-Penn. Port Washington, NY: Kennikat.

Billingsley, Andrew. 1992. *Climbing Jacob's Ladder: The Enduring Legacy of African-American Families.* New York: Simon & Schuster.

Brown, Elsa Barkley. 1995. "What Has Happened Here: The Politics of Difference in Women's History and Feminist Politics." Pp. 39-54 in *"We Specialize in the Wholly Impossible": A Reader in Black Women's History,* edited by Darlene Clark Hine, Linda Reed, and Wilma King. Brooklyn: Carlson.

———. 1994. "Negotiating and Transforming the Public Sphere: African American Political Life in the Transition from Slavery to Freedom." *Public Culture* 7:107-46.

Chautevert, Melinda. 1997. *Marching Together: The Women of the Brotherhood of Sleeping Car Porters.* Urbana: University of Illinois Press.

Clark-Lewis, Elizabeth. 1991. "This Work Had an End": African-American Domestic Workers in Washington, D.C., 1910-1940." Pp. 195-208 in *Women and Power in American History: A Reader,* Vol. 2, *From 1870,* edited by Kathryn K. Sklar and Thomas Dublin. Englewood Cliffs, NJ: Prentice Hall.

Duron, Clementina. 1984. "Mexican Women and Labor Conflict in Los Angeles: The ILGWU Dressmakers' Strike of 1933." *Aztlan: Journal of Chicano Studies Research* 5:145-61.

Franklin, V. P. 1984. *Black Self-Determination: A Cultural History of the Faith of the Fathers.* Westport, CT: Lawrence Hill.

Giddings, Paula. 1984. *When and Where I Enter: The Impact of Black Women on Race and Sex in America.* New York: William Morrow.

Glenn, Evelyn Nakano. 1985. "Racial Ethnic Women's Labor: The Intersection of Race, Gender, and Class Oppression." *Review of Radical Political Economics* 17:86-108.

Guerin-Gonzales, Camille. 1994. "Conversing across Boundaries of Race, Ethnicity, Class, Gender, and Region: Latino and Latina Labor History." *Labor History* 35:547-63.

Gwaltney, John Langston. 1971. *Drylongso: A Self-Portrait of Black America.* New York: Random House.

Harley, Sharon. 1981. "Black Women in the District of Columbia 1890-1920; Their Economic, Social and Institutional Activities." Ph.D. dissertation, Howard University.

———. 1991. "When Your Work Is Not Who You Are: The Development of a Working-Class Consciousness among Afro-American Women." Pp. 42-55 in *Gender, Class, Race, and Reform in the Progressive Era,* edited by Noralee Frankel and Nancy S. Dye. Lexington: University Press of Kentucky.

Harley, Sharon and Rosalyn Terborg-Penn, eds. 1978. *The Afro-American Woman: Struggles and Images.* Port Washington, NY: Kennikat.

Higginbotham, Elizabeth. 1994. "Black Professional Women: Job Ceiling and Employment Sectors." Pp. 113-31 in *Women of Color in U.S. Society,* edited by Maxine Baca Zinn and Bonnie Thornton Dill. Philadelphia: Temple University Press.

Higginbotham, Evelyn Brooks. 1993. *Righteous Discontent: The Women's Movement in the Black Baptist Church, 1880-1920.* Cambridge, MA: Harvard University Press.

———. 1995. "African-American Women's History and the Metalanguage of Race." Pp. 3-24 in *"We Specialize in the Wholly Impossible": A Reader in Black Women's History,* edited by Darlene Clark Hine, Linda Reed, and Wilma King. Brooklyn: Carlson.

Hunter, Tera W. 1995. "Domination and Resistance: The Politics of Wage Household Labor in New South Atlanta." Pp. 343-57 in *"We Specialize in the Wholly Impossible": A Reader in Black Women's History,* edited by Darlene Clark Hine, Linda Reed, and Wilma King. Brooklyn: Carlson.

———. 1997. *To Joy My Freedom: Southern Black Women, Lives and Labor after the Civil War.* Cambridge, MA: Harvard University Press.

Jackson, Giles B. and D. Webster Davis. [1908] 1971. *The Industrial History of the Negro Race of the United States.* New York: Books for Libraries.

Janiewski, Dolores, E. 1985. *Sisterhood Denied: Race, Gender, and Class in a New South Community.* Philadelphia: Temple University Press.

Jones, Jacqueline. 1985. *Labor of Love, Labor of Sorrow: Black Women, Work, and the Family from Slavery to the Present.* New York: Basic Books.

Kelley, Robin D. G. 1994. *Race Rebels: Culture, Politics, and the Black Working Class.* New York: Free Press.

Kessler-Harris, Alice. 1982. *Out to Work: A History of Wage-Earning Women in the United States.* New York: Oxford University Press.

Mann, Susan A. 1990. "Slavery, Sharecropping, and Sexual Inequality." Pp. 133-57 in *Black Women in America,* edited by Michelene R. Malson, Elisabeth Mudimbe-Boyi, Jean F. O'Barr, and Mary Wyer. Chicago: University of Chicago Press.

Marks, Carole C. 1993. "The Bone and Sinew of the Race: Black Women, Domestic Service and Labor Migration." *Marriage and Family Review* 19:149-73.

Miller, Kelly. 1908. *Race Adjustments: Essays on the Negro in America.* New York: Neale.

Moynihan, Daniel Patrick. 1965. *The Negro Family: The Case for National Action.* Washington, DC: U.S. Department of Labor, Office of Policy Planning and Research.

Reagon, Bernice Johnson. 1990. "Women as Culture Carriers in the Civil Rights Movement: Fannie Lou Hamer." In *Women in the Civil Rights Movement,* edited by Vicki L. Crawford, Jacqueline A. Rouse, and Barbara Woods. Bloomington: Indiana University Press.

Romero, Mary. 1992. *Maid in the U.S.A.* New York: Routledge.

Shimatsu, Yoichi and Patricia Lee. 1989. "Dust and Dishes: Organizing Workers." Pp. 386-94 in *Making Waves: An Anthology of Writings by and about Asian American Women,* edited by Asian Women United of California. Boston: Beacon.

Steady, Filomina C. 1981. "Female Employment and Family Organization in West Africa." Pp. 49-64 in *The Black Woman Cross-Culturally,* edited by Filomina C. Steady. Cambridge, MA: Schenkman.

Terborg-Penn, Rosalyn. 1985. "Survival Strategies among African American Women Workers: A Continuing Process." Pp. 139-55 in *Women, Work and Protest: A Century of U.S. Women's Labor History,* edited by Ruth Milkman. Boston: Routledge & Kegan Paul.

Terborg-Penn, Rosalyn, Sharon Harley, and Andrea Benton Rushing, eds. 1988. *Women in Africa and the African Diaspora.* Washington, DC: Howard University Press.

Tienda, Marta and Jennifer Glass. 1985. "Household Structure and Labor Force Participation of Black, Hispanic, and White Mothers." *Demography* 22:381-94.

White, Deborah Gray. 1985. *Ar'n't I a Woman? Female Slaves in the Plantation South.* New York: W. W. Norton.

———. 1990. "Female Slaves: Sex Roles and Status in the Antebellum Plantation South." Pp. 22-33 in *Unequal Sisters: A Multicultural Reader in U.S. Women's History,* edited by Ellen C. DuBois and Vicki L. Ruiz. New York: Routledge.

Zavella, Patricia. 1987. *Women's Work and Chicano Families: Cannery Workers of the Santa Clara Valley.* Ithaca, NY: Cornell University Press.

# PART II

# Manufacturing and Domestic Service

Both factory work and private household work have played a significant part in the employment histories of women from working-class, working-poor, immigrant, and minority ethnic/racial communities. Moreover, over the past century the two kinds of occupations have been closely related, with household labor providing labor market elasticity and absorbing some of the reserve army of the unemployed during downturns in the business cycle. Although laborers in factories are frequently exposed to health hazards not found in private households, employment in factories offers autonomy and other attractions that are absent from domestic service. Factory work has traditionally offered women independence, better pay than domestic work, and social security, medical, and other benefits. However, factory jobs have not been universally available.

Racial and ethnic hierarchies have been replicated in the composition of factory and domestic workforces. When factory jobs were first opened to women in the United States, native-born White women were the first group to leave domestic service en masse; they were quickly followed by European immigrant women. Even after emancipation, Black women dominated in domestic work in the South, but in the Northeast they eventually entered the factories and replaced European immigrant women. The ethnic and racial change was most dramatic between 1890 and 1920, when the number of White female servants declined by one-third and the number of Black female domestics increased by 43%. Between 1910 and 1920, foreign-born women declined from 46% to 36% of the domestic labor force. In the Southwest, domestic service dominated the field of possibilities for Mexican and Mexican American women through World War II.

Evidence of the function of domestic service in absorbing surplus labor can be seen in times of economic crisis. The Depression temporarily reversed the invasion-succession process described above. By 1930, native-born White women had increased their share of the domestic labor market to 20%, and foreign-born women had increased to 41%. Thus, in the early 1930s, we find an anomalous situation in which three out of every five domestics in the Deep South were White. This was a short-term perturbation of the dominant trend, however. By 1940, native-born White women had returned to their families or had found better jobs; they constituted only 11% of the domestic labor force. Today, racial hierarchies continue to shape domestic occupations. Both inside and outside the underground economy, women of color, many of whom are immigrants, hold the majority of low-paid positions. Latina immigrant women are the largest group entering the occupation, particularly in major urban areas, including Washington, D.C., New York, Chicago, and Los Angeles.

Manufacturing and domestic service offer ideal sites for examining the impacts of ethnicity and race on the class experiences of working women. But the ethnicity-, race-, and class-related experiences of women employed in manufacturing and domestic service are only one focus of the studies in this section. Each of the following chapters also inquires into other mitigating factors. Joyce Chinen's discussion in Chapter 3, concerning the manufacture of Hawaiian "alohawear," frames the issues in an industry evolving out of colonialism and immigration resulting from the labor needs of capitalism. In Chapter 4, Louise Lamphere and Patricia Zavella investigate the levels of resistance among workers who share similar class positions in manufacturing but differ in ethnicity. In Chapter 5, Pierrette Hondagneu-Sotelo includes citizenship status in her study of working-class immigrant Mexican women's experiences in the labor force.

Chapters 3 and 4 report findings from research on different aspects of the manufacturing sector and the family lives of working women. Chinen employs a macro-level analysis of the garment industry to describe the historical development of a gendered and racialized workforce within a region that is not predominantly White. She traces the process by which indigenous cloth production became commodified while simultaneously the skilled labor force in Hawaii was becoming proletarianized. Placing the creation of alohawear in a historical context, Chinen outlines the role that colonialization played in shaping the hierarchy of workers and the connection to Hawaii's booming tourist industry. She identifies three different groups of workers in order to highlight important ethnic, racial, immigrant, class, and age characteristics: old-timers, recent immigrants, and young locals. She then shows how these groups have changed over time. The impact of the industry's colonial history in shaping its structure becomes evident in contemporary descriptions of young locals who receive state-supported vocational-technical education in the field of fashion design at community colleges and state universities. They are hired in design, pattern making, and grading, which serves to separate them from the other women workers without allowing them entrée to positions of management or ownership or to other highly paid professional jobs in the industry. Chinen identifies potential mechanisms for unionization and collective resistance, but she suggests that most resistance remains at an individual level.

In Chapter 4, Lamphere and Zavella present a microanalysis of management control and forms of resistance in apparel and electronics firms in a region that has become increasingly White since U.S. colonization. Focusing on issues of resistance, the labor process, and management control in apparel and electronics firms in Albuquerque, New Mexico, the authors investigate a range of resistance strategies and management control methods. Their study encompasses three plants employing non-immigrant, English-speaking, and high school-educated Chicanas and White women. These women work side by side in the plants, receiving similar wages, benefits, promotions, and job security. Lamphere and Zavella compare levels of resistance within hierarchical management and participative structures to the workers' economic role in their families, arguing that neither race/ethnicity nor the workers' financial contributions to their families' livelihoods determine individual or collective resistance strategies. The hypothesis that workers with the greatest economic need would be least likely to resist was not supported by their study. Instead, hierarchical management was met by individual rather than collective resistance, and the participative structure was resisted by both individual and collective strategies. The structure of the labor process and plantwide work culture offered different inducements to workers, who responded from their place in the production process.

In the final chapter in this section, Hondagneu-Sotelo investigates the importance of citizenship alongside race, class, and gender in analyzing women's access to formal and informal labor markets. In her study of undocumented Mexican immigrant women employed as private household workers, she demonstrates how legislation shapes workers' legal status and thus constrains employment options, making Latina immigrants distinctively disenfranchised and vulnerable in U.S. society. Exploring the employment strategies of Mexican immigrant women in the San Francisco Bay Area, Sotelo describes how industries are able to exist in both formal and informal sectors by exploiting workers' lack of legal status. Simultaneously, her study illustrates how immigrants create employment opportunities and regulate the informal sector through social networks established in the immigrant community. By analyzing the effects of the 1986 Immigration Reform and Control Act on individual choices, Hondagneu-Sotelo makes visible the fluidity of citizenship that can change formally within a worker's lifetime and informally through the establishment of community ties. Comparing the circumstances under which the Mexican immigrant women she studied accepted live-in positions with how they moved into day work employed by several employers, she demonstrates the efficacy of resistance strategies and community ties in mobilizing resources to improve working conditions. Subcontracting arrangements between immigrant women constitute one very effective strategy for mitigating the effect of undocumentation over time. Women with more experience and established employer networks provide training and employment leads to less experienced women in exchange for labor, thus increasing the experienced women's pay. Constantly adapting to legislative constraints and changing conditions, immigrant women struggle individually to improve their working conditions and employment options.

# 3

# The Evolution of Alohawear: Colonialism, Race, Ethnicity, Class, and Gender in Hawaii's Garment Industry

## JOYCE N. CHINEN

This chapter examines the situation of Asian Pacific American women who work in garment production in Hawaii. It describes the historical development and current labor force of the garment manufacturing industry in Hawaii vis-à-vis other locales and then examines the consequences that employment in the garment industry has had for contemporary workers. Although women have been the primary producers of clothing throughout Hawaiian history, changes in the process of clothing production have meant that the racial and ethnic characteristics of these women workers have shifted over time. This chapter argues that both oppression and empowerment characterize the lives of women who work in this industry.

AUTHOR'S NOTE: I thank Mary Romero, Elizabeth Higginbotham, Ann Stromberg, Barbara Gutek, Laurie Larwood, and the anonymous reviewers of this volume for their helpful comments on earlier drafts of my chapter.

Hawaii tourism brochures depict White heterosexual vacationers against a backdrop of beaches, sunsets, and rain forests. Attired in "alohawear"—comfortable, colorfully printed sport shirts and dresses—tourists relax while people of color serve them. In this chapter, I examine the garment manufacturing industry in Hawaii and its predominantly non-White female labor force, guided by four questions: How have women of color, particularly Asian Pacific American women, become the labor force of this industry? What are their working conditions? How do the workers experience, understand, and respond to their working conditions? How do these workers' domestic and marketplace lives interact?

Hawaii's multiethnic population, labor force participation rates of married women which have been consistently higher than those in the rest of the United States throughout much of the 20th century (Chinen 1984; Geschwender and Carroll-Seguin 1988; Bill 1995), and historically transformed state forms (i.e., from chiefdoms to kingdom, to republic, to U.S. territory, to U.S. state) provide a good social laboratory in which to study how political, economic, cultural, and social forces converge to construct racial/ethnic, gender, and class relations. After discussing the literature that informs this study, I will briefly describe my methodology. I will then provide some background on Hawaii and on how the garment industry developed there, and then discuss their relevance for the contemporary situation of garment workers. Finally, I will discuss some of the garment workers' own perspectives on their marketplace and household work.

This study stems from historical studies of U.S. garment workers and from the recent literature on racial formation (Omi and Winant 1994) and feminist studies (Collins 1990; Glenn 1992; Romero 1992). Although contemporary garment workers in Hawaii and the continental United States are predominantly people of color, the racialization of the labor force occurred relatively late in the 20th century, and was built upon the ethnic base formed by Jewish, Italian, and other mostly Southern and Eastern Europeans.

In colonial America, clothing production was a gendered, household-based activity; it moved to factories in the late 18th and early 19th centuries, incorporating native-born Euro-American girls into wage work. Mass production of ready-to-wear clothing became possible in the mid-19th and early 20th centuries with the technological development of the sewing machine, the incorporation of uneducated native-born and immigrant Euro-American women into the industry's labor force (i.e., it became both *proletarianized* and *gendered*), and the industry's institutionalization of factory and contractor firm arrangements (Kessler-Harris 1982; Jensen and Davidson 1984; Amott and Matthaei 1991). The large-scale strikes and labor organizing drives across the nation in many different industries, known as the Great Uprisings, in the period of 1900 to the 1930s brought unionization to the industrial labor force. This movement improved pay and working conditions, but the increasing availability of cheaper labor outside of the industrial Northeast since the 1970s has brought deindustrialization and restructuring.

In the *maquiladoras* (contracting firms) along the U.S.-Mexico border, the export-processing zones in Asia and Latin America, and the newly returning sweatshops in the garment industry centers of New York, San Francisco, and Los Angeles, exploitative conditions like those that preceded unionization have reappeared in the late 20th century. Fueled by global competition, computerized management information systems, communications technology, and capital mobility, these unstable, undesirable, low-wage jobs are filled by Third World laborers and immigrant women and men of color (Chapkis and Enloe 1983; Jensen and Davidson 1984; Lamphere 1987; Enloe 1989; Tiano 1990; Louie 1992; Bonacich, Cheng, Chinchilla, Hamilton, and Ong 1994).

These changes in the organization of garment production and in the composition of the industry's labor force point out how economic and political forces socially construct racial and gender categories (Omi and Winant 1994), and how women's work experiences reflect that gender, race/ethnicity, and class are "interconnected, historical processes of domination and subordination" (Amott and Matthaei 1991, p. 11).

However, domination and subordination are not only socially constructed, they are also only part of the story for racial/ethnic minority working-class women; resistance and empowerment are also important elements. Collins (1990) notes that oppression occurs at several levels: individual consciousness, group or community, and institutional or societal. She also shows that in occupying subordinated statuses, African American women have created an experience-based epistemology that includes a consciousness of *both* oppression *and* empowerment. The resulting "Black feminist thought" includes the individual's refusal to accept her subjugator's worldview, the reliance on and building of community in response to oppression, and sometimes challenges to established institutions.

## METHODS

I used primary and secondary data sources to examine changes in Hawaii's garment industry. For most of the historical analysis prior to 1970, I relied on a comprehensive descriptive history of the Hawaiian garment industry by Fundaburk (1965). My analyses of the situation since the 1970s are based on archival sources, such as state government documents, and on semistructured interviews that I conducted with four state agency officials and 37 manufacturing firm owners and managers in the 1984-1986 period. The interviews and government documents provided information on state activities, firm histories, changes in firms' production processes, and the effects of state actions on the firms. Additionally, once I had identified patterns and effects, I selected two representative manufacturing firms from which I interviewed a sample of workers ($N = 25$). Throughout this chapter, I use the pseudonyms "Casually Chic" and "Tropical Sunsets" to refer to these two firms.

With management's permission, I gave a 10-minute presentation at each of the two factories in which I introduced myself and the research project to the workers during their 30-minute lunch break and solicited volunteers by passing around a sign-up sheet. I then contacted and interviewed the volunteers on weekends or after work, either at the respondents' homes or at a nearby coffee shop. The semistructured interviews ran about 2-3 hours in length and covered the respondents' family and educational backgrounds, employment histories, and working conditions, including any changes in the past 5 years and the consequences of those changes on their work and home lives. Pseudonyms are used throughout this chapter to preserve the respondents' anonymity and confidentiality.

My sample of 25 garment industry workers represents about 25% of each firm's employees and approximates the existing demographic distributions within both of the firms, based on the information provided by the managers in the earlier interviews. The sample consists of 23 women and 2 men, with an age range of 22 to 73 years. The ethnic distribution is as follows: 14 Japanese, 5 Filipina, 2 Chinese, 1 Caucasian, and 3 mixed race. The garment industry labor force in Hawaii is composed of three distinct Asian Pacific groups that reflect changes in labor force recruitment: I refer to these groups here as *old-timers, recent immigrants,* and *young locals.* The old-timers were Nisei (second-generation Japanese American), and at the time of the interviews in 1986, most were in their 60s. Most had no more than 8 years of formal schooling, and had spent most of their employed lives (more than 20 years) in the garment industry, having entered during the industry's growth years. They had been married for more than 25 years to spouses who were retired from largely skilled blue-collar jobs. All but one had adult children.

All but one of the recent immigrants were Filipina, and all but one were married. Ranging in age from 25 to 45, most had immigrated to join their families in Hawaii in the 1970s, after the 1965 immigration law lifted the restrictive quotas imposed on Asian countries. Most had completed high school, and a few even had some college education. However, though they spoke English, a few had difficulty with the language. Many had dressmaking skills that they had learned in the Philippines, and family and friends provided initial employment leads.

In contrast to the old-timers and the recent immigrants, the young locals were generally under 30 years of age, unmarried, third-generation Asian or Pacific Americans, and tended to be children of interethnic parentage. Most lived in extended kin households, partly because of Hawaii's expensive housing situation and partly because of family situations that included abuse by or illness of a family member. Additionally, most of the young locals had received formal technical training for jobs in the garment industry from a local state-supported community college and had entered the industry through the education-industry network (i.e., through instructors or former students with whom they had forged friendships in their fashion technology classes).

## BACKGROUND ON HAWAII

Hawaii is the only state in the United States where White people are a numerical minority. In 1990, 33.4% of the state's population were *haole* (Caucasian), but about 30% of those were transient. About 2.5% were African American and .5% were Native American. Of the 63% Asian and Pacific Island American population, Japanese predominated, making up 22.3% of the population, followed by Filipinos at 15.2%, Native Hawaiians at 12.5%, Chinese at 6.2%, Koreans at 2.2%, Samoans at 1.4%, Vietnamese at 0.5%, and other Asian Pacific groups at 1.5% (U.S. Bureau of the Census 1992, Table 3), although the Hawaii Health Surveillance Program's sample survey suggests that part-Hawaiians have been undercounted and places their proportion at 18.0% (Hawaii Department of Business, Economic Development, and Tourism 1994,

p. 37). Several important social, political, and economic factors have shaped this multiracial, multiethnic society (Daws 1968; Fuchs 1961; Kuykendall 1938, 1953; Beechert 1985; Dorton 1986; Kent 1983; Trask 1984; Manicas 1995).

Before Hawaii became the 50th U.S. state in 1959, it was a territory of the United States, a republic, and, still earlier, an independent kingdom. Located in the northern Pacific, the Hawaiian Islands were settled before 500 A.D. by migrating Polynesians. By 1778, when British Captain James Cook "discovered" these islands, the Hawaiian population, conservatively estimated to be 250,000 (Schmitt 1977; Nordyke 1989), or nearly a million by more radical historians (Stannard 1989), was organized into four major chiefdoms. Massive depopulation followed Hawaii's integration into the East-West mercantile capitalist trade. Its chiefdoms were consolidated into a kingdom in 1795, and by 1832, its population had fallen to about 130,000 because of introduced diseases, warfare, and forced neglect of traditional food production for commodity production (Beechert 1985; Stannard 1989; Kent 1983).

New England Congregationalists and emerging business interests laid the foundation for the American colonization of Hawaii. By the mid-1800s, they had reshaped the political system along U.S. lines, dismantled the traditional land tenure system, and developed the infrastructure for capitalist agriculture. Five heavily interlocked corporations, known as the Big Five, dominated the political economy. When Hawaiians tried to reassert control in 1893, business interests, aided by the U.S. military, overthrew the Hawaiian monarchy, set up a republic, and engineered the 1898 annexation of Hawaii by the United States.

From the mid-1800s through the 1930s, Hawaii's sugar plantation system imported labor from all parts of the world, but especially from Asia. Chinese, Japanese, Korean, and Filipino laborers were successively incorporated into the plantation labor force, while Hawaiians were increasingly pushed to the marginal sectors of the economy. This produced a racially and ethnically stratified, plantation-dominated society: Euro-American (*haole*) elites; various European immigrants as managers, technicians, and supervisors; and Asians as workers (Geschwender, Carroll-Seguin, and Brill 1988; Fuchs 1961; Manicas 1995). Members of each ethnic group gradually left the plantations for better opportunities in urban areas, but it was the labor movement and the rise of the Democratic Party that truly transformed Hawaii's political economy after World War II.

Hawaii's Democratic Party (a coalition of organized labor, returning Japanese American veterans, and party stalwarts) seized political power in the 1950s and helped to raise the socioeconomic status of the descendants of Asian immigrant labor. The Big Five corporations (the old business oligarchy) responded by moving operations overseas, with continental U.S. and foreign capital, mostly from Japan, filling the void. Tourism and the military have now eclipsed the sugar and pineapple industries. Since the 1960s, massive in-migration from the continental United States, Asia (the Philippines, Korea, China, Hong Kong, Taiwan, and Southeast Asia), and from the Pacific Basin (Samoa, Tonga, and Micronesia) has added to the ethnic stratification of the islands. Because land ownership is highly concentrated and most goods imported, housing is expensive and the cost of living is about 35% higher than the U.S. average; thus most households in Hawaii require multiple earners (Chinen 1984; Geschwender and Carroll-Seguin 1988). Finally, encroaching urbanization and the successes of progressive social movements of the 1970s-1980s have led Native Hawaiians to organize around land, water, religious practice, and, increasingly, sovereignty issues (Trask 1984). The historical and current conditions of the garment manufacturing industry should be viewed within this sociohistorical context.

## HISTORICAL DEVELOPMENT OF HAWAII'S GARMENT INDUSTRY

The development of Hawaii's garment industry both parallels and deviates from that of the mainland U.S. garment industry. In Hawaii, the industry has proceeded through four periods (the preindustrial, early industrial, World War II to statehood, and the contemporary era), with each period bringing changes in the social organization of production (Fundaburk 1965; Chinen 1989).

### Preindustrial Period

Native Hawaiian clothing in the preindustrial period before Western contact was fashioned from *kapa,* a fibrous cloth produced from the inner bark of mulberry plants that was soaked in water, pounded, formed into sheets, and block printed. Women used indigenous materials and intergenerationally transmitted technical knowledge and skills to produce this highly valued cloth for use by members of the extended family (so the cloth had use value) rather than for sale in a market to derive profits (giving it exchange value).

Integration into the East-West mercantile capitalist trade introduced foreign fabrics of silk, satin, and gingham into Hawaii. The missionaries' puritanical dress code forced Hawaiians into suits and long, unfitted dresses called *muumuu* and introduced sewing as a production technique. Dressmaking remained mostly household based, but tailor shops gradually appeared in urban areas in the latter half of the 19th century. They sporadically employed mostly Portuguese immigrants as needlewomen and paid them $1.00-$3.00 for an 8½-hour day, three to six times a year (Blascoer 1912). Thus the social organization of garment production changed from Native Hawaiian women using indigenous materials and traditional techniques for household use, to using Western fabric sources and styles, dressmaking or tailoring techniques, and the wage labor of European immigrant women for sale to customers for profit.

**Early Industrial Period (1922-1940)**

Four developments characterize the early industrial period of garment manufacturing in Hawaii: the establishment of the first clothing factory in 1922, the growth in imported and ready-made clothing, the birth of tourism, and the proliferation of home sewing.

Proletarianization occurs when skilled work that was formerly autonomously performed is transformed, separating conception and execution functions, with salaried managers performing the former functions and wage workers performing the latter functions under the direction of managers (Mills 1956). The establishment of clothing factories beginning in 1922 signaled the proletarianization of garment producers as they became wage workers.

Additionally, once the social organization for mass-produced ready-to-wear apparel was available, the markets for these products expanded from primarily agricultural workers' clothing and military uniforms to encompass brightly printed "aloha" shirts and dresses for the developing tourist and continental U.S. export markets. Although the labor force was still female, its racial-ethnic composition changed from predominantly European (Portuguese) to increasingly Asian, as Japanese and Chinese workers moved out of the plantations and into urban areas. Most of these workers were young Japanese American women informally instructed in dressmaking by the small entrepreneurial sewing schools that proliferated in the 1920s-1950s.

## World War II to Statehood

Martial law, imposed on Hawaii from 1941 to 1944, restricted "non-essential" shipping between Hawaii and the continental United States. Garment manufacturers were unable to get their products to their export markets, and retailers faced difficulty securing merchandise. Manufacturers adapted to the crisis by subduing their prints and producing for the local retail market, and retailers by marketing more locally produced clothing. This wholesaler-retailer arrangement became the foundation for postwar growth in the industry.

Garment manufacturing firms multiplied after the war as innovations in fabric, design, and printing technology stimulated the market for alohawear both locally and abroad. Asian women, mostly Nisei, dominated the garment industry's labor force, because nearly 40% of Hawaii's 1940 population was Japanese. These women were channeled into this industry because they possessed both limited formal education and dressmaking skills intended for use in their future homemaking roles. After getting married and having children, they returned to become the part of the workforce referred to here as the old-timers.

In 1949, the Hawaii Garment Manufacturers Guild, a trade association, was formed to address marketing and labor force creation. Between 1955 and 1964, the industry grew rapidly. Its annual wholesale volume climbed from $7 million to $20 million, expanding in both local and export markets. Securing labor and capital was a major concern and became even more problematic with export market expansion. However, access to capital eased somewhat when the 1954 Democrat-dominated legislature increased the number of bank charters and opened up the banking industry in Hawaii. Unlike their continental U.S. counterparts, garment workers in Hawaii remained mostly nonunionized.

## Contemporary Situation

After statehood was obtained in 1959, tourism became Hawaii's leading industry, supporting related industries such as alohawear and other souvenir manufacturing. Throughout the 1960s, expanding markets and low capital and technology requirements encouraged garment firms to proliferate. This aggravated competition, depressed prices, and reduced profitability. By the mid-1970s, these patterns, coupled with growing foreign imports and knockoffs (imitations) of locally successful designs, caused established markets to decline. Individually, Hawaiian garment manufacturers responded to this crisis by segmenting and/or specializing in men's, women's, or children's upscale or budget product markets; formalizing operations within the workplace; contracting out sewing (including to home sewers); and extending firm operations into the retail area. These efforts were met with limited success.

In 1977, faced with declining tax revenue and jobs, the state of Hawaii's Department of Planning and Economic Development (DPED) brought together members of the Fashion Guild trade association in two seminars. The director of the DPED's Economic Division reminded the attenders that "the State cannot deal with you individually. . . . We could do all sorts of things for this industry together if you support your organization." The seminars provided the impetus for a DPED-underwritten comprehensive $100,000 study of the local garment industry for the industry's trade organization (Kurt Salmon and Associates 1979), the findings and recommendations of which were to justify state-subsidized product marketing and production programs. In the marketing area, DPED underwrote part of the cost of putting on trade shows that featured Hawaiian products locally, on the mainland United States, and in Europe.

On the production side, the Garment Industry Training Program (GITP), which operated from 1980 to 1983, was designed to enhance the knowledge base and skills of both management and workers in the industry. It trained new power machine operators for the industry (most of whom were immigrants or refugees); provided production seminars on costing, contracting, marker making, and so on; and offered subsidized industrial engineering services to eight firms. Finally, the GITP facilitated rationalizing fashion education in the state-supported 2-year (technical) and 4-year (baccalaureate) higher-education institutions.

My interviews with manufacturing firm owners indicate that newer firms with clearer and more future-oriented market niches were more likely than older firms to have received the industrial engineering services and to have benefited from the state's activities (Chinen 1989). For example, Casually Chic, which was started in 1974 as a partnership between two friends who had both been trained in and held degrees from the Fashion Design and Merchandising Program at University of Hawaii, had expanded its operations to two plants and had received several fashion industry design awards. This firm had applied for and received industrial engineering consulting services. In contrast, Tropical Sunsets had been started toward the end of World War II by a couple and their friends without any sewing or industrial background because "the Army and Navy guys—they would go down to Hotel Street and buy all kinds of souvenirs—they would buy anything." The company's business and workforce had expanded during the boom years of the 1950s and 1960s, but had been severely reduced in the 1970s, from more than 65 workers to 28, and from 5 to 4 days of production per week. The state, therefore, was supporting the rationalization and expansion of those firms whose production, marketing, and sales were most likely to grow.

## WORKING CONDITIONS
## OF GARMENT WORKERS

The relationship of the state to the firms in which workers are employed is also important. Although the proportions of recent immigrants in the two firms examined here are about equal, a greater proportion of young locals are employed at Casually Chic, the successfully developing firm, than at Tropical Sunsets. Most of these younger, fashion technology-trained workers reported that they had been referred to their present jobs by their instructors or former classmates. Thus successfully developing firms enjoyed an advantage in terms of access to the newly developed pool of skilled labor.

Despite differences in their firms' trajectories, workers in both firms were paid very low wages. In June 1986, the average hourly wage for the garment industry was $4.53, or only $1.18 over the minimum wage (Hawaii Department of Labor and Industrial Relations, 1986; Hawaii Department of Business, Economic Development, and Tourism 1988). When asked about their feelings about their wage levels in their inter-views, most workers said that they felt their wages should be higher. Sharon, who sews for Casually Chic, summed up the sentiments of many workers when she said, "Our job is a skilled job—for the amount of things we have to do, I think it's really underpaid."

Hawaii's garment workers' complaints about their low wages are not based in idle dissatisfaction or perceptual problems. Table 3.1 shows that although garment industry pay increased from $89.08 per week in 1972 to $169.37 per week in 1986, when these workers were inter-viewed, the relative gap between garment workers' pay and the amount required to sustain even a low-income budget for a family of four had increased by 10% during this period. Thus garment workers had to

**TABLE 3.1** Household Budgets for Family of Four, 1972 and 1986

| | 1972 | | 1986 | |
|---|---|---|---|---|
| | Yearly $ | Weekly $ | Yearly $ | Weekly $ |
| **Type of budget** | | | | |
| Low | 9,118 | 175.34 | 21,534 | 414.12 |
| Intermediate | 13,617 | 261.86 | 34,032 | 654.46 |
| High | 20,579 | 395.75 | 53,793 | 1,034.48 |
| **Garment industry wages** | | 89.08 | | 169.37 |
| **% gap between garment industry and low budget** | | 49.2 | | 59.1 |

SOURCES: Hawaii Department of Business, Economic Development, and Tourism (1984, p. 372) and Hawaii Department of Labor and Industrial Relations (1986, pp. 77-79E).

contend not only with generally low wages, but also with increases in the cost of living that had outpaced increases in their wages.

In addition, most of what is included in the workers' meager benefits packages is required by state law. Because of the 1974 State of Hawaii Pre-paid Health Insurance Act, which mandates that employers offer health insurance to employees working more than 20 hours per week, all of the garment workers have access to health insurance, workers' compensation, and eight paid holidays. Beyond that, the benefits paid to workers vary by the firm for which they work. Benefits are only slightly better at Casually Chic, which offers life insurance and profit-sharing programs; Tropical Sunsets does not. However, workers reported that they had not received any profit sharing in the previous 2 years. Workers at both firms also reported that they enjoy informal benefits, such as discount prices on surplus fabric. Additionally, at Casually Chic, workers have permission to use the garment patterns and the power machines for their personal sewing before or after work hours.

The increasing volatility in markets, sales, and profitability that has intensified competition in the garment industry at both the local and global levels (Bonacich et al. 1994) has also increased stress among garment workers, albeit in different ways. At Casually Chic, 6-day workweeks are common. For these workers, this means larger paychecks, but also physical exhaustion from mandatory overtime and heavy production quotas. At Tropical Sunsets, fewer work hours per week (with the workweek reduced to 4 days) meant shrinking paychecks and increased anxieties about eventual job loss.

Additionally, although safety and health hazards exist in both firms, the crowding and heavy production volume made them more prevalent at Casually Chic. In my interviews with firm owners/managers, I observed that this plant appeared to be much more congested than other plants I visited. My observations were supported by the concerns of workers such as Laura, a layer and cutter at Casually Chic, who had already accidentally cut herself: "The aisles are narrow, and people constantly walk behind you. The fabric is slippery and [pieces] can slip on the floor, and we sweep [the floors] only during the 2:30 break. There are big bolts [of fabric] under the table and they stick out—it's dangerous."

Others workers noted that fumes from increasingly used synthetic fabrics and dyes may be responsible for health problems. Occupational health studies have linked the inhalation of fabric dust to byssinosis (brown lung disease). Sheila, a seamstress at Casually Chic, discussed these and other problems in her work environment:

> The dust, [it's] certain material only, mostly flock material. [Wearing] the kerchief helps. Six to seven out of the twelve [workers in the sewing area] off and on use kerchiefs. [Also, the] chemicals on the fabrics. My eyes water and get red from the smell. It was cold when I was on the old machine [because] it was right by the vent where the cold air comes. I had to cut my buys' old socks to put over [points to her wrists]. It was like rheumatism.

## WORKERS' RESPONSES
## TO THESE CONDITIONS

If low wages, meager benefits, and high stress characterize working conditions in the garment industry in Hawaii, why do workers remain in these jobs? The reasons differ for each of the three groups of workers. Limited economic opportunities are only part of their story, for woven throughout the interviews are themes of intrinsic satisfaction in their work, personal accomplishment, and empowerment.

Some, like Rosita, who works in the design department of Casually Chic, emphasized "the creativity of the work—trying to come out with something out of this cloth." Even Sharon, who works further down on the production hierarchy, looked forward to sample-making assignments. She said, "The best part is sewing samples. I like to do one-of-a-kind; some are challenging, not one whole day of doing the same thing."

Positive relations with their coworkers were another reason women gave for continuing in their jobs. Scholars suggest that workers with low financial compensation and little opportunity for upward mobility because of their gendered workplaces tend to view good social relations with their coworkers as an important element of their "working conditions" (Miller 1980; Kanter 1982; Hodson 1989). Although most workers do not carry these friendships beyond the work setting, their discussions during coffee and lunch breaks (called "talk story") provide opportunities for sharing and mutual affirmation. For example, the fact that many old-timers reported that their discussions were of their favorite Japanese television program, *Oshin* (a serial depicting a poor woman's life, her perseverance in the face of hardship and suffering), suggests that the program's theme resonated with these women.

In most work settings, class consciousness and worker resistance are defined by the presence or absence of public expressions of protest or labor organization. Although neither of these describes the responses of the garment workers I interviewed, subtle forms of collective resistance had occurred. For example, 34-year-old Sheila's thoughts about leaving the industry included two components: her own situated consciousness of wanting more for herself, and her older coworkers' encouraging her to consider other options. She said, "I want to do something different, I'm getting tired of sewing, plus the older ladies tell me, 'You don't want to stay in this industry—no future.' "

Although deceptively unprovocative, these worker interactions can accumulate to produce collective actions. When Rose and her coworkers in Casually Chic's finishing department discovered that incentive rates were being adjusted upward whenever workers exceeded the 100% set by time-motion studies, they individually decided it was not worthwhile to participate in the incentive system. I learned from the firm's production manager that even with the incentive system in place, the rates averaged "around 70% most of the time." A similar decrease in production rates occurred at Tropical Sunsets when management attempted to switch the organization of production from "whole garment" to "section work." Although management figured that rationalizing production through section work would boost production, workers figured out that they would be saddled with other people's mistakes and have less control over their own work. The workers did not formally protest, but they slowed the pace of their work so that management was forced to go back to the old system.

## WORKPLACE-HOUSEHOLD RELATIONSHIP

Hawaii's garment workers also gain a sense of accomplishment that they can carry into their domestic lives. The high cost of living in Hawaii requires multiple earners and pooling of resources within a household for sheer economic survival. Nearly all the old-timers reported that they owned their own homes. In Hawaii, where housing is extremely expensive and the median purchase price of an existing single-family home was $177,600 in 1987 (Hawaii Department of Business, Economic Development, and Tourism 1988, p. 563), these older women's meager wages contributed significantly to payment of their household mortgages and expenses. The recent immigrants and young locals were more likely to be renting than to be buying homes, but their earnings were similarly essential and valued.

Both old-timer and recent immigrant women reported that they perform most of the domestic work in their households, but their marketplace work meant that the amount and organization of their domestic work had been modified to meet their employment schedules. Because factories operate from 7:00 a.m. and most left home at 5:00 a.m., their household work was limited to either the weekends or the few hours after dinner. For example, these women mentioned that instead of being saddled with preparing separate daily menus, they either cooked soups and stews so that leftovers could be stretched over several days or had their families eat out several times a week (i.e., purchase meals). Lillian and other old-timers spoke of getting their husbands, many of whom were retired, to help with vacuuming, washing or drying dishes, and some housework. Although these practices are minor modifications, they also indicate that women's market work has reduced their domestic workload.

These strategies were less evident among the young locals, both because most were unmarried and because there was more variation within this group. Their domestic work was influenced by their youth, their working-class backgrounds, and their relatively fluid family situations. Although a gender-based division of labor characterized their households, their domestic contributions were more likely to be in "assisting" rather than "managing" domestic work. Thus they "helped" with the laundry and child care and with driving family members to and from various engagements. However, their youth, the necessity of their financial contribution to the household, and the heavy work schedules most young locals shouldered by working at Casually Chic actually prevented them from taking on more domestic work.

The situations of all three groups make it clear that the interrelationship between household and marketplace is actively negotiated by women in their performance of marketplace and domestic roles. It also influences how they feel about their work and themselves. Although occupying subordinate positions in both arenas, most women workers still play off their work in the two spheres and derive a measure of satisfaction from both of them.

## SUMMARY AND CONCLUSION

Both continuing and changing social patterns characterize the Hawaiian garment industry and its workers. The most enduring pattern is that women are the producers of apparel. However, changes in apparel production from 1778 onward reflect the colonization of Hawaii and the replacement of a subsistence-based indigenous economy by a market-oriented one. Thus the indigenous process of apparel production performed by Native Hawaiian women was supplanted by imported Western fabric and dressmaking techniques.

As foreigners reformulated Hawaii's political economy, proletarianization and later racialization of the apparel production workforce occurred; that is, European, primarily Portuguese, women were the early workers, but as the industry developed and rationalized its production process, garment manufacturing work became dominated by women of color, mostly Nisei women. As it progressed, the garment industry's labor force has undergone ethnic succession, differentiation, and stratification. Nisei women are being replaced by two different groups, recent immigrants and young locals. In these two groups can be seen not only the continuing use of women of color in the garment industry workforce, but also increasingly their racial/ethnic stratification. Recent immigrant women fill mostly less-skilled, lower-paying production jobs on the shop floor, such as sewing, whereas young locals fill the more technical production jobs, such as designing, pattern making, and grading. This social hierarchy has been facilitated by state-supported vocational-technical education and training programs that were initiated as local and global competition and restructuring intensified within the garment industry.

The low returns on employment received by recent immigrants and young locals are tied to the condition of the industry at this historical moment, and to the workers' particular locations in Hawaii's social structure. The social conditions of recent immigrants in Hawaii's garment industry parallel those of many racial/ethnic minority immigrant groups in the United States, who, constrained by limited resources, opportunities, and language proficiency, are resigned to taking low-paying jobs associated with this industry. Young locals, most of whom are third-generation Asian and Pacific American, have been culturally assimilated to Hawaiian society. For them, placement in this low-wage industry occurs because of the demands of their relatively problematic working-class families, high housing costs, and their state-supported vocational-technical education.

The social formation of Hawaii's garment industry labor market represents the melding of several factors. These include historically based forms and actions of the state vis-à-vis the economy. These, in turn, facilitate racial/ethnic and gender-based social constructions that define and locate groups in different positions within the garment production process. However low their earnings might be, these Asian Pacific American women's material contributions to their households empower them in their homes, reducing and restructuring their domestic work. Conversely, their status in their families permits them to withstand and even challenge higher levels of exploitation in their work places, both individually and for other workers. In short, through the garment industry in Hawaii we are able to see a tenuous balance between the contradictory conditions of oppression and empowerment enacted by these three groups of working-class women.

## REFERENCES

Amott, Teresa L. and Julie A. Matthaei. 1991. *Race, Gender, and Work: A Multicultural Economic History of Women in the United States.* Boston: South End.

Beechert, Edward D. 1985. *Working in Hawaii: A Labor History.* Honolulu: University of Hawaii Press.

Bill, Teresa. 1995. "Overview." Pp. 1-3 in *Into the Marketplace: Working-Class Women in 20th Century Hawai'i,* edited by P. Matsueda. Honolulu: Hawaii Committee for the Humanities.

Blascoer, Frances. 1912. *The Industrial Condition of Women and Girls in Honolulu: A Social Study.* Honolulu: Paradise of the Pacific.

Bonacich, Edna, Lucie Cheng, Norma Chinchilla, Nora Hamilton, and Paul Ong, eds. 1994. *Global Production: The Apparel Industry in the Pacific Rim.* Philadelphia: Temple University Press.

Chapkis, Wendy and Cynthia Enloe. 1983. *Of Common Cloth: Women in the Global Textile Industry.* Washington, DC: Transnational Institute.

Chinen, Joyce N. 1984. "Working Wives and the Socioeconomic Status of Ethnic Groups in Hawaii." *Humboldt Journal of Social Relations* 11:87-103.

———. 1989. "New Patterns in the Garment Industry: State Intervention, Women and Work in Hawaii." Ph.D. dissertation, University of Hawaii at Manoa, Honolulu.

Collins, Patricia Hill. 1990. *Black Feminist Thought: Knowledge, Consciousness, and the Politics of Empowerment.* New York: Routledge, Chapman & Hall.

Daws, Gavin. 1968. *Shoal of Time.* New York: Macmillan.

Dorton (Kameeleihiwa), Lilikala. 1986. "Land and the Promise of Capitalism." Ph.D. dissertation, University of Hawaii at Manoa, Honolulu.

Enloe, Cynthia. 1989. *Bananas, Beaches, and Bases: Making Feminist Sense of International Politics.* Berkeley: University of California Press.

Fuchs, Lawrence. 1961. *Hawaii Pono: A Social History.* New York: Harcourt Brace Jovanovich.

Fundaburk, Emma Lila. 1965. *The Garment Manufacturing Industry in Hawaii.* Honolulu: University of Hawaii, Economic Research Center.

Geschwender, James A. and Rita Carroll-Seguin. 1988. "Asian American Success in Hawaii: Myth, Reality, or Artifact of Women's Labor?" Pp. 187-207 in *Racism, Sexism, and the World-System: Studies in the Political Economy of the World-System,* edited by Joan Smith, Jane Collins, Terence K. Hopkins, and Akbar Muhammad. Westport, CT: Greenwood.

Geschwender, James A., Rita Carroll-Seguin, and Howard Brill. 1988. "The Portuguese and Haoles of Hawaii: Implications for the Origin of Ethnicity." *American Sociological Review* 53:515-27.

Glenn, Evelyn Nakano. 1992. "From Servitude to Service Work: Historical Continuities in the Racial Division of Paid Reproductive Labor. *Signs: Journal of Women in Culture and Society* 18:1-43.

Hawaii Department of Business, Economic Development, and Tourism. 1984. *State of Hawaii Data Book.* November. Honolulu: Author.

———. 1988. *State of Hawaii Data Book.* November. Honolulu: Author.

———. 1994. *State of Hawaii Data Book.* June. Honolulu: Author.

Hawaii Department of Labor and Industrial Relations, Research and Statistics Office. 1986. *Hours and Earnings, 1972-1986.* Honolulu: Author.

Hodson, Randy. 1989. "Gender Differences in Job Satisfaction: Why Aren't Women More Dissatisfied?" *Sociological Quarterly* 30:385-99.

Jensen, Joan M. and Sara Davidson, eds. 1984. *A Needle, a Bobbin, a Strike: Women Needleworkers in America.* Philadelphia: Temple University Press.

Kanter, Rosabeth Moss. 1982. "The Impact of Hierarchical Structures on the Work Behavior of Women and Men." Pp. 234-47 in *Women and Work: Problems and Perspectives,* edited by Rachael Kahn-Hut, Arlene Kaplan Daniels, and Richard Colvard. New York: Oxford University Press.

Kent, Noel J. 1983. *Hawaii: Islands under the Influence.* New York: Monthly Review Press.

Kessler-Harris, Alice. 1982. *Out to Work: A History of Wage-Earning Women in the United States.* New York: Oxford University Press.

Kuykendall, Ralph. 1938. *The Hawaiian Kingdom: 1778-1854.* Honolulu: University of Hawaii Press.

———. 1953. *The Hawaiian Kingdom: 1854-1874.* Honolulu: University of Hawaii Press.

Lamphere, Louise. 1987. *From Working Daughters to Working Mothers: Immigrant Women in a New England Industrial Community.* Ithaca, NY: Cornell University Press.

Louie, Miriam C. 1992. "Immigrant Asian Women in Bay Area Garment Sweatshops: 'After Sewing, Laundry, Cleaning and Cooking, I Have No Breath Left to Sing.' " *Amerasia Journal* 18:1-26.

Manicas, Peter, ed. 1995. *Social Process in Hawaii: A Reader,* 2nd ed. New York: McGraw-Hill.

Miller, Joanne. 1980. "Individual and Occupational Determinants of Job Satisfaction: A Focus on Gender Differences." *Sociology of Work and Occupations* 7:337-66.

Mills, C. Wright. 1956. *White Collar.* New York: Oxford University Press.

Nordyke, Eleanor C. 1989. *The Peopling of Hawai'i,* 2nd ed. Honolulu: University of Hawaii Press.

Omi, Michael and Howard Winant. 1994. *Racial Formation in the United States: 1960-1990,* 2nd ed. New York: Routledge.

Romero, Mary. 1992. *Maid in the U.S.A.* New York: Routledge.

Kurt Salmon and Associates. 1979. *Garment Manufacturing in Hawaii.* Prepared for Hawaii Department of Planning and Economic Development, Honolulu.

Schmitt, Robert. 1977. *Historical Statistics of Hawaii.* Honolulu: University of Hawaii Press.

Stannard, David E. 1989. *Before the Horror: The Population of Hawai'i on the Eve of Western Contact.* Honolulu: University of Hawaii, Social Science Research Institute.

Trask, Haunani-Kay. 1984. "Hawaiians, American Colonization, and the Quest for Independence." *Social Process in Hawaii* 31:101-36.

Tiano, Susan. 1990. "Maquiladora Women: A New Category of Workers?" Pp. 192-223 in *Women Workers and Global Restructuring,* edited by Kathryn Ward. Ithaca, NY: ILR Press.

U.S. Bureau of the Census. 1992. *1990 Census of the Population, General Population Characteristics, Hawaii.* CP-1-13. Washington, DC: Government Printing Office.

# 4

# Women's Resistance in the Sun Belt: Anglos and Hispanas Respond to Managerial Control

## LOUISE LAMPHERE
## PATRICIA ZAVELLA

This chapter focuses on women's resistance to management control and its relation to ethnic difference in apparel and electronics firms in New Mexico. Anglo and Hispana women's acts of individual, collective, and minimal resistance at three different plants are examined. The analysis and findings are based on intensive interviews with 53 working mothers and their husbands. The authors found that resistance developed differently in each of the three work settings and that Hispana and Anglo women had more similarities on the jobs than differences. The findings also suggest that the extent to which women are responsible for providing for their families has no relationship to their level of resistance to managerial control.

Over the past 20 years, the composition of the industrial labor force in the United States has changed as more women have continued to work while rearing children, and semiskilled and skilled jobs have been increasingly filled by people of color and immigrant workers, especially women. At the same time, U.S. manufacturing has experienced a radical restructuring, primarily characterized by the decline of heavy industry, the movement of light industry to the South and West as well as to the Third World, and the advent of Japanese management techniques as a way of shoring up U.S. productivity. In this climate, women have been seen as more docile workers than men, and managers have deliberately attempted to control women's labor through various strategies and practices. To understand the conditions under which women consent to or resist managerial control, we need a complex analysis of women's position as industrial workers, one that takes account of restructured and relocated industries, the new array of management practices, and the diversity among women workers.

This chapter focuses on women's resistance to management control and its relation to ethnic difference in apparel and electronics firms in Albuquerque, New Mexico. These factories were part of "Sun Belt industrialization," the building and expansion of manufacturing facilities in the West and South that began in the early 1980s. In Albuquerque, many of these new facilities were enthusiastic innovators in the growth of "participative policies" that were catching on in U.S. firms a decade ago. We examine women's resistance in three plants that illustrate the range of resistance strategies we found. These responses range from individual strategies of resistance at Leslie Pants, an apparel factory with hierarchical management; to collective resistance through a union drive at HealthTech, a plant that makes surgical sutures and has a participative structure; to minimal resistance and a climate of consent at Howard Electronics, a participative plant that manufactures electronic thermostats.

We look at the strategies and tactics for resisting management control that have been developed by both Anglo and Mexican American women.[1] The racial/ethnic affiliation of the workers is important in these workplaces, for the workforce is predominantly Hispana. We argue that women of different racial/ethnic backgrounds had similar work experiences and resistance strategies in particular workplaces, and that women's resistance was shaped by management policies, the labor process, and the wage structure rather than racial/ethnic differences per se. In this period when ethnicity/race is seen as a source of major divisions among workers, it is important to understand when women have common reactions to their work situations and to build models that illuminate the complexity and variability in women's perceptions and behavior on the job.

The heart of our project consisted of intensive interviews with working mothers and their husbands. In all, we interviewed 53 young mothers employed in electronics and apparel plants, including 37 Hispanas and 16 Anglos; of these, 38 were married and 15 were single mothers. We located our interviewees through a variety of sources: sympathetic plant managers who referred us to the personnel manager or plant nurse for names of potential interviewees, suggestions by union officers, contacts through friends or colleagues, and names of other working mothers through women we had already interviewed. Because we were unable to get access to plant records, and union membership lists did not indicate whether workers were mothers of small children, we relied on a "snowball sample" based on contacts with both workers and managers. Interviews were conducted separately with women and their spouses in their homes and involved two long, tape-recorded sessions for both the husband and the wife.[2] In writing this chapter, we have utilized the 31 interviews from three plants (Leslie Pants, HealthTech, and Howard Electronics) because these represent the range of management systems and worker strategies we found within the study.

All of the mothers we interviewed had children younger than school age, and most of them had entered the labor force during high school and continued to work after marriage. When their children were born, many returned to work after their 6-week maternity leaves expired. These Sun Belt mothers, then, were committed to remaining in the labor force and juggled the demands of work and family lives.

In Albuquerque these industrial workers occupy a relatively privileged place in the local economy. The electronics and apparel plants studied were built between 1972 and 1982; they were branch plants of larger multinational companies. The workforce was not an immigrant one, but consisted primarily of high school-educated workers. A handful of the women had some vocational training at the local community college or through the military. Our Hispana informants were predominantly third-generation U.S. citizens whose first language was English. Within the larger Albuquerque economy, predominantly male jobs in construction and service are much more vulnerable than predominantly female jobs. Most of the women were earning between $5.00 and $6.50 an hour in 1982, but the importance of their paychecks to their families varied depending on their husbands' wages and job status. Of the 38 couples we interviewed, in 30 (79%) the wives were coproviders or mainstay providers; that is, they earned almost as much as their husbands or had the more stable job in the family—the one with the good benefits that was less likely to be lost during recessionary layoffs.[3]

## BUILDING A FRAMEWORK TO STUDY
## RESISTANCE IN THE CONTEXT
## OF MANAGEMENT POLICIES

Since 1975, the U.S. economy has undergone a structural transformation as many industrial plants have begun to close or to move their operations abroad. Women in these industries, such as apparel, textiles, electrical products, and shoes, have often been faced with layoffs and job loss (Rosen 1987). At the same time, working-class families have become more dependent on female wages, and wives have stayed in the labor force while their children are young, often going back to work after a 6-week maternity leave.

Managers have begun to transform the workplace in response to foreign competition, attempting to make U.S. companies more productive. Borrowing management techniques developed in Japan after the American occupation and building on the "quality of work life" (QWL) movement of the 1970s, corporations have turned to various forms of "participative management," instituting quality circles, team structures, and various forms of open-door management.

Following Perkins, Nieva, and Lawler (1983, pp. 5-15), we define participative management in terms of the wide range of personnel and management policies that characterize "high-involvement plants." Such firms have flat organizational structure, with few levels between the plant manager and shop-floor workers; a mini-enterprise or team work structure; and a strong emphasis on egalitarianism in the way work and leisure areas are designed. There is usually a commitment to employee stability, heavy emphasis on training, pay based on the attainment of "skill levels," and job enrichment whereby workers have some control over the organization of work. Our interviewees came from seven different plants: three with traditional hierarchical management structures and four that were of the high-involvement type. These latter four firms did not to have strict assembly lines, allowed workers to rotate jobs, and did not enforce quotas or use piece-rate systems. Often there were equal benefits for blue-collar and white-collar employees, no time clocks, no special parking places for management, and a plantwide work culture designed to build a loyal workforce. Two of these plants organized production in teams, with facilitators rather than supervisors.

Many commentators, particularly management consultants and business school professors, have been enthusiastic about the potential of participative management techniques to reform more hierarchical and traditional management structures and to revolutionize the U.S. workplace at all levels (see Peters 1987, pp. 282-89; Ouchi 1981). Others have seen the darker side of the QWL movement, naming line speedup, just-in-time inventory control, and manipulative team meetings a system of "management by stress" (Parker and Slaughter 1988, pp. 16-30).[4]

Robert Howard (1985) emphasizes the manipulative aspects of participative management where workers are led to "feel in control" but where power remains with management (pp. 127-29). Guillermo Grenier (1988) expands on this theme and emphasizes the ways in which teams are used to "debureaucratize control." Although power differences are de-emphasized in company rhetoric, a manager's authority is in fact widened and peer pressure is used to create a compliant workforce:

> The trick is to make workers feel that their ideas count and their originality is valued while disguising the expansion of managerial prerogatives in the manipulative arena of pop psychology. By depending less on impersonal rules and more on personality characteristics, today's manager effectively de-bureaucratizes the control mechanism of the firm. (Grenier 1988, p. 131)

In this chapter, we take a position similar to Grenier's, as will become clear in our discussion of women's resistance at HealthTech. However, we also want to examine one of several workplaces we studied where resistance did not erupt into a struggle over a union drive, where management participative policies were less ambitious and global, and where women, on the surface at least, appreciate the positive aspects of nonhierarchical management. Our argument here is not that participative management has lost its manipulative character, or that there are not subtle pressures for workers to be loyal to the firm, but that women pick and choose from among the panoply of management practices, voicing favorable responses especially concerning those that help mediate the contradictions they face as workers *and* mothers. Indeed, they still may engage in individual tactics and strategies of resistance when it comes to gaining some control over the labor process.

Our approach to resistance owes much to a number of scholars who have analyzed the workplace and work culture. Susan Porter Benson

(1986), for example, implicitly includes the notion of resistance in her definition of work culture as "the ideology and practice with which workers stake out a relatively autonomous sphere of action on the job" (p. 228). Benson, who developed her ideas in collaboration with Barbara Melosh, sees work cultures as "a realm of informal, customary values and rules that mediates the formal authority structure of the workplace and distances workers from its impact." She argues that "work culture is created as workers confront the limitations or exploit the possibilities of their jobs. . . . Generated partly in response to specific working conditions, work culture includes both adaptation and resistance to these structural constraints" (p. 228; see also Melosh 1982).

Following Richard Edwards (1979), we see the labor process and management policies as systems of control. They involve the exercise of power and, as such, always promote resistance. As Michel Foucault (1980) suggests, "There are no relations of power without resistances; the latter are all the more real and effective because they are formed right at the point where relations of power are exercised; resistance to power does not have to come from elsewhere to be real, nor is it inexorably frustrated through being the compatriot of power. It exists all the more by being in the same place as power" (p. 142). The exercise of power at the point of production also brings up issues of consent, accommodation, quiescence, and approval, issues that have been explored by Michael Burawoy (1979) and Nina Shapiro-Perl (1979). Resistance can include a number of individualistic tactics, the sorts of "everyday resistance" or "weapons of the weak" described by James Scott (1985) in his study of Malay peasants.

In examining resistance on the shop floor, we use the language of "tactics and strategies," emphasizing the simultaneously positive and reactive nature of resistance. Workers are both attempting to carve out a space where they can control the labor process and resisting management's system of control. It is important to note, as Dorrine Kondo (1990) reminds us, that individual actions may simultaneously include resistance and consent. In other words, these strategies may invoke subversion and the attempt to control the production process but simultaneously bind workers more firmly to management's control mechanisms and to compliance with the firm's policies (pp. 223-24).

For those researchers who have focused on particular workplaces where both White women and women of color are employed, women's tactics and strategies on the job have emerged as a central theme. Using individualized strategies, women have resisted the fragmentation of their labor processes (Lamphere 1979; Sacks and Remy 1984) and have attempted to gain control and autonomy within particular work sites or in relationship to individual employers (Glenn 1986; Rollins 1985; Romero 1992). Some women have struggled to "bring the family to work" so as to "humanize the workplace" (Lamphere 1985, 1987), whereas others have consented to exploitative conditions in part because of their economic vulnerability and family constraints (Shapiro-Perl 1984).

Other researchers have demonstrated how women of color and White women have engaged in collective resistance, including joining labor organizations in service and clerical settings (Costello 1991; Milkman 1985; Sacks 1984), striking for union recognition in canneries and the garment industry (Ruiz 1987; Coyle, Hershatter, and Honig 1980), and successfully pursuing race and sex discrimination suits in canneries (Zavella 1987, 1988). These collective actions ultimately created significant changes in particular work sites or in large sectors of some industries. Only a few researchers, however, have examined how women of different racial groups in the same work site have engaged in individual or collective resistance (Ruiz 1987; Sacks 1988).

Our research, conducted in 1982 and 1983 during a period of national recession, focuses on Hispana and Anglo women who are electronics and apparel workers in the same factories. We describe below the women's resistance in the three firms (one hierarchical and two participative). Resistance ranges from individual strategies and tactics (those that attempt to preserve a woman worker's control over the labor process) to full-blown collective efforts to unionize. There is variability both among plants and among the women in each plant's labor force.

Thus we seek to situate resistance along a continuum and to recognize that resistance, consent, and unarticulated quiescence form a range of responses to new forms of management practice. In our study, the women themselves often made contradictory assessments of their work situations. On the one hand, they appreciated management policies that helped them mediate the tensions they experience being mothers and workers (policies such as flextime) or that promised a more egalitarian workplace (open-door management). On the other hand, the women had a sharp sense of the importance of wresting control over their work from management. These seemingly contradictory responses—both appreciation of the "positive" aspects of participative management and a practice of resistance—took various forms, depending on the firm's organization of work, its pay system, its management policies, and the plant work culture that evolved.

In our study we found that, more than either her provider role or her racial/ethnic status per se, a woman's position in the labor process, her struggles with her job, and her particular relationship with supervisors and other management were important in the woman's development of work strategies. To illustrate the variety of environments in which resistance and accommodation emerge in a field of contradictory power relations, we will discuss three different plants: an apparel factory with hierarchical management, a health products plant with a new participatory management that experienced a very bitter union drive, and a thermostat factory where participative policies have been installed successfully.

## INDIVIDUAL TACTICS IN AN APPAREL PLANT

At Leslie Pants, women workers confronted a system of hierarchical control. Like most apparel plants, Leslie was organized into several lines, where bundles of pants progressed from one sewer to the next. The small parts, such as pockets and belt loops, are assembled first, then the side pockets, fly, belt, and side seams are sewn later. Each section of the line is supervised by a "floor lady," and workers are paid a piece rate. The essence of the piece-rate system is that a worker's wages depend on the level of efficiency she reaches. Efficiency is defined as the number of hip pockets, belt loops, or the like sewn in a day to reach a base rate of 100% efficiency, which in 1982 was $4.25 an hour. Achieving efficiency takes a great deal of hand/eye coordination and an ability to pace oneself throughout the day; a worker must always keep an eye on how many bundles need to be done in order to maintain or increase her level of production. Individuals develop their own sets of tactics and strategies for gaining a measure of control over their work.

Although these tactics can be seen as a measure of resistance—an attempt to keep from capitulating entirely to management's methods of extracting production from workers—they also ensnare women in the system itself, keeping them working to improve their percentages. As they do so, women are encouraged by the system of rewards held out by management and by the lively work culture created by managers, aimed at building a loyal workforce.

The cases of Dolores Baca, a Hispana, and Mary Pike, an Anglo, illustrate the ways that women can be more or less successful in developing tactics and strategies for dealing with the piece-rate system. For both, resistance never became a confrontation with management, but was part of a "mixed consciousness" illuminating the field of contradictory power relations, where a sharp sense of how to exercise some control over one's work was simultaneously placed alongside an appreciation for management incentives, health benefits, profit sharing, and company celebrations.

Dolores Baca, a coprovider, had worked in the plant for 8 years. Her husband, Albert, was a grocery store stocker, and Dolores's job at Leslie Pants was important in stabilizing their marriage. Both she and Albert preferred that he provide economic support while she remain at home to care for their infant daughter: "I wish I could stay home and take care of the baby. But we can't afford it, you know. So I got to work and my mother takes care of my baby." Albert agreed with her assessment: "I really wish that she could stay home, you know, instead of [the baby] having to stay with her grandma." In 1982, Dolores was working on belt loops, but had been trained to hem pants as well. She was making $5.37 an hour and had recently reached 110%; she was trying to maintain a new level of 120%, so her wages would increase.

Similarly, Mary Pike, an Anglo coprovider, struggled to keep her piece-rate average up to 78% on the new job (elastic waist bands) she was assigned after returning from her pregnancy leave. Mary had been employed for only a year and returned 6 weeks after her baby was born because "I had to go back and start getting the paychecks." Her husband, Don, had lost his high-paying job in the New Mexico oil fields and had been fortunate to find a job at Leslie Pants in another city. But that factory closed and they both transferred to Albuquerque: "When they announced they were closing the plant, I was in tears. Here I was about 3 months pregnant, losing all the insurance, and both my husband and I were losing jobs. I was really scared. It was a hard blow just to go to Leslie Pants after he'd been working on the oil rig, making $11 an hour, and we had bought this trailer." Mary made $5.11 an hour, and her job at Leslie Pants was crucial for her family's survival.

During training or retraining, both Dolores and Mary developed tactics to deal with the piece-rate system, which pushes workers to produce as quickly as possible, but where work has to be accurate or it will be returned for repairs, resulting in lost time and wages. This begins first when a woman is introduced to "the method" or routine for doing a job, which is written up in a manual called a "blue book." Dolores had worked out a way to bypass the method and developed her own tricks of the trade:

> They do expect for you to go by "the method," that's what the instructor is for. To show you the method and how to do it in order to be faster. Sometimes you're doing that, but sometimes you think, "I can do it this other way, and it'll be faster for me." But they do come around and check you to see if you're on your [prescribed] method. Once I see her coming I right away go back to my [prescribed] method, you know. But to me doing it the way where I feel more comfortable and faster at it, I do it that way.[5]

Mary, in contrast, had problems mastering her new job of sewing on elastic waist bands. One of her biggest problems was dealing with cutting-room mistakes, in this case "shaded parts." She absorbed the mistakes herself, doing repairs when garments were returned to her. "If they're shaded, the parts, like say the bands are dark brown and the pants are a little beige or something, if you sew it on, you get it back. You get pretty quick at ripping out too. But it does take a long time to make repairs on the operation." Dolores, facing a similar problem, used the strategy of going to her supervisor: "Like now we've been having problems with our loops. They've been like overlapped. And we've been having trouble with that because they're too fat on the bottom and we can't fold them and they don't look right like that, you know, [so we] throw them away. So we've been having problems with that, but we do go straight to our supervisor or line manager." Here the supervisor was crucial in getting new loops, so that Dolores and other workers on the same operation would not lose pay.

Dolores's tactics, which included devising her own method and getting help from her supervisor, allowed her to maintain her piece-rate average, whereas Mary, trying to cope with some of the same problems, used similar individual strategies but was struggling rather than succeeding.

Dolores was typical of several women we interviewed who were experienced workers, employed at Leslie Pants for between three and nine years. They were in jobs they knew well and were not struggling with work difficulties. Mary was one of several workers who were having problems. These women tended to be relatively new workers who were also being retrained on new jobs while they were simultaneously experiencing machine difficulties or trouble with cutting-room mistakes.

The piece-rate system could potentially produce competition among workers where it is difficult even to meet the piece rates (Lamphere 1987), yet that did not seem to happen here. Instead, many women expressed an individualized ideology that "how much you earn is really up to you." Mary, for example, did not emphasize competition among workers, but acknowledged that cutting-room mistakes or machine problems got in the way of her producing more quickly.

The piece-rate system acts almost "automatically" to extract labor from workers as they push each day to increase their pay. At Leslie Pants, management's major intervention was to buttress the piece rate with a system of rewards and incentives, as well as with good benefits. Each trainee or worker who was being retrained graduated from the program when she reached 100% efficiency, but further recognition was given to those who reached 110% and 120%. Graduations were held on Thursdays; those being recognized were presented with diplomas and were given soft drinks or coffee and brownies during the morning break. As Dolores Baca described the system, "First they give you little flags, and then with 100% you get a pin that says Leslie Pants and then you get a flag that says 100% [which goes above the worker's machine]. And then your 110, you get another pin and your flag for 110." Dolores, who had just received her pin for reaching 100% on belt loops, said that the recognition made her feel "proud, happy, 'cause you're working so hard 'cause, you know, you want to make money, see. And you feel happy that you have already made it and you know you can make it every day and you can make some money, you know."

When a worker maintained 130% for 7 weeks, she joined the President's Club. An 8 × 10 color photo of each member of the club was posted on the wall in the front entryway to the shop floor. Members were taken out to lunch yearly by the plant manager and thanked for their efforts on behalf of the plant. Dolores, as well as other interviewees, was very positive about the President's Club: "I like it but you got to work, you got to work hard to get into it." Some women, like Tony Sena, emphasized how difficult it was to maintain high levels of production because of daily layoffs during the recession or disruptions in the production process. Tony was trying to achieve 110% on hang pockets, but had difficulty accruing the 32 hours per week for 2 weeks necessary to get the award, because she had been sent home early several days a week due a reduced number of orders. Nevertheless, reactions to the reward system were positive; some interviewees showed us their certificates and pins. Unlike the Rhode Island apparel plant studied by

Lamphere (1987), at Leslie there was no sense that the system was an unnecessary embarrassment that merely showcased management's goals. Instead, workers felt that the plant really depended on the 130% workers to keep production up.

In some apparel plants, a piece-rate system combined with strong supervisory control can create worker competition or disgruntlement with supervisors (Lamphere 1987). At Leslie Pants, preventing this divisiveness was crucial to management, which sought to keep up worker morale by creating a strong plantwide work culture. This included sponsorship of nonwork activities that ranged from picnics to raffles, as well as contests at Halloween and Christmas. By co-opting workers' organizational skills and cultivating worker participation in plant activities, the firm prevented the growth of a strong women's work culture of resistance. The plant manager was quite clear about this when he noted, "If a manager takes care of his people, then there are no problems." Otherwise one might "tap out" the available labor pool or encourage unionization.

Management was very successful at creating a labor force that contained a number of high producers (members of the President's Club). On the whole, tactics or strategies to control their own labor remained at an individual level, between a woman and her work, her machine, and her supervisor. The lack of a strong set of resistance strategies at a collective level was a result of management's ability to make the piece rate system palatable through nonmonetary rewards, such as membership in the President's Club, and monetary incentives, such as good benefits and a profit-sharing plan. Morale and loyalty were further encouraged through a wide range of company-sponsored picnics, raffles, and other forms of entertainment. Resistance did not go very far, and co-optation was characteristic as the women came to see their goals as consonant with those of the company.

## PARTICIPATIVE MANAGEMENT, TEAMS, AND A UNION DRIVE

Our second example is HealthTech, the firm that in 1982 represented the most participative of the plants we studied and, at the same time, the plant that generated the most conflict over the nature of participative management. HealthTech produces surgical sutures, and most workers were engaged in swaging (pronounced "swedging"), attaching surgical thread to curved needles and winding the thread to ready it for packaging. During the course of our interviews, the company was the site of a union drive. The drive met with a great deal of company resistance, and in May 1983, the union was defeated in an election by a two-to-one margin.

We focus here particularly on the experiences of three women we interviewed: Lucille Sanchez, an anti-union activist and Hispana mother of three; Bonnie Anderson, an Anglo mother of three who was a union supporter; and Annette Griego, a Hispana single parent and strong union supporter. We use these three cases to show how a woman's place in the production process, her relationship with "facilitators," and her family situation influenced her participation in the union drive as a form of resistance. In addition, we draw attention to the process of the drive itself and the dialectical relationship that evolved as workers responded to management tactics and vice versa.[6]

Coprovider Lucille Sanchez's husband was a truck driver for a local beverage company who earned slightly more than Lucille's hourly wage. She believed that her job paid well and had good security, which was very important to her. She first stated, "I like everything about that job." Then she recalled that she did not like the rotating shifts. "[My husband] doesn't like me to work but he knows that I have to. If it was up to him, he'd rather have me home, especially since we had the last baby." She agreed with her husband that it would be better if she remained at home, taking care of their three children, but she continued working mainly for economic reasons.

Unlike Lucille, Bonnie Anderson was a mainstay provider. Her husband, a cement truck driver, had been laid off for 8 months in 1982 because of the recession in the construction industry. Bonnie's wages and benefits were the main source of support for her spouse and three sons. She worked at HealthTech as a swager, using a machine to attach surgical thread to curved needles. She enjoyed her job because of good coworkers and the challenge of beating the clock, but did not like it that when her machine broke down, it was counted against her. She characterized her job as having relatively good job security, but not good pay, and the possibilities for promotion were difficult because whether "they liked me" would play a big role in her getting a better job. She was strongly committed to working. "It was hard for me to give it up," she said, but she also believed that "if [a woman] has got kids, I think it's important for her to stay home, if she enjoys it. [But] sometimes you can stay home with your kids and not be a good mother. But I think your kids are important." Her husband "always backed me, whatever I wanted to do, he would back me. If I wanted to work, fine, if I didn't that was okay too." Once he was laid off, however, her job became crucial for family support.

Annette Griego, a young widow, was the sole provider for herself and her son, although she shared household expenses with her sister and sister's boyfriend. She had became pregnant at 16, married her son's father, and then began living with her divorced mother after her own marital separation and then her husband's suicide. Annette began living with her sister soon after the birth of her son in 1978; she started working at HealthTech in 1981.

At the time of our interview, Annette was part of a committee that had just become "above ground" and had passed out a union leaflet, which caused a lot of tension at work. Her facilitator quit holding team meetings because the team talked about pro-union issues. Annette was strongly committed to her job. She liked her coworkers, and the fact that "management isn't always on your back . . . cause we don't let them get on our back," indicating a strong sense of collective resistance. She did not like that workers were pressured to work fast (in order to attain 110% efficiency), yet if they made their quota or even went over, there was no reward. "I don't like that about the job—you can work your hardest and do twice as much as the person next to you and you can be getting the same pay." She appreciated the good benefits, that the plant was in a convenient location for her commute to work, and that the company "makeup policy" allowed workers to make up missed work. The disadvantages of the job were the low pay, the pressure to work faster, and the management's attempts to get workers to produce more than at their other plants that were unionized: "As it is, our [production] numbers are too high. They're comparing us to the other plant. But you backtrack and say if we compare them to the other plant, they are making 40-50% more. They only have to make 67% and then after that it's all bonus and incentive. Not only that, they have downtime—anytime you're not swaging, you get downtime. We don't get that."

Annette also had a difficult time coping with HealthTech's policy of rotating shifts—alternating between working first and second shifts every 2 weeks. Annette's sister also alternated three shifts as manager of a fast-food place. Annette divided child care with her live-in sister and her mother (who lived 20 miles from Albuquerque), and had a complicated system that sometimes meant that her son spent the night at his grandmother's home. Characterizing this arrangement, she said, "Sometimes things get kind of hectic."

The "team concept" at HealthTech entailed a massive restructuring of management-worker relations. Each team had a "facilitator"—not a supervisor or "boss" who meted out rewards and punishments, but rather someone who focused on the interpersonal relationships within the team. In addition, the hiring prerogatives of management were shared with the team. Two team members interviewed prospective employees, and if the evaluation was negative, the person usually was not hired. Teams were also involved in evaluation for raises and even firing. Team meetings were supposed to be occasions when team members could discuss ways in which they could help each other meet the production targets that resulted in reaching 100% efficiency at the end of a 12- or 18-month period.

There was, however, a contradiction between management's participative ideology and its practice. It was this contradiction that brought about the union drive. Workers in channel and drill swaging (who were attaching surgical needles to thread) had difficulty meeting weekly efficiency levels as they were being trained. They were working on machines that had come from another plant and that often broke down. They were penalized for down time and couldn't "keep their numbers up." Team meetings for those under several of the facilitators became "just one big tattletale session." As Bonnie, one of the first workers hired in the new plant, who was assigned to channel swaging (Team A), explained, the facilitator "was always on us about numbers. It was always his job if our numbers didn't come up. And why did we do so poorly that week. We'd have to go around the table" (to explain why their numbers reached only 67% rather than 80% efficiency, for example). "I hated that. It was so embarrassing. It really was." Bonnie also found it difficult to participate in the firing of a teammate—for example, someone who was "a good worker and a good person" but whose numbers "weren't there" because he had some trouble with his machine.

The problem for Annette was that she was having machine difficulties and her numbers were low: "When they first started using gut in channel swaging, I was the first one to work with it. I had to learn. The facilitator had me trying different dyes to find out which dyes the needles worked best with and stuff like that. So my numbers dropped then too." These difficulties were probably related to Annette's view that as long as they were working under a learning curve, with higher rates expected as their training progressed, they should have been paid on a piece-rate or bonus system. She also felt the numbers were too high: "They are always comparing us to the other plant. But their swagers have been there an average of 15-20 years and we've only been swaging a year or a year and a half."

Lucille's difficulties did not occur in the beginning; they only became noticeable when she needed to maintain 100% efficiency during her "demonstration period" of 13 weeks. She learned both the drill swaging technique and how to wind the sutures quickly; she was asked to train new employees in the drill department in March. She continued training until December 1981 and then began a period of 13 weeks' "demonstration" in winding:

> Well, in the winding department it took several weeks and I was performing like at 97 or 98%. I couldn't get over that 98 or 99 hump. My last week in demonstration is when I went on a daily basis to 117, 124, and that averaged out to make up for the other weeks when I hadn't made the 100%. So, I took a big step without realizing what position I was putting myself into, and then not only that I was the first person to demonstrate. That made the pressure more severe. You know, there was lots of people behind you and lots of people against you. It was really hard.

Lucille felt that other team members were not supportive and that she was not given credit or praise for finishing her demonstration (and getting a raise). However, this did not dampen her overall enthusiasm for her job; she gave her work top ratings on all aspects, from pay to supervisor and job security.

Women in channel swaging and drill swaging responded to the labor process and pay system differently. Many, especially in the more demanding channel department, developed tactics to deal with the pressures of producing, but also came to feel that the numbers were too high, that it would be difficult to go through demonstration, and even that a piece rate system that would reward faster production would be fairer. Women in drill swaging, like Lucille, had less difficulty learning the technique, but most felt pressure to work harder to attain 100% efficiency, working quickly while avoiding defects.

Within a year of when the plant opened, workers like Bonnie and Annette in the channel and drill swaging teams had come to feel that workers were unfairly treated and that the team concept was not really "participation." They had begun to see through company ideology and feel that their participation was really only on the surface and under the control of management. They formed an organizing committee and contacted Amalgamated Clothing and Textile Workers Union, with the goal of forming a union.

Management's response occurred at the levels of both ideology and tactics that sanctioned union activists, divided them from other workers, and prevented new workers from voting for the union. In terms of ideology, management used notions of participation and democracy to discredit unionism. They argued that a union would interfere with the effort to get everyone to participate and the company would "lose flexibility" in implementing the high-involvement design. One company document stated, "We give everyone a chance to represent themselves without a 'third party' such as a union."

Management responded swiftly to the campaign. Team meetings became the arena in which the facilitator could mold anti-union opinions, often calling on those who had already taken an anti-union stance to pressure their peers. For example, one facilitator at a team meeting provoked an anti-union discussion of the Coors strike in Colorado, using comments from a female personnel administrator whom he had invited to a meeting to voice pro-company sentiments. Lucille, a member of his team, became a vocal supporter of the company and helped organize an anti-union committee. At team meetings she was always available to chime in with her anti-union opinions. In another team, this same facilitator was effective in isolating one of the pro-union women and turning others against her. He allowed and even encouraged her best friend to demand this woman's resignation from the newly formed Compensation Committee because she was "untrustworthy" and unable to represent her coworkers' opinions because she was a union activist. At a larger meeting later that week, he asked her to stand up and be identified, further embarrassing her and singling her out as a "troublemaker." She felt she was "being harassed for her political opinion" and eventually resigned.

About 4 months after the campaign started, the management planned two firings and then later fired another two women—all members of the union organizing committee. The firings created a climate of fear that the union was never really able to overcome, even though activists filed unfair labor practice grievances for these firings and for another firing that took place later. Facilitators carefully screened new employees and hired only anti-union recruits. They continued to isolate union supporters, breaking up conversations between activists and other workers and branding pro-union workers as "losers" and pro-company workers as "winners."

During the last two months of the campaign, management stepped up its efforts, sending anti-union memos home with paychecks, showing anti-union films, initiating a Union Strike Contest (asking employees to guess how many strikes the union had engaged in between 1975 and 1983), and pushing the campaign motto, "Be a Winner! Vote No." In such a climate, it is not surprising that the union lost, getting only 71 votes; 141 employees voted against the union.

Whereas men in the plant were evenly divided on the union issue (22 for and 23 against), women voted against the union 72% to 29%. Furthermore, only 24% of the Hispanas voted for the union, whereas 40% of the non-Mexican American women (Anglos, Blacks, and Asian Americans, about 22 altogether) did so. Many Hispanas and several Anglo and Black women who had earlier been supportive of the union backed away during the last few months of the campaign. (For example, 37 Hispanas and 7 Anglo and Black women had signed a petition sponsored by union supporters asking the company to investigate a bad smell that was pervading the plant; later, they did not vote for the union. Had they continued to support the union, the union would have won.)

Although the gap between participative philosophy and company practice, along with difficulties at the point of production, produced the union drive, company tactics created a climate of fear, making the company rhetoric about the team concept and not needing a "third party" seem a safer avenue. For many of the women, this was the best job they had ever had, and it was too important to risk.

## PARTICIPATIVE MANAGEMENT AND MAKING THERMOSTATS

At other plants in Albuquerque, managers have been able to implement participative management in ways that have pushed the contradictions between management ideology and shop-floor practice in a different direction. Women in these plants have not broken open the contradiction and revealed the gaps between "participation" and the power exercised by management. Instead, women have held in tension their critique of the demands placed on them and their sense of management's willingness to incorporate worker views on the production process and thus downplay the hierarchy of decision making. Interviewees expressed appreciation for an open-door policy, job rotation, the chance to talk with the plant manager over coffee, and the ability to vote on a plantwide holiday schedule. Howard Electronics, which produces electronic thermostats, is an example of this kind of plant. By 1991, the plant had developed a team structure that went even further than the one at HealthTech. Rather than having two assembly lines, the plant now has a number of teams, one for each part of the assembly process. Each team has a facilitator and meets weekly, as do the teams at HealthTech; however, in addition, members of each team are cross-trained on all the jobs for which the team is responsible. Most important, the teams manage their own budgets, keep track of production, and conduct their own quality control. Teams have replaced supervisors, and indeed, many middle-level management positions have been eliminated.

Anita Alvarez was an electronics assembler at Howard in 1982. She had electronics training and had previously worked at two other electronics factories. When her husband became unemployed, she applied at Howard and for a while was a mainstay provider. At the time of our interview, her husband was employed as a custodian and she was a coprovider. She characterized her job as having good pay and job security, but found opportunities for promotions "pretty hard."

In 1982, women at Howard reported on the ways in which management incorporated their views and was flexible in enforcing quotas or absence regulations. Anita, who had faced an unrealistic quota of testing 200 liquid crystal displays an hour, talked to her supervisor, who told her, "That's all right, you just do the work, and if you can't put it out, you can't." It was not surprising that she felt "the advantage is probably that I can say whatever I feel like, and they'll listen to me. If I have changes I want to make, I'll go up there and I'll say it and they'll listen. . . . [The firm is] like one big family."

Linda Henry, an Anglo single parent and sole provider, worked at Howard Electronics as an assembly operator, inserting electronic components on the printed circuit boards ("stuffing boards") on the thermostats. She had worked previously for 14 years as a dental assistant, but left that occupation because the benefits were much better at Howard. To Linda, the most important aspects of a job were good pay, job security, and opportunities for promotion. She was satisfied with her pay and job security, but worried that she would not be able to advance at Howard because "it's hard without the basic training." She was committed to her job because "for the position I'm in [as a single parent] with my two little children, I need the job security and I need the good pay. And I mainly need the free benefits which we have."

Linda delivered a cogent critique of the way in which management had raised the rates on stuffing boards four times over the previous year, thus making it impossible for her to make any incentive pay. Instead of being resentful, she emphasized the plant's participative policies: "They made it a point to come out and talk to you every day, and they made it a point to see how you like it and if you were happy. . . . They didn't segregate you like, say, they were the office and you were the factory."

Both Anita and Linda emphasized their supervisors' efforts to create a friendly and egalitarian atmosphere. As Anita said, "You don't find very many supervisors that come and sit down and eat lunch with you and act like he's not even a supervisor, you know." Even those we interviewed who were more critical of the plant emphasized the job security, good pay, and benefits the plant offered.

For English-speaking Hispanas and Anglos who are products of the U.S. public school system, participative management draws upon a number of notions inherent in American cultural descriptions of the self in a democratic society. Self-sufficiency, responsibility, "team spirit," and competition (for awards such as Team of the Week and Team of the Month), as well as quality, are all stressed in the pamphlet each Howard team has written for visitors who tour the plant. The ideology of participation and management's "listening to what I have to say" both evoke a sense of democracy and egalitarianism.[7]

In workplaces such as Howard, women come to see themselves as "individuals," "team members," employees who have "ownership of quality," and not as women who are being pushed to higher and higher levels of production. In a political economy such as that in Albuquerque, where there are few good jobs for women, this is a powerful and highly seductive system. Some of these jobs may disappear due to plant buyouts, declines in military spending, and future recessions in the electronics industry, but the few women who hold the jobs that remain will continue to appreciate the advantages of working in "new participatory plants."

## CONCLUSION

In our research, we found that Mexican American and White women had similar reasons for entering the labor force to begin with, and they were placed in comparable positions without regard to their ethnicity. All of these women were in the lowest but most numerous positions in each plant, working as sewing operators and electronics assemblers. Although the majority of the labor force was made up of Hispanas, these women had been raised and educated in the United States, much like their Anglo counterparts, had similar job training, and worked in departments that were not segregated by ethnicity or race. Thus all the women experienced the same features of their jobs—whether the wages and benefits were good, whether there was job security and possibilities for promotion—in similar terms.

Moreover, we found no neat relationship between a woman's provider role and her resistance to managerial control. One might expect that those women in the most dire economic circumstances, the sole and mainstay providers, would be the most conservative, the least likely to rock the boat at work. Instead, we found that some of the most vulnerable of our informants—those who had the most to lose, such as single-parent Annette Griego at HealthTech and mainstay provider Bonnie Anderson, were the most militant. In contrast to other single parents in their firms and to most of the Hispana married women—who could rely on their spouses' wages—Annette and Bonnie withstood management's harassment and were active union supporters. Anglo and Hispana women alike (including coprovider Lucille Sanchez) voted against unionization. Both of the married interviewees at Leslie Pants, one a Hispana coprovider and one an Anglo mainstay provider, felt ambivalent about their work, but both worked hard to try to increase their wages through partial acceptance of the company's piece-rate and reward culture. And at Howard Electronics, where participative management had been successfully introduced, where management allowed some worker say over the speed of the work and workers were treated with respect, both Anita Alvarez, the Hispana coprovider, and Linda Henry, the Anglo single parent, were relatively satisfied with their jobs, although they both realized there were few opportunities for advancement.

Resistance developed very differently in each of these three settings. At Leslie Pants, the hierarchical apparel plant, tactics and strategies used by workers to control their own work remained very much at the individual level, as women carved out their own approaches to the piece-rate system, at the same time accepting and becoming part of management's overall reward structure and plantwide work culture. In contrast, at HealthTech, which operated through a similar set of learning curves but without piece rates, workers forged similar individual tactics but also came to resist at a group level the firm's new participative structure and ideology. And finally, at Howard, a more flexible production process and participative features again kept tactics to an individual level while pulling women into a system that drew successfully on American cultural notions of participation, self-sufficiency, and egalitarianism.

We have shown that women's work in each of these factories posed different constraints, depending on a woman's place in the production process, management's attempts to create a firm work culture, and management's degree of success in creating conditions in which women could gain some control over their labor. Although all of these women were confined to "women's jobs," each had originally sought work in factories that were regarded as places that offered good jobs, and each strategized in her everyday work to make the most of the opportunities provided. In this sense, Hispanas and Anglos had more similar experiences of work in Sun Belt factories than they had differences on the job.

## NOTES

1. We use *Mexican American* and *Hispana* interchangeably. For a discussion of ethnic identity among our sample, see Lamphere, Zavella, Gonzáles, and Evans (1993) and Zavella (1993).

2. Louise Lamphere interviewed Anglo women, and Patricia Zavella and Jennifer Martinez interviewed Hispanas. Anglo husbands were interviewed by Felipe Gonzáles and Victor Mancha, and Gary Lemons talked with Anglo husbands.

3. In our sample, 11 Hispano and 8 Anglo couples were coproviders, 7 Hispano and 4 Anglo couples were mainstay providers, and 15 women were sole providers. In an additional 8 couples (7 Hispano and 1 Anglo), the women were secondary providers, but none of them are discussed here. The term *secondary provider* is derived from Hood (1983); it indicates that the woman's contribution to family income is significantly less (usually at least 30% less) than her spouse's income. We do not wish to imply that such a woman's wages are "pin money" or not important.

4. Others, particularly Rehder and Smith (1986) and Brown and Reich (1989), have been much more positive about the NUMMI plant, playing down issues of line speed and stress and emphasizing increased worker involvement (including the active presence of the union) and productivity.

5. As Jennie Garcia, an interviewee who had been an instructor for 4 years, noted, not all instructors insist that their trainees follow the blue book: "If you see that somebody's making their goal and is producing more . . . why do anything?"

6. See Lamphere and Grenier (1988) for a more detailed explanation of why the union drive failed.

7. In 1992, Leslie Pants broke with tradition in the apparel industry and converted its assembly-line organization to a team structure. Each team of 36 operators is organized into miniteams of 4 to 8 workers who each learn two or three operations and help one another maintain quality control. Management pays a flat hourly rate of $7.30 an hour, plus a bonus of 30 cents an hour if the team produces fewer than 2.9 flaws in every 100 pairs of pants. The company instituted the new system to improve quality and boost worker morale. Perhaps Leslie Pants will be able to follow Howard Electronics in the successful implementation of a participative management style.

## REFERENCES

Benson, Susan Porter. 1986. *Counter Cultures: Saleswomen, Managers, and Customers in American Department Stores, 1890-1940.* Urbana: University of Illinois Press.

Brown, Claire and Michael Reich. 1989. "When Does Union-Management Cooperation Work? A Look at NUMMI and GM-Van Nuys." *California Management Review* 31(4):26-44.

Burawoy, Michael. 1979. *Manufacturing Consent: Changes in the Labor Process under Monopoly Capitalism.* Chicago: University of Chicago Press.

Costello, Cynthia B. 1991. *We're Worth It! Women and Collective Action in the Insurance Work Place.* Urbana: University of Illinois Press.

Coyle, Laurie, Gail Hershatter, and Emily Honig. 1980. "Women at Farah: An Unfinished Story." Pp. 117-44 in *Mexican Women in the United States: Struggles Past and Present,* edited by M. Mora and A. del Castillo. Los Angeles: University of California, Chicano Studies Research Center.

Edwards, Richard. 1979. *Contested Terrain: The Transformation of the Workplace in the Twentieth Century.* New York: Basic Books.

Foucault, Michel. 1980. *Power/Knowledge: Selected Interviews and Other Writings,* translated by C. Gordon, L. Marshall, J. Mepham, and K. Soper. New York: Pantheon.

Glenn, Evelyn Nakano. 1986. *Issei, Nisei, War Bride: Three Generations of Japanese American Women in Domestic Service.* Philadelphia: Temple University Press.

Grenier, Guillermo J. 1988. *Inhuman Relations: Quality Circles and Anti-Unionism in American Industry.* Philadelphia: Temple University Press.

Hood, Jane. 1983. *Becoming a Two-Job Family: Role Bargaining in Dual Worker Households.* New York: Praeger.

Howard, Robert. 1985. *Brave New Workplace.* New York: Penguin.

Kondo, Dorinne K. 1990. *Crafting Selves: Power, Gender, and Discourses of Identity in a Japanese Workplace.* Chicago: University of Chicago Press.

Lamphere, Louise. 1979. "Fighting the Piece Rate System: New Dimensions of an Old Struggle in the Apparel Industry." Pp. 257-76 in *Case Studies in the Labor Process,* edited by A. Zimbalist. New York: Monthly Review Press.

————. 1985. "Bringing the Family to Work: Women's Culture on the Shop Floor." *Feminist Studies* 11:519-40.

————. 1987. *From Working Daughters to Working Mothers: Immigrant Women in a New England Industrial Community.* Ithaca, NY: Cornell University Press.

Lamphere, Louise and Guillermo Grenier. 1988. "Women, Unions, and Participative Management: Organizing in the Sunbelt." Pp. 227-56 in *Women and the Politics of Empowerment: Perspectives from the Workplace and the Community,* edited by Ann Bookman and Sandra Morgen. Philadelphia: Temple University Press.

Lamphere, Louise, Patricia Zavella, Felipe Gonzáles, and Peter B. Evans. 1993. *Sunbelt Working Mothers: Reconciling Family and Factory.* Ithaca, NY: Cornell University Press.

Melosh, Barbara. 1982. *The Physician's Hand: Work Culture and Conflict in American Nursing.* Philadelphia: Temple University Press.

Milkman, Ruth, ed. 1985. *Women, Work, and Protest: A Century of U.S. Women's Labor History.* Boston: Routledge & Kegan Paul.

Ouchi, William G. 1981. *Theory Z: How American Business Can Meet the Japanese Challenge.* Reading, MA: Addison-Wesley.

Parker, Mike and Jane Slaughter. 1988. *Choosing Sides: Unions and the Team Concept.* Boston: South End.

Perkins, Dennis N. T., Veronica Nieva, and Edward Lawler. 1983. *Managing Creation: The Challenge of Building a New Organization.* New York: John Wiley.

Peters, Thomas J. 1987. *Thriving on Chaos: Handbook for a Management Revolution.* New York: Alfred A. Knopf.

Rehder, Robert R. and Marta Medaris Smith. 1986. "Kaizen and the Art of Labor Relations." *New Management,* October.

Rollins, Judith. 1985. *Between Women: Domestics and Their Employers.* Philadelphia: Temple University Press.

Romero, Mary. 1992. *Maid in the U.S.A.* New York: Routledge.

Rosen, Ellen Israel. 1987. *Bitter Choices: Blue-Collar Women in and out of Work.* Chicago: University of Chicago Press.

Ruiz, Vicki L. 1987. *Cannery Women, Cannery Lives: Mexican Women, Unionization and the California Food Processing Industry, 1930-1950.* Albuquerque: University of New Mexico Press.

Sacks, Karen Brodkin. 1984. "Computers, Ward Secretaries, and a Walkout in a Southern Hospital." Pp. 173-92 in *My Troubles Are Going to Have Trouble with Me: Everyday Trials and Triumphs of Women Workers,* edited by Karen Brodkin Sacks and Dorothy Remy. New Brunswick, NJ: Rutgers University Press.

————. 1988. *Caring by the Hour: Women, Work, and Organizing at Duke Medical Center.* Urbana: University of Illinois Press.

Sacks, Karen Brodkin and Dorothy Remy, eds. 1984. *My Troubles Are Going to Have Trouble with Me: Everyday Trials and Triumphs of Women Workers.* New Brunswick, NJ: Rutgers University Press.

Scott, James C. 1985. *Weapons of the Weak: The Everyday Forms of Peasant Resistance.* New Haven, CT: Yale University Press.

Shapiro-Perl, Nina. 1979. "Labor Process and Class Relations in the Costume Jewelry Industry: A Study in Women's Work." Ph.D. dissertation, University of Connecticut, Storrs, Department of Anthropology.

————. 1984. "Resistance Strategies: The Routine Struggle for Bread and Roses." Pp. 193-208 in *My Troubles Are Going to Have Trouble with Me: Everyday Trials and Triumphs of Women Workers,* edited by Karen Brodkin Sacks and Dorothy Remy. New Brunswick, NJ: Rutgers University Press.

Zavella, Patricia. 1987. *Women's Work and Chicano Families: Cannery Workers of the Santa Clara Valley.* Ithaca, NY: Cornell University Press.

————. 1988. "The Politics of Race and Gender: Organizing Chicana Cannery Workers in Northern California." Pp. 202-24 in *Women and the Politics of Empowerment: Perspectives from the Workplace and the Community,* edited by Ann Bookman and Sandra Morgen. Philadelphia: Temple University Press.

————. 1993. "Feminist Insider Dilemmas: Constructing Identity with Chicana Informants." *Frontiers: A Journal of Women's Studies* 13(3):53-76.

# 5

# Working "Without Papers" in the United States: Toward the Integration of Legal Status in Frameworks of Race, Class, and Gender

## PIERRETTE HONDAGNEU-SOTELO

Although undocumented legal status joins with relations of race, class, and gender to block employment opportunities for immigrant women in the formal sector of the U.S. economy, it does not necessarily hinder these women's progression within the informal sector. Mexican undocumented immigrant women doing paid domestic work, over time, obtain jobs that offer more autonomy, greater flexibility, and higher pay. Although these women are still denied the right to reside or move within the nation-state legally and the legal rights of employment and social entitlements available to citizens and legal residents, the contrast between the work experiences of undocumented Mexican immigrant women in live-in positions and those in job work situations suggests that the effects of undocumented legal status are mitigated by time and the establishment of community ties.

In this chapter, I discuss how legal status, together with race, class, and gender, funnels undocumented Latina immigrant women into informal sector labor markets and shapes their job experiences. In particular, the case of paid domestic workers illustrates how undocumented legal status compounds the scarcity and the substandard quality of employment opportunities faced by poor women of color. In spite of this, the undocumented Mexican immigrant women whom I studied manage to use social networks to construct more or less steady employment where they have some autonomy, flexibility, and better earning potential than they do in other jobs. Undocumented legal status constrains their employment, but as the women gain access to community resources over time, being "without papers" becomes less of a hindrance. Social networks in the immigrant community mitigate some of the disadvantages of undocumented legal status, as they allow women informally to regulate and improve an unregulated, informal sector occupation.

Latina immigrant women work in numerous industries, but many are concentrated in three occupations located in the informal sector of the economy: assembly, street vending, and paid domestic work. Mexican, Cuban, and Dominican immigrant women work in garment and other assembly work in factories, homes, and sweatshops (Soldatenko 1991; Fernandez-Kelly and Garcia 1992; Pessar 1984). In Los Angeles, Guatemalan, Salvadoran, and Mexican immigrant women create employment for themselves as street vendors of food, beverages, clothing, jewelry, audiocassettes, and other items (Sirola 1992). And Latina and Caribbean immigrant women take jobs as paid domestic workers and as nannies (Colen 1989; Hondagneu-Sotelo 1994; Ruiz 1987; Salzinger 1991; Simon and De Ley 1984; Solorzano-Torres 1987; Trevizo 1990).

Women of color and immigrant women have a long history of doing paid domestic work in the United States (Glenn 1986; Rollins 1985; Romero 1992; Dill 1994). Although domestic work is sometimes performed by male college students, unemployed aerospace workers, and elite British nannies, the majority of new entrants to the occupation are immigrant women from the Caribbean, Mexico, and Central America. The number of paid domestic workers in the United States and the number of Latina immigrants in the occupation are unknown, but in areas such as Southern California and south Texas, paid domestic work is virtually institutionalized as an occupation performed by Latina immigrant women (Romero 1992; Ruiz 1987). Female U.S. citizens of color are still in the occupation, but as Glenn (1992) indicates, since the end of World War II many of them have shifted employment to some form of "public reproductive labor" that occurs in the formal sector of the economy, to jobs that are located in large institutions. Racial/ethnic minority women are disproportionately represented in jobs as cooks, cafeteria workers, janitors, hotel maids, and nurse's aids in convalescent homes and other institutional settings (Glenn 1992). Although these jobs leave much to be desired, they are an improvement over paid domestic work because they are regulated jobs that offer some minimal level of benefits and are not based on relations of servitude.

In the following sections, I argue that the absence of U.S. citizenship status is an important feature that, together with relations of race, class, and gender, blocks employment opportunities for immigrant women. I also discuss some of the ramifications of undocumented legal status. I then describe the research I conducted with undocumented Mexican immigrant women, and explore how undocumented legal status intersects with these women's employment in paid domestic work in live-in situations, where employment occurs at the place of residence, and in "job work" arrangements, where domestic workers clean different houses on different days. Contrasting the experiences of the live-ins and the job workers indicates some of the constraints of undocumented legal status and suggests that the effects of undocumented legal status are mitigated by time and the establishment of community ties.

## LEGAL STATUS IN THE MATRIX
## OF RACE, CLASS, AND GENDER

A substantial body of literature testifies to the complex ways in which race, class, and gender shape employment opportunities and experiences for women of color. No longer are race, ethnicity, gender, and class relations understood as static, independent entities whose consequences can be summarized in monistic theories or additive models. Rather, they are seen as intersecting systems of power relations that produce different outcomes in different historical and political contexts (Collins 1990; King 1988).

Chandra Mohanty (1991) argues that women's lives are shaped by immigration, nationality, and citizenship together with race, class, and gender. Citizenship and immigration policies reflect economic interests. These policies are also informed by racism, sexism, and heterosexism, as particular groups are singled out and excluded in citizenship legislation. Formal exclusion, however, does not hinder employment. In fact, legal disenfranchisement may make a group of workers more attractive to employers. In this regard, Robert J. Thomas's (1985) study of agricultural workers demonstrates the complex ways in which citizenship status stratifies labor markets. And research from Canada suggests that citizenship status now mediates "the entire matrix of relations pertaining to paid domestic labor on an international scale" (Bakan and Stasiulis 1995, p. 303).

In this chapter, I use the remarks of Mohanty (1991), Thomas (1985), and Bakan and Stasiulis (1995) as a point of departure to discuss the employment experiences of undocumented Mexican immigrant women. The theoretical point I wish to contribute to the discussion of systems of race, class, and gender is relatively straightforward: Citizenship or legal status is a significant analytic category that might fruitfully be incorporated in our analyses of women's employment in the United States. As multiethnic societies are created through transnational processes and mass immigration, legal status becomes an increasingly important axis of inequality.

Both feminist scholarship and the literature on race and ethnicity provide important clues for the analytic treatment of legal status. First, it is important to look at legal status as a social and political construction, as a category that is legislatively constructed and that assumes meaning within a particular set of social relations. In the United States, a hierarchy of citizenship statuses has been created by immigration legislation and by post-1965 immigration.

A second characteristic of legal status, one that follows directly from its social construction, is that it is a fluid category. The meaning of a particular legal status varies regionally and historically. For example, the salience of unauthorized legal status rises to the surface during mass deportation campaigns that target particular groups. Moreover, legal status is a fluid category because a person may experience various legal statuses over a lifetime. New immigrants to the United States, for example, may begin their stays with undocumented or unauthorized legal status, but may over the course of time gain access to some form of temporary or permanent legal status, and perhaps eventually to naturalized citizenship. The ability to move between categories is predicated on both changes in immigration legislation and the ability to meet legislative criteria.

Third, legal status is not a variable that can be neatly measured; rather, it is a category that is contextually defined. Although legal status may be conceptualized along a hierarchical continuum that spans native-born citizenship, naturalized citizenship, legal permanent residence, temporary legal status, and unauthorized or "illegal" status, the effects of falling into one of these categories are not automatic. Citizenship status assumes meaning within the matrix of class, race, and gender, and within a particular social and historical context. Post-1965 immigration to the United States stems principally from Asia, Latin America, and the Caribbean, and because immigrants from these areas are often identified by their language and phenotypical features, racial categorization exacerbates their visibility in the workplace as possible immigrants without legal status. Legal status underlines and exacerbates racial/ethnic difference and inequality. By contrast, Swedish au pairs or Irish immigrants who work without authorized legal status are better able to "pass" and hide their legal status because of their racial privilege. In the following section, I focus on characteristics of the most disenfranchised category of legal status, the undocumented category, in order to explore how it affects employment.

## WHAT DOES IT MEAN TO
## WORK "WITHOUT PAPERS"?

Three critical factors distinguish undocumented immigrants and refugees from citizens and immigrants with legal status: an outlawed presence, the criminalization of employment, and exclusion from social entitlements. Undocumented immigrants are, first of all, denied the right to enter the nation-state's boundaries, or to move or reside within the territory of the nation-state legally. They enter surreptitiously, crossing on foot at night or hidden in trucks, or on commercial jets using falsified documents; or they may enter with authorized temporary legal status, on a tourist or student visa, and then overstay visa extensions. Their existence within the national-political territory is outlawed, they live in fear of detection, and in all public and bureaucratic settings, they must attempt to "pass" as legally authorized persons.

Expulsion by the dominant group is the ultimate negative sanction for undocumented immigrants. Harsher than segregation, and perhaps surpassed only by slavery and extermination through genocide, the forcible removal of unauthorized immigrants occurs in both individual and mass actions. Mass deportations are common during economic downturns. Mass expulsions based on legal status are intertwined with racial categorization and economic interests. Employer demand, however, often runs counter to official government policies. Restrictionist immigration laws do not necessarily stop, and may even fuel, the willingness of employers to hire undocumented immigrant women for household work. Employers who want to pay the least amount possible may prefer undocumented domestic workers.

A second feature distinguishing undocumented immigrant status is that since passage of the 1986 Immigration Reform and Control Act (IRCA), unauthorized immigrants have no legal right to employment in the United States. IRCA's employer sanctions provisions criminalize work for undocumented immigrant workers and the employers who knowingly hire them. These restrictions attempt to erase the presence of undocumented immigrants by removing their ability to survive economically.

IRCA effectively moves immigrant restriction from the border to the workplace. Although workers with undocumented status still find employment in the formal sector by using false documents, the imposition of illegality complicates the entire process of securing work. With the implementation of this legislation, the cost of obtaining and the quality of fraudulent documents has risen, and undocumented workers typically face an extended waiting period in finding jobs (Bach and Brill 1990). Moreover, criminalization of employment effectively ensures that unauthorized workers have no political basis from which to denounce unfair working conditions and subminimum wages, as it denies them the political right of protest. For these reasons, cities with large undocumented immigrant populations have witnessed the expansion of non-regulated, informal sector work (Grossman Brezin 1989). Although this trend was already under way in the major immigrant cities, the criminalization of formal sector work for undocumented immigrants fueled informal sector growth.

A third feature distinguishing undocumented legal status is the denial of social entitlements, including tax-supported programs that undocumented immigrants help to support financially. Undocumented immigrants may not receive food stamps, Aid to Families with Dependent Children (AFDC), public housing assistance, or unemployment insurance. Many of these restrictions also apply to legal residents who obtained legal status through one of the two legalization programs under IRCA. Although these new legal residents obtained legal rights to enter, reside, and work in the United States, they were prohibited from accepting government assistance, including unemployment compensation, AFDC, and food stamps, for five years after obtaining legalization. Still, undocumented immigrants are able to make limited use of government resources if they have U.S. citizen children.

Denied alternatives, undocumented immigrants lack the option of turning down jobs with substandard working conditions and pay. Restrictions on social entitlement eligibility for undocumented immigrant workers mean that they need to accept any job on any terms. Government verification of legal status for social entitlements thus saves some sectors of private capital from having to provide standard wages, benefits, or better working conditions for employees.

The features of undocumented legal status, outlawed presence, criminalization of employment, and denial of social entitlements together limit employment options and make undocumented immigrants vulnerable in their relations with their employers and among themselves. These features influence the relationship between undocumented legal status and paid domestic work in several ways. An outlawed presence—and the resulting constant fear of detection, apprehension, and deportation—makes employment in a private household *more* appealing to undocumented immigrants than public employment. And, as noted above, the criminalization of employment imposed by IRCA's employer sanctions has increased the ranks of undocumented workers within informal sector employment, such as paid domestic work, where formal regulations are rarely enforced. Finally, the denial of social entitlements limits the ability of undocumented immigrant workers to confront their employers directly and militate for changes in their workplaces.

Paid domestic work is increasingly performed by Latina and Caribbean immigrant women, many of whom lack authorized legal status. They constitute a group of workers who, due to their class, race, gender, and legal status, are among the most disenfranchised and vulnerable in our society. Given the conjuncture of these circumstances, which exacerbate the asymmetry in the employer-employee relationship, how do immigrant women strategize to improve their employment as domestics? Looking at undocumented immigrant women domestic workers not as hapless victims but as purposeful social actors offers some clues.

## METHODOLOGY

My research on domestic employment derives from a larger study on migration patterns and changing gender relations among Mexican undocumented immigrant women and men (Hondagneu-Sotelo 1994).

Researching a population that is criminalized by the imposition of "illegal status" is not easy. First, it can be difficult to locate subjects, as their livelihoods depend on their keeping their unauthorized immigration status a secret. Second, obtaining subjects' consent for participation in a research project involving documentation can be problematic. Who, after all, asks questions and engages in surveillance in the immigrant's world? Priests, police, and Immigration and Naturalization Service (INS) agents are likely candidates for these activities. Further, in-depth interviews and participant observation, the methods I used, are very intrusive.

I was able to locate participants for the study through contacts I had previously established by working in the community. The timing of my project also assisted in this endeavor, as research began in November 1986, just as IRCA passed, and continued until May 1988. The new legislation proved fortuitous for my research, as it effectively divided undocumented immigrants into "paper chasers" who would be eligible for amnesty-legalization and "paper forgers," a group of people driven by the law to falsify documents in order to secure employment. In community meetings, public informational forums, and among neighbors, the legislation effectively made undocumented immigrants "come out." My activism and personal reciprocity also assisted my research goals because they enabled me to develop a level of trust with some immigrant women and to collect detailed information about the women's citizenship, work status, and participation in the underground economy.

The study was conducted in a Mexican immigrant community located in the San Francisco Bay Area. The well-defined immigrant barrio where these people reside is one of the poorest areas in the county. The barrio, however, is bordered by both middle-class and very affluent residential areas, and the women seek domestic employment in these surrounding communities. The data derive from informal conversations and participant observation that occurred in various public and private locales, supplemented by interviews with 17 undocumented immigrant women with recent experience as non-live-in domestic workers. All interactions and interviews were conducted in Spanish.

It is not possible to use conventional random sampling techniques when researching undocumented immigrants in the United States, thus I used a nonrandom snowball method to select 44 study participants. Of the 24 women in the study, 17 had experience as paid domestic workers, but none was currently working as a live-in.

The majority of the 17 women interviewed were between 30 and 50 years old, although one woman had begun working as a domestic worker in the United States at the age of 15 and another was still energetically working at the age of 71. Fifteen of the women were currently married or living in consensual unions. The sample reflects diverse class and occupational origins: 10 of the women came from rural, peasant backgrounds; 4 came from urban, working-class origins; and the remaining 3 came from urban, middle-class backgrounds in Mexico. These women chose to do paid domestic work because, as undocumented female workers, they had few employment options in the local economy and because domestic work offered more flexible hours and potentially higher pay than other job alternatives. Much of the material below comes from my observations of these women's conversations and interactions with other immigrant women in the community.

## DOING PAID DOMESTIC
## WORK "WITHOUT PAPERS"

Low status, lack of guaranteed benefits and job security, relatively low wages, indefinite hours, and the absence of formal labor contracts locate domestic work near the bottom of the occupational hierarchy. A primary defining feature of the job is the intensely personalized, particularistic relationship established between employer and employee. In the asymmetrical relationship with her employer, various symbolic markers of subordination serve to remind the domestic worker of her inferior position (Rollins 1985; Glenn 1986; Kaplan 1987; Palmer 1989).

Paid domestic work is organized in various ways, and although there is no linear path between them, these might be considered in a hierarchy, with live-in employment at the bottom (Romero 1987). In live-in employment, characterized in part by "payment in kind" in the form of room and board, there is no separation between the employee's work site and residence, so the domestic worker remains vulnerable to manipulation by the employer's personalistic appeals to family ideology—to see herself "like one of the family" (Young 1987). In daily work, the domestic worker is employed in the same household on a daily basis, but returns to her own home at night to live with her family, in her own community, so that work hours are more clearly circumscribed (Glenn 1986). These type of arrangements were established by Black women in the Northeast after World War I (Katzman 1981; Clark-Lewis 1995), and today the daily work arrangement is most common for domestic workers who care for young children in the homes of their employers (Wrigley 1991). Finally, in arrangements that Mary Romero (1988) terms "job work," domestic workers clean different houses on different days, sometimes cleaning two to three houses in a single day, and instead of receiving an hourly wage, they are a paid a flat fee in exchange for their cleaning services. In job work arrangements, domestic workers generally work without supervision and are able to sell their services as expert, professional cleaners.

In the remainder of this chapter, I compare the experiences of Mexican undocumented immigrant women in live-in situations with those in job work arrangements. None of the 17 undocumented immigrant women I interviewed were currently working as live-in domestics, but 7 of them had initially found employment as live-ins when they arrived in the United States.

## LIVE-IN WORK

Women unaccompanied by either spouses or parents encounter a restricted range of jobs and residential situations. Seven of the interviewed women's first jobs entailed live-in residential arrangements with their employers. Milagros A., Francisca M., Maria M., Maria Alicia N., Mariana V., and Margarita C. all initially worked as live-in domestics, and Maria del Carmen O. simultaneously worked as a restaurant cook and lived with her employers' family.

Historically, live-in employment has been a common form of incorporation into a new urban society for single women migrants (Katzman 1981). Because the live-in employee typically does not spend earnings on rent, transportation, food, or utilities, she may initially view all of her earnings as savings, as Mariana V. did: "I thought it would suit me and my needs. I didn't have to spend money on food or on rent. Everything I earned was for me, not for my bills." Margarita C. echoed this with sentiments of gratitude: "They gave me everything—food, a bed and a roof over my head. . . . I didn't have to buy much. It immediately seemed very good to me, and as the family were Latinos, that is, of Mexican parents, and they spoke Spanish, it seemed magnificent to me."

These women initially rationalized their low pay because it freed them of living expenses, but such work is very poorly remunerated. Both Francisca M., who first migrated while she was separated from her husband, and Margarita C., who migrated while single, worked as live-in domestics for Latino families in the San Francisco Bay Area in 1975. In exchange for a daily schedule that spanned at least from dawn until the evening, Francisca earned $25 dollars a week and Margarita $40. Calculated on the basis of a 5-day-a-week, 12-hour workday schedule, their approximate hourly wages were, respectively, 42 and 67 cents. Their experiences are not uncommon; a survey conducted among return migrant women in Mexico in 1978 and 1979 revealed that 97% of women who had been domestic workers reported earning less than $10 a day (Kossoudji and Ranney 1984). "Payment in kind" is one solution for newly arrived immigrant women who lack other job alternatives because of their undocumented legal status, and who lack the support of kin, but the quality of room and board, as we will see later, is often substandard.

In live-in arrangements, neither the job's tasks nor the workday schedule is clearly defined, so, as Glenn (1986) has noted, there is "no clear line between work and non-work time" (p. 141). Because she resides with the employer, a live-in domestic worker's job does not necessarily begin with breakfast preparation and end with washing dinner dishes: She may be awakened in the middle of the night to clean a dog's vomit, called to serve a meal at irregular hours, or expected to provide baby-sitting for her employer's relatives. Although a live-in domestic worker receives concrete, tangible room and board "privileges" and cash payment, there is an effective "hidden exchange" whereby the employee puts forth an ill-defined workday. This mystifies or obscures the missing wages.

One of the defining features of domestic work is the highly personalistic relationship established between employer and employee, and most studies agree that this is generally intensified in live-in employment (Rollins 1985; Glenn 1986). Because they live with their employers, live-in domestics are deprived of lives that include normal social interactions with friends and kin. Employers may assume a benevolent, protective, maternalistic stance toward their employees, posturing as surrogate families in order to sustain the live-in domestic worker's loyalty and dependence.

Undocumented legal status exacerbates this dimension of dependence and submission. One of the ways in which this is experienced in live-in jobs is through the promise of the employer's "sponsoring" the acquisition of legal status (Colen 1989). In some cases, the vulnerability that comes with undocumented legal status exacerbates sentiments of family belonging and total dependence. When employers make offers or promises to sponsor the domestic worker's application for legal permanent residence, employees may respond with gratitude, regardless of whether the promises are realized. Maria M. first migrated to California when she was single and had worked as a live-in. She nostalgically invoked the illusion of familial belonging with her employer:

> I really wanted to stay in the U.S. back then, because the lady I worked for told me to stay, she said she would fix my [immigration] papers. . . . She really loved me a lot because she told me she was going to Washington, that I was going with her, that she would arrange for my papers first. . . . Today there are few people like that woman, because in reality, now the Americanas keep the Latinas around only for their own convenience, back then it was different. Back then, there were sincere people and that woman treated me like a sister instead of like a servant. Look, I had my nap, I had my lunch, and I had my outings with her, of course I went as the baby-sitter. But really, we would go shopping, we would go to restaurants—we were like sisters.

Although Maria insisted that "back then" employers were kinder, she was in fact comparing a much more intensely personalized live-in arrangement with her current paid domestic employment, where she worked for several different employers on different days. For Maria M., having been "like a sister instead of like a servant" was also intertwined with the possibility that through dependence on her employer, she would obtain legal status. Some 20 years later, Maria M. was still undocumented and trying to obtain legal status.

For newly arrived single immigrant women without kin or family in the United States, live-in jobs hold the promise of protection, security, and emotional support. The first job held by Milagros A. was as a live-in domestic/baby-sitter for a professional Latina who was a single parent. Milagros stayed in that job for 5 years, cleaning house, cooking, and raising the child until he was old enough to enter kindergarten. She related that her employer provided the consideration and compassion that she had not received from her own adult children, whom she felt had abandoned her. She recalled: "I liked my new life here. She [the employer] paid me well. But more than that, she gave me compassion and understanding, when my children, they've practically forgotten about me! [starts crying]."

Not all of these women characterized their Latino employers as benevolent. Even in situations where employer and employee were kin related, the live-in domestic workers remained in disadvantaged positions largely due to their undocumented legal status, lack of experience in the new society, and lack of social resources. Margarita C. believed that when her aunt and uncle had employed her sister as a live-in, they intentionally deterred her sister from establishing employment or social relations elsewhere because they benefited from her services. Margarita alleged that these confining arrangements were common among kin:

> My aunt imprisoned her. . . . When there were advertisements on the radio for a baby-sitter or someone to clean house, or whatever, my aunt would say, "No, no, you are here caring for my children." . . . Relatives, just because they help you to cross, because they make themselves responsible for us in some form, they also take advantage of us, they abuse us and they also don't allow us to search for work elsewhere. They know we don't have the papers to work elsewhere. They don't let us buy a car, they don't let us separate from them because we are helping them as a baby-sitter, or as the person who cleans the house and cooks. . . . The aunt or the relative works, she comes home and the meal is already made. So why is she going to help her look for a job elsewhere? . . . She also doesn't allow her to go out with friends because the friends will say, "Are you still there [working] with so-and-so? Why don't you leave? Perhaps they will pay you more elsewhere." . . . My aunt had my sister there almost like a prisoner in her house.

Regardless of whether they felt "like a sister" or "like a prisoner" in live-in arrangements, these women chose live-in work because it lessened the risks they would be exposed to as women and as undocumented immigrants. Live-in employment seemed to promise protection. Compounding the risks of harassment, arrest, and deportation imposed by an "illegal" presence in the country, being young, unmarried women unaccompanied by family or kin made them easy prey for those who might take advantage of their sexuality. Not only men, but women as well could take advantage of one's circumstances, as Mariana V. discovered during her first year in the United States, when an older, more experienced immigrant woman suggested prostitution to her:

> Then that same woman, the one who brought me to that job, she wanted to use me to make business. [Interviewer: What kind of business?] Well, sell me, or I don't know what she wanted. Because she saw that I was alone, that I didn't have family here, well, she didn't know if I had family here

or not, since I was renting [a room] in a house. So she would say to me: "Woman, fix up your appearance, put on some makeup, find a man and everything will change. Fix your teeth." My teeth were different then, one was missing and they were a little crooked. I saw that this woman was sly, so I didn't pay any attention to her.

Stories of live-in jobs are characterized by memories of abuse and deception. With the exception of Milagros A. and Maria M., most of the women held bitter memories of their live-in jobs. Maria del Carmen O. worked as a cook and lived at the home of her restaurant employers for 3 years. Initially she also did household chores for the family and shared a bedroom with the family's daughter, but when territorial disputes over bedroom space arose, she stopped doing domestic chores and the employers moved her into their backyard, into what Maria del Carmen described as a dwelling more appropriate for an animal than for a person:

> It was like a room for a dog. My bed and my suitcase and a chair is all that fit in that room. . . . After, I started fixing it up outside. I arranged, cleaned, threw out things. Later, when my friends would visit, they were shocked at what I called my "residence." I lived there for 3 years. They [employers' family] would lock the door to the bathroom. . . . In winter, I sometimes felt as though my body would remain stiff forever . . . [due to the cold] there were nights when I couldn't sleep all night long. I'd pass my hand over my head and there would be ice.

When Maria del Carmen recalled how these primitive living conditions had caused her to catch pneumonia, she cried. On another occasion, flipping through her photo album, she showed me pictures of what she had variously described as her "residence" and as a "room for a dog." The rudimentary structure consisted of a laminated tin roof, boards for walls, and a "ceiling" that was not even high enough to allow Maria del Carmen, who was approximately 4 feet, 10 inches, to stand up while she dressed. Like other immigrant women, she tolerated these conditions because she lacked legal status, because she knew virtually no one outside of the restaurant, and because she hoped eventually to achieve her goal: "I said to myself, well, if I leave, I won't be able to save and that is what I wanted to do, to buy a house back there [in Mexico]."

Although none of the women I interviewed had employers who withheld their entire pay, many experienced some type of employer deception regarding pay. Maria Alicia N. earned $90 a week when she arrived in 1984 to work as a live-in domestic in affluent Marin County. She had accepted the job on the condition that the employer would help her find part-time domestic work on the side, but these jobs, and the income she might have earned at them, were never forthcoming. Maria del Carmen O., the woman who was recruited to work as a cook in a Mexican restaurant, earned the most, $120 a week plus room and board. Still, the pay and the living conditions were below what she had been led to expect in exchange for the services she rendered 6 days a week, 8 to 10 hours a day:

> Don't think that once I was here they paid me what they said they would. They were over one month late in paying me at all. Then they said they'd pay me $120 a week, but I told them they had promised me $160. They argued that since I didn't know how to do everything the old cook did, that's why they paid me only $120. . . . They never raised my pay. I never earned more until the new owners took over 3 years later.

Women who lived with their employers enjoyed limited contact with kin and friends. Even the words they used to describe live-in employment highlight the seclusion and social isolation of the job: *vivir encerrada* (to live locked up), *puerta cerrada* (closed door), and *adentro* (inside). Some live-in domestic workers had both Saturdays and Sundays off, but others were allowed only one day off during the week. On their days off, if they had kin nearby, the women generally went to stay with them. Although live-in employment offered protection through anonymity by obscuring legal status, working as a live-in inhibited community contact and the accumulation of social ties.

The enforced isolation during the work week made the early period of resettlement especially difficult. Mariana V. worked as a live-in maid for a Mexican family, and on the weekends, she stayed with her female cousin in Oakland. For Mariana, a short weekend with her cousin barely compensated for a week spent in solitude and servitude:

> Once I was here, life became impossible. Here I was alone, closed up in the house, whereas in Mexico I was able to walk around in the open air with my family. It was all so different. I came that [drought] year when there was no water, in 1977. Oh lord, I'd think about how back home I could swim in the river. Sometimes I cried.

Margarita C. worked as a live-in during the week, and on weekends she stayed with her three siblings and worked a second job as a motel maid. She recalled that on weekend evenings she and her sister busied themselves with various chores, so even during off-hours, there was no time for social life: "We didn't have a social life, no, there was no time. There was nothing more than work and to the house, to clean the house, buy the food and all those things one does. . . . We didn't have time to talk with anyone, and we didn't start going to the dances until much later."

Maria del Carmen O. did not have any kin, friends, or acquaintances nearby. On her weekly day off from the restaurant, she spent the day alone and had to go out to purchase her meals. She said: "I didn't have friends. I was always in the restaurant, with them [employers] and at the house. I didn't have transportation then. It was a long time before I got to know the streets."

The isolation and solitude they experienced intensified the effects of employer harassment and intimidation among these undocumented immigrant live-in employees. Several of the women reported that their employers had threatened to call the Immigration and Naturalization Service. Maria del Carmen O.'s employers warned her about singing in the shower, lest her voice attract INS suspicion. When Mariana V. wanted to go out in the evening with her boyfriend, her employers objected and enforced their objections by underlining her vulnerable legal status: "They told me that without papers, it was not safe to go out at night." Margarita C.'s employers told her that she was lucky to have a job at all, given her unauthorized status:

> It was a life without life, just work. They wanted me to do everything; to polish the floors, to bathe the dog, to cook and care for the children. I told them it was too much, but they said that since I was here as an illegal, if I didn't want to work, then I could just go back to Mexico.

Employers imposed their own rules and attempted to reinforce loyalty by reminding the women that their inferior legal status allowed them few options.

The many drawbacks to live-in work—the ill-defined and expanded work schedule, the isolation and solitude, the dependence that is engendered, the highly personalized employer-employee relationship, and deception over pay arrangements—make such arrangements tolerable for only for a limited time, generally the immigrant's initial period of resettlement. There is no linear path out of live-in employment, but as these immigrant women began to develop social ties with other immigrant women and men through attendance at church and English classes, and as they gained friends and kin in the settlement area, they were able to opt out of live-in work. Making the transition into day work allowed these women to participate in normal social relations with family and friends.

## JOB WORK

Lack of "legal papers" is a key reason these women remain in domestic work. Many of the formal sector jobs available in the local labor market, even low-paid, physically demanding ones in hospital laundries, cafeterias, and motels, require proof of legal status. This became more pronounced after the Imigration Reform and Control Act's employer sanctions went into effect in 1986. Given the limited job options for Mexican undocumented immigrant women in this particular community, the most appealing source of employment was paid domestic work performed according to job work arrangements.

Doing job work allowed women to break out of extreme relations of dependency with their employers and to establish some semblance of normal social life. If domestic workers can accumulate a sufficient number of employers, they can walk away from their least desirable jobs. Moreover, all of the women in the study agreed that the earning potential in job work outweighs the average pay for live-in and daily domestic work. Still another advantage of job work is that it allows domestic workers to set their own hours and work schedules, and flexibility is a factor much appreciated by women who have their own family and household responsibilities (Romero 1987).

Domestic work, however, even when performed under job work arrangements, is still part of the informal, unregulated sector of the economy. Although the occupation came under the purview of the Fair Labor Standards Act in 1974, regulations concerning minimum wage and working conditions are poorly enforced (Rollins 1985; Salzinger 1991). One factor that contributes to this is that the work occurs in a multitude of disparate, private household work sites. Domestic work is, as Judith Rollins (1985) has pointed out, one of the most private labor arrangements. The work itself occurs in isolation, as there are typically no coworkers, comanagers, or official guidelines to follow. The labor arrangement is made between two individuals in a private household.

Adding to the burden of conducting individual negotiations in asymmetrical employer-employee relationships, domestic workers who engage in job work arrangements need to have multiple employers, so the job search becomes more or less constant.

Although undocumented legal status helps to funnel Mexican undocumented immigrant women into jobs as domestic workers, undocumented legal status does not necessarily lead them to be hapless victims. In spite of social relations of class, race, gender, and legal status, the undocumented immigrant women that I studied worked hard to improve their own situations in paid domestic work. Although undocumented legal status left them with no legal right to work and denied them any claim to standard wages and benefits, the women very consciously tried to improve their earning potential.

Social networks were a key resource the women used to improve their jobs. They did this by trading cleaning tips; by sharing tactics about how best to negotiate pay, how to geographically arrange jobs so as to minimize daily travel, how to interact (or, more often, avoid interaction) with clients, how to leave undesirable jobs; and by sharing remedies for physical ailments caused by the work, as well as cleaning strategies to lessen these ailments. In various social settings—at picnics, baby showers, a parish legalization clinic, and in people's homes—these immigrant women engaged in lively conversations about paid domestic work. The women were quick to voice disapproval of one another's strategies and eager to recommend alternatives. These network interactions occurred spontaneously throughout the barrio in diverse social settings. Below, I focus on two aspects of these social network exchanges to show how they relate to undocumented legal status: job-finding techniques and subcontracting relations.

### Finding the Day Jobs

The women I interviewed faced two steps in locating work. They first had to locate and secure employers, and then, as undocumented immigrant workers, they had to overcome criminalization of employment. The primary method of finding jobs was through employer referrals. Employers recommended a particular domestic worker to their friends, neighbors, relatives, and coworkers. Teresa E., for example, found her first domestic job at a county medical clinic with a nurse who needed someone to clean her house every other week. This employer recommended Teresa E.'s services to her own coworkers, so that Teresa E.

eventually cleaned houses on different days of the week for three public health nurses who shared the same office but lived in different neighborhoods. Some domestic workers also found jobs through referrals received from their kin, primarily from their male kin who worked as gardeners.

The second step in securing employment is overcoming the regulations that require legal work authorization. The women that I interviewed reported that most employers in private residences do not ask to see documents verifying work authorization. Unlike employment in the formal sector of the economy, most employer-employee transactions in paid domestic work occur "under the table." The domestic workers generally received their weekly or biweekly pay in cash, which was typically either handed to them directly or left for them in an envelope. Employers did not pay social security taxes or federal or state income taxes, and employees were not eligible for unemployment or disability compensation.

Although employers did not ask for visual proof of legal status, they did sometimes inquire about their domestic workers' legal status; this became increasingly prevalent during the period in which I conducted the research. I conducted my interviews and participant observation in a volatile, transitional time, from November 1986, when the employer sanctions of IRCA went into effect, through May 1988. There was a heightened sensitivity to "illegal status" in the workplace during this period, as employers were required to fill out and keep on file "I-9" forms testifying to each new employee's work authorization.

When women received referrals from their established employers, the new prospective employers rarely inquired about legal status. Some women, however, did report difficulties when referrals did not come from one of their employers' friends. In these cases, the new employers asked the women if they had "papers." Maria G., for example, received a job lead from her brother-in-law, but when she telephoned to inquire, she was immediately asked if she had a "green card." She did not, so she did not further pursue this job prospect.

Undocumented legal status sometimes caused women to lose jobs where they had not yet established any tenure. In the spring of 1988, Tola B. started cleaning a large, two-story house that she described as unusually filthy. The employer led her to believe she would have a steady, once-a-week job, but when she asked if Tola was a citizen or legal resident, Tola told the truth. The following week, the employer telephoned to tell her that her cleaning services were no longer needed.

When Tola recounted this incident at a baptismal party in the park, her friends chastised her for not having lied about her legal status. One woman exclaimed, "What? You told her the truth? No, no, that's wrong. You have to tell them what they want to hear. They don't want to see your papers, they just want to hear you say that you have them." The other women nodded in agreement, and one added, "If they want me to be with papers, well, then that's how I present myself."

For Tola B. and the women to whom she recounted the incident, there appeared to be two morals to the story. First, the incident underlined how important it is not to reveal one's undocumented legal status. Revealing undocumented legal status can prevent or terminate employment, even in paid domestic work. And second, this case illustrated for the women the risk of taking on a new job where the house has not been recently cleaned. The hardest and dirtiest work is typically performed on the first visit, and domestic workers may be abruptly dismissed after the initial cleaning. In exchanges such as this one that occurred at the park, the women were teaching one another the normative behavior required to survive as an undocumented immigrant in the domestic work occupation.

Because job work requires that domestic workers acquire and maintain a number of different jobs, many of the undocumented immigrant women were constantly on the lookout for more jobs. Part of the occupation seems to be the search for more jobs and for jobs with better working conditions and pay, so the issues of concealment and detection of legal status arise constantly.

## Subcontracting Arrangements

Many undocumented immigrant women, especially those who are newly arrived, who are not well connected to kin networks, and who may be trying to get out of live-in work, find that it is difficult to secure their first engagements in job work. For this reason, they may first subcontract their services to other, more experienced and well-established immigrant women who have steady customers for domestic work. This provides an important apprenticeship and a potential springboard to independent contracting. Romero (1987) discusses the important training and recruitment functions of these apprenticeships among Chicana domestic workers in Denver. Although subcontracting can be beneficial to both parties, it is not a relationship characterized by altruism or harmony of interests.

In the community I studied, the informal subcontracting relationship was generally established between two Mexican undocumented immigrant women. Although these two women generally shared the same legal status, gender, race/ethnicity, and relative class position, they were differentiated by the length of time they had been in the United States and by the social network resources they had accumulated here. A newly arrived immigrant women who is "without papers" and is trying to break into job work is in a much weaker position than one who has been here a long time and is well established.

To illustrate the contrast between newly arrived and long-term, established undocumented immigrant women, I will examine the experiences of one woman who entered the occupation as a live-in and then became a subcontracted domestic worker. She was able to break out and establish clients of her own, and ultimately established a thriving route of employers, cleaning as many as 15 or 16 houses a week. In order to maintain her busy route, she took on, at different times, several undocumented immigrant women as subcontracted workers. This woman, Maria Alicia, secured her initial live-in job with the help of a female acquaintance. When the job did not yield the leads for domestic day work she had expected, Maria Alicia quit and began working alongside another immigrant women who promised to help Maria Alicia find her own *casas* (houses). Maria Alicia jumped at this chance, but she earned no wages as a domestic work helper. She recalled these days as being "full of exhaustion, anxiety, and nerves" as the job leads that she had expected were not forthcoming.

> I helped her to work a lot, and she did not pay me. Nothing, nothing. I would help her do three or four houses a day. No, no, no, no, they were giving me nothing. It would have been better had I never accepted. Then she started taking me to work with her daughter, so I said, well here I am going to charge. All I asked of her is that she understand that I am desperate, I need work.

After several months, she located a steady housecleaning job from another immigrant woman, but she held reserved appreciation for this favor: "I am grateful [to her], but she also wanted to get out of that job and she charged me [a fee] for it." When she secured this 25-hour-a-week job at an hourly rate of $5, she brought her three children from Mexico.

Maria Alicia gradually accumulated a number of different *casas* to clean on different days of the week. As she accumulated more houses, at different times she herself took on a number of "helpers" so that she could continue to add more houses and earnings to her weekly work schedule. These subcontracted workers were usually newly arrived kin or friends who were also undocumented immigrant women. Rather than recalling her experiences as a "helper" who was subcontracted to assist another paid domestic worker, she cited three recent incidents where her own hired "helpers" had not performed up to the standard she set. She now blames her sister for being too dependent and unassertive, her friend for being irresponsible and lazy, and her boyfriend's sister for being unwilling to work hard and initially accepting a low level of pay.

The subcontracting relationship embodies and reproduces inequality among paid domestic workers. Although she remains bitter about entering the occupation by working as a subcontracted helper, Maria Alicia now identifies with her position as a relatively successful domestic worker who occasionally takes on her own helpers. Her official legal status as an undocumented immigrant has not changed, but she has overcome some of the liabilities associated with it as she has accumulated experience, utilized network resources, and sometimes hires her own helpers.

For newly arrived undocumented immigrant women who lack sufficient contacts with employers, subcontracting provides an important means of entry into the occupation. For well-established domestic workers, the subcontracting relationship is a way to yield enough labor to cover an increasing number of lucrative jobs; that is, it is a way to advance one's own tenuous, but improving, economic situation. Domestic work is neither a static occupation nor a route to jobs in the formal sector of the economy. Even in the absence of formal occupational regulations and legal status protections, domestic workers can move up the ranks from live-in to job work, gradually finding employers who offer higher pay and better working conditions, accumulating more casas to clean, and eventually, perhaps, their own "hired help" to assist them in their employment.

## CONCLUSION

Although Zoë Baird's failed nomination for U.S. attorney general in the early months of the Clinton presidency placed Latina immigrant nannies and domestic workers in the national spotlight, the concerns of these Latina immigrant women were hardly mentioned in the Senate hearings or in the media coverage. In this chapter I have sought to foreground these women's voices and experiences with domestic work in order to elucidate the role of a neglected analytic category, legal status, in the study of women's labor force participation. I suggest that rather than attempting to isolate legal status as a measurable variable, it is more illuminating to examine how unauthorized legal status, together with race, class, and gender, changes over time and imposes different constraints in distinct contexts of domestic employment.

Live-in and job work arrangements are two very different types of domestic employment, and undocumented legal status assumes a specific meaning within the particular context of employment. Undocumented women employed as live-in domestic workers, who live and work in isolation from their families and communities, find that their unauthorized legal status, together with their lack of social resources, disposes them to take undesirable live-in jobs. Once in these positions, women with unauthorized legal status may be coerced to stay there. In these highly personalistic arrangements, employers may threaten to call the INS authorities, restrict aspects of daily life, or promise to sponsor applications for legal residency in return for submission, loyalty, and hard work. The undocumented legal status of live-in employees gives their employers extra leverage.

In job work arrangements, undocumented legal status becomes less of a liability. It is less "noticeable" and not as immediately telling as race, class, and gender. Employers may ask their domestic workers if they are here legally, and they may ask for documentary proof of legal residence, but there are no phenotypical or distinctive markers that denote legal status with certainty. Concealment of unauthorized legal status is achieved more readily than in live-in jobs, which are characterized by more personalistic and intrusive employer-employee relations. Finally, subcontracting work relations between undocumented immigrant women suggest that time and experience differentiate the effects of unauthorized legal status.

Undocumented legal status hinders these women's entrance and mobility in the formal sector of the economy, but it does not necessarily hinder their progression within the informal sector. Although these women are still denied the right to reside or move within the nation-state legally, and denied the legal rights of employment and social entitlements available to citizens and legal residents, they still manage to improve their employment. As the women accumulate experience and become enmeshed in community social networks with kin and friends, they are no longer as vulnerable as they were when they were newly arrived undocumented immigrants. Social network exchanges help to mitigate disadvantages of race, class, gender, and legal status. No simple dichotomy of undocumented immigrant women as workplace victims or as agents of resistance can capture the nuances of their lived experience and mobility within the domestic work occupation.

## REFERENCES

Bach, Robert L. and Howard Brill. 1990. "Shifting the Burden: The Impacts of IRCA on U.S. Labor Markets." Interim Report to the Division of Immigration Policy and Research, U.S. Department of Labor, February.

Bakan, Abigail B. and Daiva K. Stasiulis. 1995. "Making the Match: Domestic Placement Agencies and the Racialization of Women's Household Work." *Signs: Journal of Women in Culture and Society* 20:303-35.

Clark-Lewis, Elizabeth. 1995. *Living In, Living Out: African American Domestics in Washington, D.C., 1910-1940.* Washington, DC: Smithsonian Institution Press.

Colen, Shellee. 1989. " 'Just a Little Respect': West Indian Domestic Workers in New York City." Pp. 171-94 in *Muchachas No More: Household Workers in Latin America and the Caribbean,* edited by E. M. Chaney and M. Garcia Castro. Philadelphia: Temple University Press.

Collins, Patricia Hill. 1990. *Black Feminist Thought: Knowledge, Consciousness, and the Politics of Empowerment.* New York: Routledge, Chapman & Hall.

Dill, Bonnie Thornton. 1994. *Across the Boundaries of Race and Class.* New York: Garland.

Fernandez-Kelly, Maria Patricia and Anna M. Garcia. 1992. "Power Surrendered, Power Restored: The Politics of Work and Family among Hispanic Garment Workers in California and Florida." Pp. 130-49 in *Women, Politics, and Change,* edited by L. A. Tilly and P. Gurin. New York: Russell Sage Foundation.

Glenn, Evelyn Nakano. 1986. *Issei, Nisei, War Bride: Three Generations of Japanese American Women in Domestic Service.* Philadelphia: Temple University Press.

———. 1992. "From Servitude to Service Work: Historical Continuities in the Racial Division of Paid Reproductive Labor." *Signs: Journal of Women in Culture and Society* 18:1-43.

Grossman Brezin, Eliot Lee. 1989. "El Impacto del 'IRCA' Sobre la Comunidad Mexicana y Centroamericana en Los Angeles, California: El Caso de los Jornaleros." Paper presented at "Seminario Sobre la Migración Internacional en Mexico: Estado Actual y Perspectivas," organized by Consejo Nacional de Población, Cocoyoc, Morelos, Mexico, October 4-6.

Hondagneu-Sotelo, Pierrette. 1994. *Gendered Transitions: Mexican Experiences of Immigration.* Berkeley: University of California Press.

Kaplan, Elaine Bell. 1987. " 'I Don't Do No Windows': Competition between the Domestic Worker and the Housewife." Pp. 92-105 in *Competition: A Feminist Taboo?* edited by V. Miner and H. Longino. New York: Feminist Press.

Katzman, David M. 1981. *Seven Days a Week: Women and Domestic Service in Industrializing America.* Urbana: University of Illinois Press.

King, Deborah K. 1988. "Multiple Jeopardy, Multiple Consciousness: The Content of a Black Feminist Ideology." *Signs: Journal of Women in Culture and Society* 14:42-72.

Kossoudji, Sherrie A. and Susan I. Ranney. 1984. "The Labor Market Experience of Female Migrants: The Case of Temporary Mexican Migration to the U.S." *International Migration Review* 18:1120-43.

Mohanty, Chandra Talpade. 1991. "Cartographies of Struggle: Third World Women and the Politics of Feminism." Pp. 1-47 in *Third World Women and the Politics of Feminism*, edited by C. T. Mohanty, A. Russo, and L. Torres. Bloomington: Indiana University Press.

Palmer, Phyllis. 1989. *Domesticity and Dirt: Housewives and Domestic Servants in the United States, 1920-1945*. Philadelphia: Temple University Press.

Pessar, Patricia. 1984. "The Linkage between the Household and the Workplace in the Experience of Dominican Women in the U.S." *International Migration Review* 18:1188-1212.

Rollins, Judith. 1985. *Between Women: Domestics and Their Employers*. Philadelphia: Temple University Press.

Romero, Mary. 1987. "Domestic Service in the Transition from Rural to Urban Life: The Case of la Chicana." *Women's Studies* 13:199-222.

———. 1988. "Chicanas Modernize Domestic Service." *Qualitative Sociology* 11:319-34.

———. 1992. *Maid in the U.S.A.* New York: Routledge.

Ruiz, Vicki L. 1987. "By the Day or the Week: Mexicana Domestic Workers in El Paso." Pp. 61-76 in *Women on the U.S.-Mexico Border: Responses to Change*, edited by V. L. Ruiz and S. Tiano. Boston: Allen & Unwin.

Salzinger, Leslie. 1991. "A Maid by Any Other Name: The Transformation of 'Dirty Work' by Central American Immigrants." Pp. 139-60 in *Ethnography Unbound: Power and Resistance in the Modern Metropolis*, edited by M. Burawoy, A. Burton, A. A. Ferguson, K. J. Fox, J. Gamson, N. Gartrell, L. Hurst, C. Kurzman, L. Salzinger, J. Schiffman, and S. Ui. Berkeley: University of California Press.

Simon, Rita J. and Margo Corona De Ley. 1984. "The Work Experience of Undocumented Mexican Women Migrants in Los Angeles." *International Migration Review* 18:1212-29.

Sirola, Paula S. 1992. "Beyond Survival: Latino Immigrant Street Vendors in the Los Angeles Informal Sector." Paper presented at the International Congress of the Latin American Studies Association, Los Angeles, September 24-27.

Soldatenko, Maria Angelina. 1991. "Organizing Latina Garment Workers in Los Angeles." *Aztlan: Journal of Chicano Studies Research* 20:73-96.

Solorzano-Torres, Rosalia. 1987. "Female Mexican Immigrants in San Diego County." Pp. 41-60 in *Women on the U.S.-Mexico Border: Responses to Change*, edited by V. L. Ruiz and S. Tiano. Boston: Allen & Unwin.

Thomas, Robert J. 1985. *Citizenship, Gender and Work: Social Organization of Industrial Agriculture*. Berkeley: University of California Press.

Trevizo, Dolores. 1990. "Latina Baby-'Watchers' and the Commodification of Care." Master's thesis, University of California, Los Angeles, Department of Sociology.

Wrigley, Julia. 1991. "Feminists and Domestic Workers" (review essay). *Feminist Studies* 17:317-29.

Young, Grace Esther. 1987. "The Myth of Being 'Like a Daughter.' " *Latin American Perspectives* 14:365-80.

# PART III

# Health Care, Professions, Managerial Positions, and Entrepreneurship

The chapters in this section capture some of the varied work settings of women in health care, the professions, managerial positions, and entrepreneurial ventures and introduce the circumstances of some middle-class women. Increasingly, women are moving into professional and managerial occupations, augmenting their numbers in entrepreneurship, and even defining new work settings in line with feminist values. The meanings for women's lives behind these impressive statistics can be examined only through empirical research. The three chapters that follow address some specific questions that provide insights into central advances in women's positions. They also teach us that social class, race, and ethnicity are key in differentiating how women experience these advances.

In Chapter 6, Sandra Morgen, an anthropologist who has studied the women's health movement, directly addresses social class differences. When middle-class Euro-American women want to build a women's health center, coalitions are necessary. In Morgen's case study, middle-class Euro-American women reached out to working-class women within the same racial group. As she describes the resulting interactions, we can see what social class means. Morgen explores the meaning of social class in this work setting, where building bridges between working- and middle-class women was essential for success. She draws upon written materials and interviews with four women to bring to highlight the different ways that social class, and politics, shape perceptions and, as a consequence, interactions across class lines. Morgen presents multiple interpretations of events and, rather than privileging any of them, details how they were shaped by social location in the larger society and the specific clinic. Her work also highlights the power embedded in social class positions, regardless of whether or not people want to acknowledge it. She reveals the power to define situations that comes with middle-class privilege and how it is often taken for granted by those who have it, yet clearly visible to those who do not. There are many lessons in Morgen's chapter for the art of coalition building. It demonstrates the level at which we have to listen to people, even if we do not share their views, and the sorts of questions that are necessary for self-reflection about our own circumstances.

Whereas Morgen explores the role of social class in shaping different perceptions, Lynn Weber and Elizabeth Higginbotham, in Chapter 7, look at women with similar structural locations—that is, employed in professional and managerial occupations—and explore racial differences in the views of their experiences in work settings. Their samples of Black and White women from Memphis are matched to explore the workplace experiences of women with shared levels of educational attainment, work experience, and social class background. Their study reveals that Black and White women who enter professional and managerial careers in this job market face different circumstances, as racism and sexism still play a major role in many workplaces.

Weber and Higginbotham asked the members of their sample to respond to systematic questions, allowing them space for detailed answers; their chapter looks explicitly at the women's perceptions of race- and gender-based obstacles in their occupations. The racial differences in viewpoints are significant, and the authors discuss these thoroughly. A key point for all readers, however, is the degree to which many of these Black and White women noted differential treatment in their workplaces attributed to gender; the additional barrier of race makes these settings even more problematic for many Black women. Like many other women in this baby boom cohort, these educated women are career oriented but have to develop their work lives in places where stereotypical views of women are still commonplace.

Although Weber and Higginbotham's respondents differ in how they see and acknowledge racism as a central issue in their workplaces, there is no clear racial divide. About a third of the White women in their study who do acknowledge race as a factor in the workplace recognize the same types of disadvantages as Black women. Again, this chapter speaks to what is necessary for building coalitions and directs our attention to the need for greater sensitivity regarding the shape of racism and sexism, even in relatively privileged workplaces.

If workers at any level think their firms, agencies, or plants have fulfilled their commitment to social justice simply by hiring people of color, women, or both, then they will miss the whole picture. Such workers may not be attentive to the daily slights, blocked mobility, lack of financial rewards, and tensions that some people experience as they continually have to prove themselves worthy. Dialogue is necessary to help us see how others experience their workplaces, even when they share space with us. Race is one of the many lenses through which workplace experiences are viewed and interpreted, but we do not have to leave our findings at that level. Social scientists can look at patterns in workplace hiring and promotion for evidence that may show some perceptions to be more valid than others.

Achieving middle-class status through entrepreneurship has long been a tradition among many immigrants, especially when mainstream avenues of achievement are blocked by racial discrimination. In the United States, Korean immigrants are one of many Asian immigrant groups to follow this pattern (Takaki 1990). Yet we do not know enough about what economic success within a racial/ethnic enclave means in terms of changes for women's lives. In Chapter 8, Pyong Gap Min, one of an increasing number of Korean social scientists studying this growing immigrant community, looks directly at the work and family intersection as he explores the impact of Korean wives' employment on marital power and status. Telephone interviews and his own experiences in the Korean American community enable him to analyze how women's roles in family entrepreneurial efforts do little to shift their power in the family and status in the community. Korean women often serve in the capacity of unpaid family workers, and their specific contributions to their family businesses are hard to discern.

Like other immigrants who operate mostly within ethnic enclaves, Korean men and women are removed from the significant changes in gender relations that characterize the mainstream United States. Min's analysis urges us to challenge social science work that does not fully address context—that is, the meaning of work in an ethnic enterprise and the gender orientation of the racial/ethnic community. We can also see how the restriction of certain immigrant groups to limited business communities may mean economic success for them, but might also retard women's abilities to advance in terms of power within their own families and the wider community.

In many respects, the following three chapters pose critical questions about middle-class occupations and positions. In U.S. society we tend to think of arriving in middle-class occupations and work settings as reaching the finish line. These chapters reveal these occupations and settings as positions from which to reassess the challenges that still face women of varied circumstances.

## REFERENCE

Takaki, Ronald. 1990. *Strangers from a Different Shore: A History of Asian Americans.* Boston: Little, Brown.

# 6

# Class Experience and Conflict in a Feminist Workplace: A Case Study

## SANDRA MORGEN

This chapter contributes to the needed project of problematizing and reconceptualizing class in social theory. It explores the complex process by which Euro-American middle- and working-class women workers in a health collective came to understand their own class placement, cross-class relationships, and class "politics" within this workplace. The chapter examines the varying experiences and interpretations of events shared by four women, two of whom identify as working class and two of whom see themselves as middle class. An analysis is presented of how these multiple interpretations of events emerged from the different experiences of coworkers as these were shaped by their structural location in society and by structural barriers to egalitarian work relations in the health clinic.

Coalitions, alliances, and work relationships between working-class and middle-class women, and between Euro-American women and women of color, have rarely been easy expressions of "sisterhood." The explanation of why this is so has been at the heart of a body of feminist scholarship that has explored the roots of differences in power, privilege, and life experience among women differently socially located by race, ethnicity, and class (e.g., Anzaldúa 1990; Collins 1990; Dill 1983; hooks 1984; Hull, Scott, and Smith 1982). The most profound insights have emerged from recent critical scholarship on race and ethnicity that has problematized and theoretically reconstructed race and ethnicity as fluid, multivalent, relational, and situated social constructions (e.g., Brown 1992; Frankenberg 1993; Mohanty 1992; Williams 1991).

In this chapter, I contribute to the necessary project of similarly problematizing and reconceptualizing class in social theory. I focus on the meaning of class among Euro-American women workers in one workplace, a health clinic organized by a cross-class coalition seeking to provide women-controlled, accessible health services in a largely Euro-American working-class community in the 1970s. I explore the complex processes by which these women came to identify by class and examine how class differences were understood and negotiated in their work lives.

In recent years, dominant theories of class have been challenged by a host of critical theorists, including feminists, who argue that class has been reified, extracted from, and elevated above other social relations of power in much social theory (e.g., Hansen and Philipson 1989). Feminist scholarship on class has demonstrated, for example, that men and women may not develop class identities or consciousness in the same ways or with all of the same "results" in action (Rapp 1982; Grella 1990); that Euro-Americans and people of color experience class differently, in ways profoundly shaped by race and ethnicity (Davis 1981; Collins 1990); and that processes of class identification are complex, rarely reducible to the indicators generally used by social scientists to assign people to classes in their research (Vanneman and Weber Cannon 1987). Some of the most innovative work on class relies heavily on in-depth interviews, autobiography, and other narrative methodologies that examine class identification and consciousness as processes in which individuals engage as they live and work in families, communities, and workplaces (Steedman 1986; Steinitz and Solomon 1986; Fantasia 1988).

Building on the insights of this emerging critical scholarship on class, I present a case study based on in-depth interviews with four women who worked for a women's health clinic in a northeastern community in the 1970s. The interviews, conducted in 1990, ranged from one hour to almost four hours. Because the interviews covered events that had taken place a decade before, I also relied heavily on documentary evidence, including written materials authored by each of the women I interviewed. I was not a participant in these events, but they took place in a location not far from, and at a time roughly coterminous with, my two years of fieldwork in another women's health clinic, itself embroiled in conflicts over class and race (Morgen 1988).

In recent years, other scholars have examined how racial, ethnic, and class divisions among women workers reflect, sustain, and sometimes challenge the racism and dominant class relations that permeate the larger society (Bookman and Morgen 1988; Glenn 1986; Lamphere 1987; Milkman 1985; Rollins 1985; Sacks 1988; Zavella 1987). This research has been conducted in the factories, offices, hospitals, and private homes where most women work. The health clinic I studied differs from these workplaces because it sought to be a women-controlled workplace that aimed to challenge hierarchical, hegemonic power relations, including oppressive class relations. Although I would not argue that this case typifies the ways women workers experience, define, and contest class in all workplaces, it does provide a unique window into processes less likely to be visible or highlighted in conventional workplaces.

## COMMUNITY WOMEN FOR HEALTH: BACKGROUND AND HISTORY

Community Women for Health (a pseudonym) was one of thousands of grassroots women's health organizations founded in the 1970s. Unlike most of these other women's health groups, Community Women for Health (CWH) was founded by an alliance of Euro-American working- and middle-class women. The working-class women who helped to found CWH belonged to a neighborhood association that had been actively involved in a variety of local political campaigns. They lived in an industrial, predominantly White working-class community that was geographically part of a large and racially diverse metropolitan area. Most of these women had low-wage jobs and were raising families, some without partners. As a rule, they were high school graduates. Before they encountered the middle-class group, their goal had been to establish an immunization clinic for children.

The middle-class founders of the group belonged to a socialist-feminist organization that was based in another community in the metropolitan area. All were Euro-American and college educated. Many had worked in health care, as providers or political activists. Few had children at the time of these events, though many were married or in long-term partnerships. Their organization believed that the women's liberation movement had been overly dominated by White and middle-class women, and they hoped to develop a cross-class women's organization to initiate change in women's health care. To meet their goal of establishing a clinic "run by women, organized nonhierarchically, which would deliver good medical care and serve as an example of the possibilities of feminism and socialism" (CWH document), they began to look for a group of working-class women with complementary goals.

CWH opened its doors as a free clinic for women and children less than a year after the two groups began discussions. Over the next five years, the clinic grew and expanded its services. Members of the original founding groups and other community members worked as a collective to staff the clinic. Most of the working-class women who were involved were paid staff members who did clerical and administrative work, health outreach, and health service delivery. Almost all of the middle-class women worked as volunteers, sharing the same duties.

The group defined itself as a collective, meaning that important decisions were reached by paid staff and volunteers through democratic processes at staff meetings. Once the clinic began to receive state money and to provide health services, it was required to name a medical director who had a medical degree. One of the founders of the clinic, a physician, assumed that position. Laws governing nonprofit organizations also required the clinic to name a board of directors, nominally the group responsible for running the organization. For most of the clinic's history the board was "on paper only"; the collective of paid staff and volunteers actually ran the clinic.

The clinic operated from a storefront in the heart of the community. Early on, the collective decided to reserve most paid positions for working-class women from the community. This decision was based on the belief that working-class women would be more likely to be actively involved with the clinic if they could be paid, because they needed to provide income for their families. Not long after the clinic's founding, a group of health professionals involved in CWH opened a mental health clinic upstairs at the facility to provide counseling services for women in the community. The income these professionals received from providing fee-for-service counseling subsidized their volunteer activities with CWH.

The documentary evidence and my interviews demonstrate that the maintenance of a cross-class women's collective was challenging, exciting, and frequently rocky. In addition to the pressures attendant to keeping the clinic open with limited funds, the staff and volunteers often faced internal disagreements about clinic policies, working conditions, and overall direction. These disagreements ranged from differences of opinion about what color the clinic's walls should be to how paid staff should be supervised; opinions were divided about free versus low-fee services, the meaning of accountability to the community, and work and leadership styles.

These difficulties came to a head in the late 1970s, when the mainly middle-class board of CWH met secretly and decided to fire the paid staff of the clinic, all working-class women, and close the clinic to reorganize. Staff members were notified by registered mail that they were fired and eligible for three weeks' severance pay. Furious about both the process and the outcome of the board's decision, the staff organized a large community meeting to challenge the board's decision. At the meeting, the staff members labeled the decision to fire them as undemocratic, an example of middle-class women depriving working-class women and the community of "community control." By the meeting's end, the board members had resigned, staff members had regained their jobs, and CWH became a working-class-run health clinic for the next two years, until it closed.

## CLASS POLITICS WITHIN
## COMMUNITY WOMEN FOR HEALTH

How did an organization that began as an alliance of middle- and working-class women who shared the goal of empowering working-class women as clients and staff reach the point where a predominantly middle class board fired an exclusively working-class staff? To what extent were the divisions that culminated in this climax primarily about class? How did class background, identity, and consciousness affect the experiences women had working in this organization? These are the questions I explored in examining the archival and interview material. This case suggests that, despite good intentions, considerable attention to class issues, and the adoption of institutional goals and practices designed to equalize power relations between middle- and working-class women, class differences were often painfully evident in the relationships between them. Moreover, conflicts about working conditions and clinic policies often reproduced hegemonic class relations despite political aims and claims to the contrary.

To unravel the meaning and experiences of class and class conflict in CWH, I first examine the climactic moment when the history of divisions culminated in a power struggle for control of CWH. I then examine the voices and perspectives of four women: two who identify as middle-class, Margaret and Liz; and two who see themselves as working-class, Betsy and Jesse (all names are pseudonyms, and details are changed to protect identities). Then, I offer my own perspective on the complex class dynamics at work in this case.

Soon after these events (which took place in the late 1970s), a community newspaper printed three letters about the crisis. One viewpoint was expressed by the group of five staff members who had been fired and were now running the clinic. They took the position that "middle-class, professional" women had usurped working-class control, especially when they used the power of a "dummy board [to fire the staff] that was never intended to have any real power" (from the letter signed by Betsy and four others). A different perspective was expressed by the clinic's medical director, Margaret, who wrote, "My objection was not that [CWH] was being run by working-class women but that in my opinion it was being run very badly and the fact that the staff was working class was no excuse."

A third letter was authored by Jesse, a founding working-class member of the collective, who had resigned shortly before the firings because she believed that the actions of some of her working-class coworkers were destroying the clinic:

> CWH didn't become the utopian socialist feminist mini-society which proved that class was no obstacle for women working together. But the problem was not class, but a defect in our ways of handling situations. . . . There was a lack of trust on the part of both community and professional women. . . . There was a lack of solidarity in political objectives. We tried to pretend we didn't need any rules.

These different perspectives, presented in letters written in the heat of the crisis, were echoed in the interviews I did 15 years later with Betsy, Margaret, Jesse, and Liz. The in-depth interviews reveal how the meaning of class and the varying interpretations of the role of class in shaping power relations emerged from a complex combination of each woman's class background and class consciousness, her political ideology, and the actual experiences she had while working at CWH.

## FOUR VOICES

Betsy was 18 when she had her first pelvic exam at CWH because "it was free and had women doctors." She found a niche there and trained to be a lab volunteer. When a clinic job became available, she left her waitress job to work at the clinic. Betsy knew she wanted a life different from those of other women in her family and community and she felt she didn't quite "fit in" with her family and friends. Although the clinic offered her an alternative, she didn't feel she "fit in" there either.

For Betsy, the working-class female world she was part of was symbolized by wearing clothes, makeup, and hairstyles that identified her as a "chick," who went out to bars with her friends from high school. It meant having a dull job and punching a clock, like her father, a factory worker. The job at the clinic meant dressing and thinking like a feminist, and making a difference in the world. Betsy found that straddling the two worlds was difficult: "During the day, I . . . wore flannel and sort of was feminist and then, in the evening, I'd go out with my . . . friends and I'd be a chick and a babe. It was very confusing to me."

Betsy was painfully aware that she had less education, fewer skills, and different life experiences and expectations from those of her middle-class coworkers. On the other hand, clinic ideology valorized the "community women," as the working-class women were called, and the political culture of the clinic emphasized the equal worth of all of its staff and volunteers. For Betsy, negotiating the ideology of equality with the everyday experience of inequality was hard: "We acted as if we were all equal. . . . But, in fact, they had a lot more advantages." In her interview Betsy detailed some of the advantages she saw the middle-class women as having: going to college, having had braces, having parents who sent you clothes, and full refrigerators. She clearly perceived the lives of middle-class women to involve fewer daily struggles than those of working-class women.

Betsy's pain and anger sharpened when she, and some of her coworkers, began to feel they were being monitored, judged, and, increasingly, treated as employees rather than coworkers by some of the middle-class women involved with the center. She dated the transformation of class differences into class conflict from specific problems that emerged after the group of mental health professionals began to offer counseling services in rooms upstairs from the clinic. She reported that conflicts arose when the women who were both CWH and counseling collective members began to engineer changes in the physical appearance of their shared space (including painting the colorful walls white) and the way the jointly used telephones were to be answered. Counseling collective members had a strong influence over decisions of the health collective, but the reverse was not true. The counseling collective was an autonomous body made up entirely of middle-class, professionally trained women. Decisions began to feel "imposed," Betsy recalled:

> All of a sudden the [counseling] collective decided they didn't like the colors [of the walls]. They wanted everything white. . . . They wanted to not only be a separate group that helped us out, but they wanted to control the health [clinic]. Control the color the walls were painted. Control what we said on the phone. . . . It just got to be it was their clinic and we were workers.

A series of explosive meetings ensued. Two middle-class women, both longtime members of the collective, resigned to protest the undemocratic decision making on the part of professional women. Their letter of resignation was a scathing critique of a "professionalism" that denied working-class women an equal voice in decisions.

According to Betsy, such problems worsened over time. For example, as part of a commitment to the empowerment of working-class women, the collective developed a policy that enabled "community women" to be paid for hours they spent taking classes. This was an important benefit, because education past high school had been beyond the financial reach of these women. However, soon after Betsy began taking a class, a new committee was established that, according to her, was to "check up on people." They explored whether employees were going to their classes and doing their jobs "right."

Betsy believed these new procedures showed disrespect for and distrust of the working-class staff and symbolized the increasing hierarchy within the staff. Suddenly, decisions the collective had made to provide education benefits to the staff and to reserve most of the paid positions for working-class women were being used against the working-class staff members. This fed her perception that the middle-class women did not see the working-class women as equals:

I think the community women never felt like they were as good. And as much as we talked about it and hashed it out, in the end that's what it boiled down to. There were questions about whether we were really doing our jobs. There were questions about whether or not community women had the same commitment to the health project as the middle-class women. . . . There was a belief [that] community women were only there for a paycheck. . . . What they did was put all community women in the paid positions. So, of course it would appear that way to the naked eye.

The feeling of being defined as employees rather than coequals in the health collective peaked when Betsy and the other paid staff were fired. She saw this action as the abuse of raw power: "I think it came down to a real power struggle in the sense that they wanted control of the health project."

Jesse, a founding member of CWH and lifelong resident of the community, was a working-class mother of four children. Jesse was attuned to differences between her life experiences and those of the middle-class women with whom she worked, but she also shared important political beliefs and experiences with them, particularly her opposition to the Vietnam War. When she first heard the socialist feminists articulate their vision of a health center, she determined that "our politics were very similar."

Jesse remembered the year of meetings before the clinic was founded as exciting, and sometimes "stormy." Although some of the working-class women were suspicious of the motives of the middle-class women from across the city, Jesse saw the groups as having complementary strengths: "People who had skills to share would share them, and the women who had community expertise would share it, and working together . . . we would learn from each other." Jesse's assessment of her relationships with the middle-class members of the collective differs from Betsy's. She felt supported and believed she gained important skills through her relationships with her professional coworkers. She took advantage of the education program the clinic provided for working-class staff and went back to college; over the years, she earned internship credits by working with the counseling collective.

Jesse acknowledged that disagreements within the staff were routinely defined by some working- and middle-class coworkers as class differences. But in her opinion, these disagreements stemmed from differences in "politics" and "work style and expectations." The problems that ultimately led her to quit resulted from the collective's unwillingness to confront or discipline a few coworkers who were not doing their jobs well. According to Jesse, the collective often hired women who lacked both the skills and the shared political commitment necessary to be effective members of the collective. These women, often former clients, needed jobs, but sometimes they suffered from problems such as alcohol abuse or domestic violence, which she saw interfering with their job performance. However, the collective was reluctant to fire anyone, even for poor job performance. For example, one woman, whose alcoholism resulted in frequent absenteeism, was the subject of group discussions for six months. In response to a proposal to fire her, Jesse remembers, "other working-class women said absolutely no . . . we have to help her. I said how? Well, we don't know. That was one of the issues I quit over."

Jesse defined the failure to confront women who were not doing their jobs well as paternalism. Although she acknowledged that it was wrong to impose political views on "community women," she believed that everyone hired should share the general political goals of CWH. Otherwise, she reasoned, the collective could not count on political commitment to motivate work discipline. In her opinion, in the absence of shared political commitment, other forms of work rules became necessary. However, when work rules were proposed, class became a "bogeyman." Those staff or board members who wanted to fire women for poor job performance were accused of indifference and not understanding the issues facing working-class women. The result was a stalemate, and polarization within the staff increased.

Margaret's perspective on the nature and roots of the problems of CWH was similar to Jesse's in crucial ways, despite differences in their class backgrounds and structural relationships to the clinic. Margaret, a White middle-class woman, helped found CWH just after finishing her residency at a prestigious hospital. When CWH applied for a clinic license, she was named medical director. Margaret understood that this title did not imply that she was to have any greater power than other women in the collective; rather, her appointment was mandated by requirements of funding agencies. Margaret was also a founding member of the counseling collective.

From Margaret's perspective, the decision to fire the paid staff and close the clinic resulted from a sharp deterioration of services, an impending financial crisis, and the widespread perception that decision-making processes "had broken down completely." As medical director and board member, she was unwilling to accept "legal and moral responsibility for a situation over which I felt I had no control." Like Jesse, Margaret believed that a failure to develop "basic points of political unity and to define our goals clearly" led to ongoing personnel crises. Like Jesse, she opposed hiring women who did not fully embrace CWH goals or who did not have the skills needed to do their jobs.

Margaret noted that a fear of conflict had historically led the collective to "sweep our differences under the rug." She believed that when conflicts emerged over personnel issues, middle-class members were accused of being "insensitive" to working-class women and of using their "class privilege" to get their way. Margaret argued that class conflict was an inadequate explanation for the problems that existed within the staff. She noted that middle- and working-class women could be found on both sides. She used Jesse as an example of a working-class woman who shared the view that a woman's class background and personal problems did not cancel out her responsibility to do her job well.

In her interview, Margaret showed considerable awareness of how her class position, and especially her medical training, shaped her attitudes and actions. She admitted to having a "take-charge" attitude that, in her mind, was filling a "power vacuum" that existed at the clinic:

> We moved into this organization that I have to say was in great disarray when we arrived. . . . We swept the floors, painted things. Part of that was the ideology that there shouldn't be an enormous division of labor along professional lines. . . . But I think once you've been through an internship and residency and you move into a situation that is chaotic, you are accustomed to certain ways. Making structure, . . . being work oriented, production oriented, not particularly process oriented. I mean I'm about as process oriented as they come for docs.

Although she acknowledges that she, and others in the counseling collective, had considerable power, she attributes this not to class, but to structural problems with collectivity that allowed individuals who put more time and energy into the clinic to have more influence: "So if you kind of last out everybody else, you got your way. So there were six of us [the counseling collective] and . . . we got our way."

From Margaret's perspective, the professionals who had made a long-term commitment to CWH sought not control, but to "get organized": by painting the walls and doing minor carpentry, searching for stable outside funding, proposing to charge sliding-scale fees instead of providing free care, and completing the paperwork that would enable them to bill Medicaid. She saw these changes not in terms of community versus professional control but as actions to get CWH "a little more organized, and a little more on a firm financial footing." From her perspective, these changes were consistent with the clinic's goals.

Margaret believed that many members of the collective had a "romanticized" view of working-class women, a view that interfered with the development of clear criteria for hiring or holding staff accountable to basic features of work discipline. She acknowledges that the decision to fire the staff and close the clinic for reorganization was undemocratic. But she saw these actions as a last desperate attempt to save the clinic, a goal she saw as being in the long-term interest of both the community and the many women who had worked to build CWH.

Liz, a middle-class woman who worked at the clinic for several years after its founding, resigned about 18 months before the mass firing. Her eight-page letter of resignation describes the actions of "professional women [who] were wrecking the clinic." She was troubled by "changes in the direction and tone of the [clinic] that . . . occurred slowly and subtly, not by mandate . . . but by unrecognized power manipulations." In this letter and her interview, Liz recounted incidents that showed how the middle-class members of the counseling collective treated their working-class coworkers with contempt and insensitivity. Liz claimed the professional women were unable to see working-class women as equals, "as anything other than a client." Liz echoed Betsy's view that the decision to paint the walls white exemplified "professionalism" and disregard for the work and desires of the working-class women to make the place their own.

Liz strongly believed that the criticisms of some of the working-class staff for not being "accountable" to work rules and time schedules resulted from narrow definitions of accountability. She argued that much of the work the working-class women did was invisible, particularly the outreach, community education, and organizing that took place outside the clinic:

> Like pushing sex education in the schools . . . these are volatile issues and pretty risky for people who live here. . . . And there was no appreciation of what that meant. . . . All the groundwork and things the community women did to make us able to do what we did . . . [the professional women] didn't see that as work. It was invisible to them. It was the most narrow sense of responsibility and accountability.

Liz believed that "what was important about class is that different people have different amounts of control over their own lives, different amounts of power in society . . . and therefore different self-interests in the system." Her understanding of class became visceral and concrete through her work at CWH:

> When I went into the [collective] I had like a certain language or analysis [of class], but I didn't really have an understanding of it. . . . I came to understand from what people from the community shared with me. You know, including their inner lives and by when somebody overstepped something. . . . I think the working-class women there had a much sharper gut understanding of the situation than I did.

Liz felt that the professional women "had blinders on," that they had a hard time seeing things from the perspective of their working-class coworkers. And because of class differences, she saw that it was hard for the working-class women to "go like a united group up against this united group of professionals. . . . They have all these articulation skills and jargonize everything."

Liz saw part of the problem as structural. Because the counseling collective functioned as a separate entity, CWH had no control over what the counseling collective did, whereas the counseling collective members functioned as a bloc and had considerable influence in CWH. Moreover, any internal disagreements of the counseling collective were closed to the view of CWH members, whereas the problems and divisions within the health collective were in full view of the counseling collective. Liz saw this as a mirror of the traditional professional-client relationship, an imbalance of disclosure and distance, with the professionals less vulnerable. She believed that some of the working-class staff sought to redress that balance by not sharing their internal problems and differences openly: "We had to do the same thing. . . . It wasn't like there weren't issues of accountability and responsibility. . . . But we couldn't be open about them because they weren't open."

Liz resigned because she believed some of the middle-class women elevated their self-interests over the goal of creating a cross-class organization to empower and serve working-class women in the community. For Liz, once the professional women's desire to "be their own bosses" traversed the line to becoming "bosses" over women they judged to be unworthy of sharing in the collective task of running the clinic, their class backgrounds had caught up with them.

## THE MEANINGS AND EXPERIENCES
## OF CLASS AND CONFLICT

In the previous section, I counterposed the voices of four women whose interpretations of shared historical events differ substantially. Each narrative articulates an analysis grounded in the experiences of that particular woman, experiences that had meaning and were felt in the context of the power relations of both the larger society and this workplace. I now offer another analysis, one meant to be positioned alongside, not "above" (as some privileged objective reading), the analyses of the four women I interviewed. My goal is not to choose one voice as authoritative. Rather, I examine how these multiple interpretations of events emerged from the different experiences of these coworkers as these were shaped by their structural location in society and the clinic.

That class is an elusive, often confusing concept for the women involved in CWH is not surprising, given the degree to which class is mystified and dominant class relations are reproduced in everyday life in U.S. society. Although CWH professed a commitment to working-class women and community empowerment, the meanings of class and class allegiances and relations were also strongly shaped by dominant relations of power and ideas about class. Even strongly felt oppositional political beliefs can be overshadowed by the heavy class lines that divide working-, middle-, and upper-class people in the larger society. Classes are segregated through housing and neighborhood patterns, differential education (separate schools, tracking, access to postsecondary education), and a host of other social structures and dynamics. Although middle- and working-class persons often work together, their employment opportunities differ, and middle-class individuals routinely have positions of authority and supervision over members of the working class. In the face of these structural realities, cross-class unity or understanding can be achieved only when those who benefit from prevailing class relations become aware and do the work of contesting those class relations, and when those subordinated by prevailing class relations have the resources, the will, and the support they need to initiate and guide those changes.

After examining many documents and interviewing my four informants, I believe it is clear that the problems at CWH did not stem from a failure of goodwill or intentions. Rather, a series of structural barriers to egalitarian work relations combined with the different stakes and understandings of women from different social locations in the class structure to create tensions and social relations that resulted from and contributed to conflicts over class.

Betsy repeatedly expressed the confusion and pain she experienced as she tried to balance CWH's stated ideological commitment to equality with her felt experience of not being equal. That disjuncture stemmed initially from her perception that the working-class staff lacked privileges and skills enjoyed by middle-class women. As conflicts pitting middle- and working-class women against each other escalated, Betsy grew angry and felt less like a coworker and more like an employee. Feeling unequal began to mean having less influence in work decisions, and finally being the object rather than the subject of decision making, when she was fired. On the other hand, Margaret and Jesse both expressed their frustration at not being able to convince the collective to fire staff who were not doing their jobs well. From their perspective, the working-class solidarity that protected some women from being fired was evidence that the paid staff did not share an overriding political commitment to CWH.

Although each of the women I interviewed cited examples of her own diminished feelings of control over important decisions, not everyone participated in the decision-making process with the same resources. Here is where some of the structural barriers to creating egalitarian cross-class relations are most evident. Because the clinic had to conform to a series of state regulations governing health organizations and nonprofit organizations, women with professional credentials or other class-related advantages (e.g., education, greater ease dealing with authority figures, and experience using the language of the bureaucracy) accrued important organizational power. Additionally, because of the dynamics of the political economy of health in the United States, operating a free clinic meant securing external funds (e.g., donations, grants, and contracts). Again, the professional women had skills and expertise not shared by most of the working-class women that enhanced the power and influence they wielded in decision making.

Theoretically, the resources and skill differences that gave a structural advantage to middle-class women were balanced by equally valued advantages brought to the organization by working-class women. But "community expertise" was often a vague, hard-to-identify resource, and, according to Liz, the professional women seemed to lack an appreciation of "the groundwork and things the community women did to make us able to do what we did."

As long as there were few lines of fissure in the organization, the delicate balance of different skills and resources did represent equal, complementary contributions to CWH. However, once disagreements arose, the balance was altered. Some resources became more important than others. Among those were the ability to articulate a position eloquently, having a solid bloc of support for one's position (e.g., the counseling collective), the ability to maintain a flow of money through the clinic, and holding positions such as medical director or board member. In each of these, working-class women were at a disadvantage. From Liz's perspective, the balance of power between the resources of professionals and community women was most undermined by the structural relationship of the counseling collective to CWH. Because the counseling collective met separately, its members could hash out their differences out of view and then function as a powerful bloc.

There were other ways differential structural relationships to the clinic shaped conflicts and the resources of different groups. For example, the decision to reserve most of the paid positions for "community women" backfired later when longtime volunteers and board members defined their own commitment to CWH solely in political terms in contradistinction to the "community women," who were portrayed as being involved "only for a paycheck." This issue became painful for the community women, who objected to having their commitment measured by middle-class women, the very class of women who were often in a position to judge them as authority figures (i.e., as teachers, nurses, doctors, social workers). At CWH, conflicts between middle- and working-class women sharpened a problem endemic in other organizations that combine volunteer and paid labor.

In the end, dominant class relations reverberated in the social relationships among staff, which were strongly influenced by structural barriers to egalitarian class relations. Some of these structural barriers were a direct result of class privileges or disadvantages that predated the women's involvement with the clinic, privileges or disadvantages that had accumulated during their lifetimes. Other barriers evolved as the unintended consequences of well-intentioned decisions, such as to reserve paid positions for working-class staff, creating both the possibility to define differential commitment and the sorting that resulted in a mainly middle-class board of directors and an almost exclusively working-class staff. Ultimately, a "management" versus "worker" scenario unfolded in ways that mirrored rather than subverted the dominant class relations of the larger society.

Up to this point, I have used the terms *community women* and *professional, working-class* and *middle-class,* respectively, as they were used by members of CWH—that is, relatively interchangeably. Here I want to suggest that the vocabulary of class can reveal the ambiguities and problems that are embodied in the conflicts presented in this case. From the very beginning of meetings between the two founding groups, the term *community women* was used by, and to refer to, the working-class women involved in CWH. The term defined what was shared by the working-class women and what differentiated them from the middle-class women: being of the community. The term *community women* often substituted for *working-class,* a term the use of which might suggest a higher degree of class consciousness or at least a greater ease with a politicized language of class. Encoded in the term *community women* is a recognition that these women had a higher stake in the community. This was both a reminder and a warning to middle-class "outsiders" to be cautious about imposing themselves where they did not belong.

On the other hand, the use of the term *professional* as code for middle-class increased during CWH's later years. Early documents are replete with the term *middle-class,* but language referring to *professionals* is unusual. This practice is in part because of the strong ideology against professionalism in the women's health movement. The term *professional* entered the vocabulary of the group as conflicts escalated, and particularly in reference to conflicts between the counseling collective and CWH. For example, Liz's letter of resignation dwells on the different interests of "community women" and "professionals," and articulates her belief that the primary interests of the professionals had been to create "a place where they can work and make a comfortable income, be their own bosses, and preferably do work that doesn't make them feel guilty." She argues that "professional self-interest" conflicted with the goal of making CWH a working-class and community-controlled organization.

It was in the context of this evolving vocabulary of class that individuals came to understand their own class placement, cross-class relationships, and "class politics" within the clinic. The issue of class placement or identification is complex, more so than is acknowledged by the standard social scientific practice of assigning class position on the basis of objective criteria such as income, education, and the occupation of an individual or household head or relationship to the means of production. Class location or position and class identity are not identical, and researchers need to investigate, rather than presume, how individuals define their class identity, including what class or classes they identify with and the salience of class identity as part of their social identity.

These women's discussion about class revealed their understanding to be relational and situated. Christine Grella (1990) found a similar pattern in her study of women and class after divorce; she concludes that for these women, "social class emerged as a process in negotiation. . . . women used social comparisons with others to evaluate their social status and to situate themselves in society" (p. 45). In other words, class identification is relational and fluid. Betsy's interview responses were laced with assessments of how she felt similar to and different from both her working-class family and friends and her middle-class coworkers. Jesse recognized how her lifelong residence in the community and her class background situated her as a "community woman." However, she also shared key political experiences and ideals with most of the middle-class members of CWH and often found herself on the same side of issues as them. Margaret noted that her direct, take-charge attitude stems, in part, from her class background, but she also saw herself as giving up key class privileges and reorienting her class loyalties by choosing to work in this community health clinic rather than in a more lucrative, prestigious job. Liz closely allied herself with the working-class staff. As one of only a few middle-class women to hold a paid position during the clinic's history, and as someone without professional training or credentials, she perceived herself as being in a structural relationship to the clinic more similar to that of the "community women" than that of the "professionals." Furthermore, Liz acknowledged that class "has always been an issue for me." Growing up in one of the biggest houses in a relatively poor section of an economically diverse suburb, and being educated in a school that practiced tracking, she often felt "at odds, either from one end or the other, in terms of class."

For Betsy, Jesse, Liz, and Margaret, class was more than a calculus of where they, as individuals, are positioned within a class structure. Class became meaningful as class identification and relations shaped power relations within the group and understandings of self in relation to others (in the group and in the larger society). Class identity emerged, solidified, and fragmented as individuals and groups perceived overlapping or divergent interests and felt understood, misunderstood, accepted, or judged by others.

Moreover, although an oppositional class analysis was at the core of the political vision of the clinic's founders, the collective neither demanded nor systematically fostered a particular political understanding of class. Although newsletters and other CWH documents expressed basic feminist and socialist principles, there was no sustained, systematic self-education provided for the staff or the larger community that would have created the foundation for a shared class politics, except in the broadest outlines. Such a process might have provided a forum for discussion of class differences that could have illuminated, or changed, some of the misunderstandings and differences between middle- and working-class coworkers.

This is not to say there were no attempts to create shared understandings of class. There were obstacles to such a process, however, including the middle-class women's awareness that it would be wrong to impose a political vision on their working-class coworkers; the demanding everyday reality of running a health clinic in a community with significant and unmet health needs; and, as time passed and conflicts escalated, a fear of fanning the flames of disharmony. My point here is to suggest that when Jesse and Margaret argued that the absence of a shared political vision was the real source of the problems, they had a point. But class differences and tensions are important reasons the processes that might have created that shared political vision did not happen.

Part of the problem was the difficulty of cross-class communication. Divisive conflicts were rarely followed by honest, constructive discussion. Rather, as Margaret admitted, differences were often "swept under the rug." A document written by one of the founders of the collective suggests that this pattern had been going on for a long time. She noted: "We were terrified of talking to working-class people because we so objectified those class differences." The result: "We did not know how to talk about those differences in a useful way and ended up . . . by only feeling guilty for who we were." On the other hand, many of the working-class women were intimidated and silenced by the language and style of their middle-class coworkers, especially by their polished, articulate, "jargonizing" talk.

In the final analysis, class differences, divisions, and conflict played a significant role in the ultimate dissolution of the cross-class alliance that had created and maintained CWH for more than five years. But it was not a simple matter of everyone playing out scripted class roles dictated solely by class background or even the larger class relations that characterize this society. Factions were not always neatly divided by class, and both middle- and working-class women brought a healthy dose of distrust of each other to their relationships.

Ultimately, although the middle-class cofounders and members of CWH genuinely sought to implement a socialist, working-class-oriented politics, they were ambivalent about losing control of the political direction of CWH. This is evident in a statement in an early CWH document: "We had a defined set of politics we wanted to communicate. . . . We did want the clinic to be eventually community controlled but we wanted that control to be by women who agreed with our politics." The desire to maintain control, to run the clinic according to their vision, was behind some of the actions professional women took to "save" the clinic. When the board fired the paid staff, they convinced themselves that the clinic's future depended on suspending community control, at least to the extent that it meant retaining the current working-class staff. From the perspective of (most of) the working-class staff, this was just one more example of hegemonic class relations in action.

## CONCLUSION

There are a number of conclusions one can draw from this case study concerning the meaning of class identities and the sources of class divisions among women workers. First, it is crucial to recognize that as long as class (and race and ethnicity) structures the resources, opportunities, and textures of relationships among women, work organizations that aim to subvert or transform dominant power relations will need to provide sustained forums in which women learn from each other and communicate directly about their different perspectives. "Better communication" means more than the airing of different views and perspectives. It requires that those who bring class or racial privilege into an organizational context be open to hearing and changing how that class or racial privilege operates to silence, marginalize, and overwhelm those without that privilege.

Second, it is unlikely that even much enhanced dialogue will result in everyone's sharing a common perspective or organizational vision. Given that, organizations must seek both to honor diversity (respecting the multiple perspectives within) and to scrutinize rigorously how different social locations shape that diversity. This will enable organizations to choose courses of action based less on the eloquence, intensity, or frequency of stated positions and more on strategic considerations that emerge from the most important organizational goals.

Finally, we must recognize that key aspects of our identities (including our class and our race, ethnicity, gender, and sexuality) are being contested, affirmed, and/or reshaped by large-scale historical processes that produce differences of power, privilege, and meaning. It is in the long-term interest of strong alliances and coalitions that groups develop ways of talking and acting that contribute to the redistribution of power and resources in both the short and the long run. That means that everyone involved has to change. Feminist theorists and activists may be more aware today of how class (and racial and ethnic) differences and conflicts divide women and undermine their political and organizational efficacy than was commonplace in the middle and late 1970s, when CWH was struggling to forge a new vision of feminist practice. However, until scholars, activists, and women at large more fully understand how class works in our everyday lives, we will undoubtedly continue to experience difficulties in forging cross-class relations and alliances in our workplaces and our shared communities.

## REFERENCES

Anzaldúa, Gloria, ed. 1990. *Making Face, Making Soul: Haciendo Caras: Creative and Critical Perspectives by Women of Color.* San Francisco: Aunt Lute.

Brown, Elsa Barkley. 1992. "What Has Happened Here: The Politics of Difference in Women's History and Feminist Politics." *Feminist Studies* 18:295-312.

Bookman, Ann and Sandra Morgen, eds. 1988. *Women and the Politics of Empowerment: Perspectives from the Workplace and the Community.* Philadelphia: Temple University Press.

Collins, Patricia Hill. (1990). *Black Feminist Thought: Knowledge, Consciousness, and the Politics of Empowerment.* New York: Routledge, Chapman & Hall.

Davis, Angela. 1981. *Women, Race and Class.* New York: Vintage.

Dill, Bonnie Thornton. 1983. "Race, Class and Gender: Prospects for an All-Inclusive Sisterhood." *Feminist Studies* 9:131-49.

Fantasia, Rick. 1988. *Cultures of Solidarity: Consciousness, Action and Contemporary American Workers.* Berkeley: University of California Press.

Frankenberg, Ruth. 1993. *White Women, Race Matters: The Social Construction of Whiteness.* Minneapolis: University of Minnesota Press.

Glenn, Evelyn Nakano. 1986. *Issei, Nisei, War Bride: Three Generations of Japanese American Women in Domestic Service.* Philadelphia: Temple University Press.

Grella, Christine. 1990. "Irreconcilable Differences: Women Defining Class after Divorce and Downward Mobility." *Gender & Society* 4:41-56.

Hansen, Karen and Ilene Philipson, eds. 1989. *Women, Class, and the Feminist Imagination: A Socialist-Feminist Reader.* Philadelphia: Temple University Press.

hooks, bell. 1984. *Feminist Theory: From Margin to Center.* Boston: South End.

Hull, Gloria, Patricia Bell Scott, and Barbara Smith, eds. 1982. *All the Women Are White, All the Blacks Are Men, But Some of Us Are Brave: Black Women's Studies.* Old Westbury, NY: Feminist Press.

Lamphere, Louise. 1987. *From Working Daughters to Working Mothers: Immigrant Women in a New England Industrial Community.* Ithaca, NY: Cornell University Press.

Milkman, Ruth, ed. 1985. *Women, Work and Protest: A Century of U.S. Women's Labor History.* Boston: Routledge & Kegan Paul.

Mohanty, Chandra Talpade. 1992. "Feminist Encounters: Locating the Politics of Experience." Pp. 74-92 in *Destabilizing Theory: Contemporary Feminist Debates,* edited by M. Barrett and A. Phillips. Stanford, CA: Stanford University Press.

Morgen, Sandra. 1988. "The Dream of Diversity, Dilemmas of Difference: Race and Class Contradictions in a Feminist Health Clinic." Pp. 370-80 in *Anthropology for the Nineties,* edited by Johnnetta B. Cole. New York: Free Press.

Rapp, Rayna. 1982. "Family and Class in Contemporary America: Notes toward an Understanding of Ideology." Pp. 168-87 in *Rethinking the Family: Some Feminist Questions,* edited by B. Thorne. New York: Longman.

Rollins, Judith. 1985. *Between Women: Domestics and Their Employers.* Philadelphia: Temple University Press.

Sacks, Karen Brodkin. 1988. *Caring by the Hour: Women, Work, and Organizing at Duke Medical Center.* Urbana: University of Illinois Press.

Steedman, Carolyn. 1986. *Landscape for a Good Woman: A Story of Two Lives.* London: Virago.

Steinitz, Victoria and Ellen Solomon. 1986. *Starting Out: Class and Community in the Lives of Working-Class Youth.* Philadelphia: Temple University Press.

Vanneman, Reeve and Lynn Weber Cannon. 1987. *The American Perception of Class.* Philadelphia: Temple University Press.

Williams, Patricia. 1991. *The Alchemy of Race and Rights.* Cambridge, MA: Harvard University Press.

Zavella, Patricia. 1987. *Women's Work and Chicano Families: Cannery Workers of the Santa Clara Valley.* Ithaca, NY: Cornell University Press.

# 7

# Black and White Professional-Managerial Women's Perceptions of Racism and Sexism in the Workplace

## LYNN WEBER
## ELIZABETH HIGGINBOTHAM

This chapter compares the perceptions of global race and gender discrimination of same-age African American and White women who are situated in the labor force in the same occupations and industries and who share educational credentials, experience, economic standing, and social class histories. This study uses a quota sample of 200 full-time employed women professionals, managers, and administrators (100 Black and 100 White) in the Memphis, Tennessee, metropolitan area. The findings indicate that the majority of White and Black respondents perceived differential treatment due to sex in their workplaces. Although a majority of the Black women also perceived differential treatment due to race, this was less often the case with the White women. And while many of these Black and White women recognized group discrimination, they were less likely to see personal disadvantage in their work settings.

AUTHORS' NOTE: The research reported in this chapter was supported by National Institute of Mental Health Grant MH 38769. We want to acknowledge the assistance of Jo Ann Ammons, Hokulani Aikau, Shannon Diamond, Sandra Marion, Stephanie Messer, Lauren Rauscher, Christine Robinson, Tonye Smith, and Yang Su. We also appreciate the comments of reviewers and colleagues.

153

It is well documented that despite recent gains, both Black and White women professionals and managers still earn far less than White men and remain segregated into segments of the workforce with limited advancement opportunities and "glass ceilings" (McGuire and Reskin 1993). Further, Black women professionals and managers earn less than White women professionals and managers (Higginbotham 1987, 1994; McGuire and Reskin 1993; Sokoloff 1992; Woody 1992). Yet our knowledge of how race and gender systems of inequality are experienced and understood by Black and White women is far less systematic and largely based on anecdotal evidence and qualitative studies of small, racially homogeneous groups of women. Understanding the ways women perceive race and gender inequity in the workplace is important for many reasons, one of the most important being the quest for common ground on which to forge collective action to redress inequities. Efforts to forge multiracial coalitions among women have often failed when women of color are expected to buy into a women's political agenda that does not reflect their sense of the problems (Baca Zinn, Weber Cannon, Higginbotham, and Dill 1986; Spelman 1988). Thus understanding the nuances in the ways that Black and White women—especially in the same structural locations and/or workplaces—perceive and respond to race and gender inequality is a critical project for social change.

Through the research presented below, we seek to contribute to that project by identifying similarities and differences in the ways that Black and White women professionals and managers perceive both race discrimination and gender discrimination in the workplace. We explore the extent to which Black and White women professionals and managers perceive discriminatory treatment in key dimensions of their work.

We review below two major types of studies that address race and gender discrimination in the workplace. First, studies of structural inequality, typically based on quantitative analyses of census data or large-scale surveys, control factors such as experience and credentials and document race and gender differences in such rewards as pay, rank, and promotions. Second, experiential studies explore women's perceptions of equity, discrimination, rewards, and opportunities. These studies are typically based on in-depth interviews with small, racially homogeneous samples. Unlike the quantitative studies, they do not typically control or analyze other factors, such as social class origins or credentials, that influence workplace perceptions.

## STRUCTURAL DISCRIMINATION
## IN RANK, PAY, AND PROMOTION

Survey and census-based research has consistently documented that professional-managerial women's authority and wages are lower than White men's (see McGuire and Reskin 1993; Sokoloff 1992; Woody 1992). Two processes are implicated. First, women have less extensive credentials (i.e., education and experience) than White men and remain clustered in traditionally female occupational categories. Most of the gap in authority and wages, however, is due to women receiving lower wages and less authority (rank) even when they have the *same* education as White men and experience and work in the *same* industries; that is, they face discrimination (McGuire and Reskin 1993; Sokoloff 1992; Woody 1992). This latter outcome is largely achieved through channeling and clustering women into sectors of the labor force that pay the least and that restrict advancement opportunities (Higginbotham 1987, 1994; Reskin and Roos 1990; Sokoloff 1992; Woody 1992). Reskin and Roos (1990) highlight one aspect of this process by documenting wage declines that occurred as White men left and women and people of color entered certain occupations, including book editing, pharmacy, and bank management. Further, they demonstrate that women are channeled into sectors, such as customer service banking, that generate no profit and restrict opportunities to move to top management. Morrison and Von Glinow (1990) report that across the labor force, the majority of women in management hold staff jobs, not the line positions from which more promotions take place.

Although recognizing that Black women experience even greater disadvantage than White women on both credentials and returns to them (McGuire and Reskin 1993), feminist scholars are often reluctant to compare the status of Black or other women of color directly with that of White women. As McGuire and Reskin (1993) caution, comparisons between Black and White women are diversionary and divisive, given that the gap between either group and White men is far larger and more significant.

On one hand, in a political sense, these cautions are surely well-taken. For example, in 1994 the *New York Times* reported the results of an analysis of census data that showed the following: Among recent college graduates with 1-5 years on the job, Black women earned $11.41

per hour, Black men earned \$11.26, White women earned \$11.38, and White men earned \$12.85 (Roberts 1994). The article highlighted the 15 cent gap between Black men and women and completely ignored the \$1.44 gap between White men and the best-off of the remaining three groups. Experts, including noted sociologists and economists, were eager to speculate on the impact of the 15 cent difference between Black men and Black women on their interpersonal relationships. Meanwhile, the \$1.44 difference between Black women and White men went unexamined. Journalistic accounts and speculations about census data, without empirical research, can be used to drive a political wedge between oppressed groups, while White male privilege is accepted as normative. Ironically, failure to analyze the dimension of race fully also leaves women politically vulnerable. This vulnerability is precisely because without understanding the commonalities and differences in the processes that produce race and gender oppression as well as perceptions of those processes, we cannot begin to work effectively together for social change.

## PERCEPTIONS OF RACE
## AND GENDER DISCRIMINATION

Qualitative, in-depth studies give us a much greater sense of interpretations, textures, and meanings and their connection to the actions that people take from their structural locations. In these studies lies the potential for understanding whether wage gaps are produced, experienced, and interpreted in the same way by White women and women of color. Yet studies of professional-managerial women's perceptions of oppression have also avoided direct comparisons of White women with women and men of color.

Both popular personal narratives (Carter 1991; Nelson 1993; Williams 1991) and qualitative research studies describe Black middle-class men's and women's everyday encounters with racial discrimination in the workplace. They vividly detail African American professionals' and managers' experiences of repeatedly having to "prove" their competence, failure to move up due to discrimination in evaluation and promotion processes, exclusion from critical networks, lack of mentoring, and feelings of marginality and isolation, as well as the unpleasant environment created by racist and sexist remarks (Bell 1990; Davis and Watson 1982; Denton 1990; Feagin and Sikes 1994; Fulbright 1986).

Most Black professional-managerial women see sexism as well as racism implicated in the discriminatory treatment they face (Bell, Denton, and Nkomo 1993; Hochschild 1993; Nkomo 1988). But how do their perceptions compare with those of White women? Are Black women equally as likely as White women to perceive sexism in professional-managerial work? Do Black and White women define the obstacles they encounter in the same ways? Certainly, lack of mentoring, feelings of marginality, and glass ceilings have been identified as obstacles by White women professionals and managers (Morrison and Von Glinow 1990; Northcraft and Gutek 1993), but do White women in the same structural locations in the workforce perceive their constraints similarly to Black women? Black women see sexism as restricting their opportunities—do White women see the ways racism oppresses their African American counterparts, or do they hold negative images of Black women? How pervasive are these varied views?

Recent scholarship on Whites and race indicates that the dominant racial ideology in the United States today is a "color-blind" ideology in which Whites not only fail to perceive racism but believe that to acknowledge racial difference is to *be racist* (Frankenberg 1993; Omi and Winant 1994). Thus White women with a color-blind ideology who perceive gender discrimination may be unlikely to perceive race discrimination in their same work environments. White people who do adhere to a "color-conscious" recognition of racial discrimination are those who can form the basis for coalitions with people of color to redress injustices (Collins 1990; Frankenberg 1993). Still others are bound to color-conscious racist ideologies, and some now see White people as racial victims in a process labeled reverse discrimination. In professional-managerial workplaces where antidiscrimination has support but affirmative action much less (e.g., Tickamyer, Scollay, Bokemeier, and Wood 1989), we know little about the extent or character of such views, and frequently men's experiences have formed the basis for the images we do have.

The literature addressing the questions of perceptions of discrimination listed above is characterized by parallel studies of racially homogeneous groups (Weber Cannon, Higginbotham, and Leung 1988) that, given the segregation of workplaces, leave us questioning whether racial differences that appear across studies are based on the different social locations of White and African American women, different treatment in the same locations, different perceptions of the same treatment, or some combination of these. Similarly, we cannot know from the existing literature whether issues such as mentoring and promotion obstacles that appear in the discussions of both Black and White women are as frequent in each group, are interpreted similarly in each group, and have the same or different effects on career plans.

The present study combines features of both structural and experiential research by looking at the interpretations and meanings attached to workplace structures by African American and White women when other key structural factors affecting workplace rewards, treatment, and perceptions are controlled. We compare the perceptions of global race and gender discrimination of same-age African American and White women who are situated in the labor force in the same occupations and industries and who share educational credentials, experience, economic standing, and social class histories.

The goal of these comparisons is twofold. First, we seek to provide the texture, interpretation, and meaning not present in large-scale demographic comparisons of salaries and labor force studies that indicate that African American women receive similar although slightly lower levels of job rewards than White women. Second, we seek to provide this interpretive picture in a qualitative study that eliminates, by a combination of controlling and matching subjects, a series of structural factors beyond race that typically confound qualitative studies based on small samples. These include age, education, employment status, occupation, industrial sector, and social class background. To do so we employ a sample of 200 women, far exceeding the 20 to 50 subjects typical of qualitative studies.

## METHODS

### Research Design

The data for this study were taken from a larger project examining the relationships among race, class background, and gender composition of occupation on a wide range of family, work, and health issues among a sample of 200 full-time employed women professionals, managers, and administrators in the Memphis, Tennessee, metropolitan area. The research instrument contained closed- and open-ended questions that elicited a general life history of each respondent, focused on family history, schooling experiences from elementary school through higher education, current employment, family and personal life, and general well-being and health. Data were collected in 1985-1987 in face-to-face interviews lasting 2½ to 3 hours each.

## Sample

We selected a sample of Black and White women who were matched on other important characteristics that affect workers' experiences and perceptions. The sample was restricted to women of the baby boom cohort (i.e., 25 to 40 years of age at the time of the study) who are college graduates who went directly from high school to college or did so within 2 years of graduation and who currently work full-time as professionals, managers, or administrators (i.e., in "middle-class" occupations; Vanneman and Weber Cannon, 1987). (For a discussion of the rationale for selecting these groups and selection procedures, see Weber Cannon et al. 1988.) All subjects were defined as currently middle class by virtue of their employment in a professional, managerial, or administrative occupation, as specified by Braverman (1974), Ehrenreich and Ehrenreich (1979), and Vanneman and Weber Cannon (1987) (see Vanneman and Weber Cannon 1987 also for exceptions). A subject was defined as upwardly mobile (from a working-class background) if neither of her parents worked in a professional or managerial occupation before the subject was 13 years old. A subject was defined as stable middle class if either of her parents worked in a professional or managerial occupation before the subject was 13.

Classification of subjects as either professional or managerial administrative was made on the basis of the designation of occupations in the 1980 census (U.S. Bureau of the Census, 1983). Managerial occupations were defined as those in the U.S. Census categories of managers and administrators, and professionals were defined as those in occupations in the professional category, excluding technicians (Braverman 1974). At the time of the study, the majority of the Black and White women had advanced degrees (master's degrees, 57 Black women, 55 White women; law degrees, 7 Black women, 8 White women; doctorates, 3 Black women, 8 White women).

We employed a quota sample that was stratified by three dimensions of inequality: race, social class background of the respondent, and the gender composition of her occupation. Each dimension was operationalized into two categories: Black and White, raised working class/ upwardly mobile and raised middle-class/middle-class stable, and female dominated and male dominated. We selected 25 cases for each of the 8 cells of this 2 × 2 × 2 design. Within each cell, subjects were selected to reflect the proportions of professionals, managers, and administrators in either male-dominated or female-dominated occupations in the Memphis standard metropolitan statistical area.

To avoid confounding race, class background, and occupation, we selected subjects so that the different race and class background categories contained women from the same or closely related occupations. We also sorted subjects into three age groupings defined by birth cohort (1956-1960, 1951-1955, and 1945-1950) to prevent overrepresentation of any age group in a race, class background, or specific occupational category.

**Procedures**

Various strategies were employed to recruit volunteers, including mailings to all 46 women's organizations listed with the public library, newspaper articles and other use of the media, as well as such labor-intensive methods as visiting organizations and talking with potential subjects and enlisting their help in reaching women. Every few weeks, volunteers who met all study parameters were sorted according to all of the stratifying variables (race, class, sex composition of occupation, professional versus managers and administrators, specific occupation, and age category). Subjects to be interviewed were then randomly selected from each pool. All the interviewers were women and the same race as the subjects.

**Measurement**

Subjects' perceptions of global race and gender discrimination and their personal experiences with discrimination were assessed using a series of open-ended questions. Categories were developed from responses and the frequencies for Black and White women are presented in Table 7.1. Exact question wordings are presented in the discussion below. All analyses are presented by race only. Separate analyses, including social class background and gender composition of occupation, did not explain any of the racial differences reported here and are not presented. This finding might suggest that for this sample of professional and managerial women, racial group membership has greater salience for such perceptions in the women's workplaces than social class background and the gender composition of their occupations.

## GLOBAL PERCEPTIONS
## OF SEXISM AND RACISM

### Sexism

We asked the interviewees, "Do you feel women are treated differently in any ways from the men in your workplace?" If the respondent's answer was yes, we asked, "In what ways?" Although a majority of respondents indicated that women are treated differently, Black women were far more likely to say so. Roughly three-fourths of the Black women (73.7%, $n = 70$) and slightly more than half of the White women (56.1%, $n = 55$) stated that they perceived different treatment of women. Among those who perceived different treatment, however, Black and White women were equally likely to mention the same four major areas of concern: treatment as inferior/subordinate, soft, emotional, helpless, and so on based on sexist stereotypes ($n = 30$); hiring and promotion discrimination ($n = 26$); necessity of "proving" themselves, working harder, needing more qualifications ($n = 16$); and lower salaries and other compensation ($n = 12$). Other areas mentioned by a few respondents included exclusion from the "old boys'" network, sexual harassment, and preferential treatment of males. Finally, four women indicated that women were treated in stereotypical ways, such as having doors opened for them, but they interpreted this behavior as preferential, not inferior treatment.

The comments of Lynn Johnson (this and all other names are pseudonyms), an African American health care administrator in a major hospital, typify the way many Black and White women described their daily struggles against traditional stereotypes of women:

> You can't be just a normal woman in that environment. They take you too much for granted and they want to treat you like you're helpless. You've got to be very aggressive, which they consider abrasive. . . . They still promote men because men "need" it and women don't "need" it. You're still fighting the same old "isms." When I'm upset, they say it's because I need a husband. When John [a coworker] is upset it's because John has so many important things on his mind. When my disposition ain't right, I'm on my menses or something. I'm serious, you go through all that!

Although wage equity has been a cornerstone of the struggle for women's rights, wages per se were not the first thing mentioned by these

**TABLE 7.1** Perceptions of Treatment, Opportunities, Rewards, and Career Goals by Race

| Race | Black | | White | | | | |
| Question | n | % | n | % | $\chi^2$ | p | N |
|---|---|---|---|---|---|---|---|
| 1. Women treated differently | 70 | 73.7 | 55 | 56.1 | 5.77 | .02 | 193 |
| 2. Blacks treated differently | 62 | 68.1 | 35 | 44.3 | 8.85 | .00 | 179 |
| 3. Subject treated unfairly due to race/sex | 42 | 42.0 | 25 | 25.0 | 5.75 | .02 | 200 |
| 4. Position deserved based on training and experience | 99 | | 96 | | 9.15 | .01 | 195 |
| Yes | 74 | 74.7 | 77 | 80.2 | | | |
| No, overqualified | 24 | 24.2 | 12 | 12.5 | | | |
| No, underqualified | 1 | 1.0 | 7 | 7.3 | | | |
| 5. Adequate pay? | 97 | | 88 | | 11.57 | .02 | 185 |
| **Yes** | | | | | | | |
| Adequate compensation | 34 | 35.1 | 52 | 59.1 | | | |
| All earn same | 16 | 16.5 | 11 | 12.5 | | | |
| **No** | | | | | | | |
| All underpaid | 17 | 17.5 | 9 | 10.2 | | | |
| Unfair evaluations | 25 | 25.8 | 12 | 13.6 | | | |
| Race or sex discrimination | 5 | 5.2 | 4 | 4.5 | | | |
| 6. Chances for promotion— based on talent, ability? | 98 | | 95 | | | | |
| **Yes** | 44 | | 45 | | | | |
| Policies are fair | 17 | 17.3 | 19 | 20.0 | | | |
| Self-confident | 17 | 17.3 | 13 | 13.7 | | | |
| Supervisor validation | 6 | 6.1 | 5 | 5.3 | | | |
| Personal experience validates | 4 | 4.1 | 8 | 8.4 | | | |

**TABLE 7.1** *Continued*

| Race | Black | | White | | | | |
|---|---|---|---|---|---|---|---|
| Question | n | % | n | % | $\chi^2$ | p | N |
| **No** | 54 | | 50 | | | | |
| Ability doesn't count | | | | | | | |
| System unfair (politics, etc.) | 20 | 20.4 | 17 | 17.9 | | | |
| Mentions racism | 8 | 8.2 | 0 | 0.0 | | | |
| Mentions sexism | 1 | 1.0 | 3 | 3.2 | | | |
| Structural obstacles | 21 | 21.4 | 26 | 27.4 | | | |
| No interest in promotion/ burned out | 4 | 4.1 | 4 | 4.2 | | | |
| **7. Current career goals** | 100 | | 97 | | 17.84 | .00 | 197 |
| Seeks new job through promotion | 24 | 24.0 | 24 | 24.7 | | | |
| New employer | 18 | 18.0 | 15 | 15.5 | | | |
| Self-employment | 15 | 15.0 | 11 | 11.3 | | | |
| Continued education/ training | 20 | 20.0 | 8 | 8.2 | | | |
| Remain in current job | 12 | 12.0 | 33 | 34.0 | | | |
| No career goals, unsure | 11 | 11.0 | 6 | 6.2% | | | |

women—Black or White. In addition to struggling against limiting stereotypes, Black and White women most often saw barriers to hiring and promotion as the crux of the inequities they faced. These barriers are especially troublesome in professional-managerial work, where expectations are that careers will be characterized by steady progress up the ladder of success (Vanneman and Weber Cannon 1987).

These women's perceptions validate recent work that has found that women's wages are most often depressed through ghettoization in lower-paying job titles and sectors of the workplace, and less through unequal pay in the same jobs, a practice explicitly prohibited by civil rights legislation (McGuire and Reskin 1993; Reskin and Roos 1990). Furthermore, in many public sector work settings, salaries are set for entire categories of workers, such as teachers or attorneys, and the main way to achieve a significant salary increase is through a promotion. Finally, one of the features of professional-managerial work is relatively high wages, and research has demonstrated that among professional-managerial women and men, job satisfaction is affected more by subjective job rewards than by salary-related factors (Phelan 1994).

Awareness of structural barriers to advancement is typified in the comments of Wendy Robinson, a White lawyer and bank trust officer:

> It's obvious that the top echelon at the bank is all male. There are a lot of vice presidents and a lot of them are female, but nonetheless, there are so many it's almost a meaningless title. All the people who have the lowest jobs are female. And all the people who have the highest jobs are male. It's just obvious.

Comments about barriers to promotion were also common in female-dominated occupations. Blair Monroe, an African American nurse supervisor, said:

> Men tend to advance rapidly. They're promoted into management positions often when they don't have as many management skills, or haven't mastered the skills as well as many females. But because they are men, and it's predominantly a female organization, they seem to just move right up the ladder.

Black women also noted a subtle process of limiting women's advancement. Differences in work assignments and responsibilities were identified by eleven Black women and only two White women as part of the process that ultimately prohibits promotion. Specifically, they mentioned that women were given token jobs, less challenging and more "secretarial" types of jobs, kept off committees and boards, and excluded from tough work that often serves as the "proving ground" for further advancement. Shirley Dayton, an African American educational specialist working in the military, talked about the sexism: "My supervisors don't expect as much from the women as they do from the men. They'll even assign the men special projects because they don't want to 'put us through it,' or tax our minds too much." Patricia Moore, an African American journalist, also saw sex bias in her workplace. She stated: "A lot of women aren't given some of the 'primo' assignments like City Hall. They [employers] think that somehow we're not as astute politically as men; since it's mostly men in the city and county administration, they figure that men would understand them better I suppose."

In short, Black women were significantly more likely to perceive gender inequities in the workplace and to demonstrate a more nuanced understanding of the dynamics of gender inequities. Yet among those who perceived inequities, both Black and White women focused on the same arenas: the limitations imposed by stereotypical images of women and discrimination in hiring and promotions. Salaries per se were much less frequently mentioned.

## Racism

There were 30 women in the sample (9 Black and 21 White) who worked in racially homogeneous workplaces. Of the remaining 170 respondents, we asked, "Do you feel Blacks are treated differently in any ways from Whites in your workplace?" In response, 68% ($n = 62$) of the Black and 44.3% ($n = 35$) of the White women indicated that Black people were treated differently, but one-third (34.3%, $n = 12$) of those White women stated that Black people receive *preferential* treatment, and some contended that White employees and/or prospective employees face "reverse discrimination." Thus among the White women, 44 (55.7%) perceived no differences in treatment, 12 (15.1%) perceived preferential treatment for Black people, and 23 (29.1%) perceived discriminatory treatment. Taken together, close to three-fourths (70.9%) of the White women perceived no negative treatment of Black people, whereas 68.1% of Black women perceived negative treatment—a striking contrast.

Interestingly, both the Black women and the White women who perceived discriminatory treatment described the discrimination as occurring in the same two areas most commonly mentioned in discussions of women's treatment: hiring and promotions ($n = 31$) and treatment based on stereotypes, in this case of Black people as inferior, incompetent, and less able, leading to disrespectful treatment by coworkers and clients ($n = 27$). A few women also mentioned salary, exclusion from social networks, and tokenism—being put in visible positions that lack power.

### Black Women

Racial discrimination in hiring and promotions was commonly cited by Black women. Cheryl Waddell, a Black medical social worker at a private hospital, said: "I think the Blacks are confined to the lower positions—lower-status positions—promotional opportunities are not as available to them as the Whites. It's not easy . . . it's definitely there." Her sentiments were echoed by Lynn Johnson, the health administrator, who said: "Oh yeah! Most definitely! Go in there and look! You know. Every last one of the maids is Black. And go look around at the nursing staff. All you got to do is look. . . . The time comes for a promotion, the White lady can have half the skills the little Black lady has. She'll get it!" Finally, Janice Freeman, a Black 36-year-old associate professor at a community college, described Black women's confrontations with negative stereotypes:

> Yes, and I hope that I'm being objective but I think that they're [Black people] treated differently because of their color and because of that other person's personal expectation of what this person can do that's ingrained in them culturally over the years or over the decades so that we have to prove more, be twice as good, and be damned near flawless to meet even their mediocre standards. And that to me is not right!

*White Women and*
*the Color-Blind Perspective*

In contrast with Black women's views, the majority of the White women (55.7%), even though they worked in integrated environments, simply did not perceive that Black people were treated any differently in the workplace. If most of the White professional-managerial women in this sample who worked in all-White environments (21%) were even less likely to perceive racial discrimination, then we can see the profound extent of middle-class White women's unawareness of racism. The position of these women represents the color-blind racial ideology that defines the dominant-culture discourse on race in the United States today (Omi and Winant 1994; Frankenberg 1993). This stance has proven to be a powerful force for the preservation of the racial status quo and a persistent barrier to a unified women's movement.

The vast majority of these White women perceived no racial discrimination, simply responding no when asked whether Blacks are treated differently in their workplaces. No further comment or elaboration appeared necessary when no differences were perceived to exist. Among those who elaborated on their responses, several explicitly presented a "color-blind" perspective, claiming not to notice race. Some women went so far as to acknowledge the difference in their perceptions from those of Blacks in their workplaces. Sharon Anderson, an occupational therapist, said, "No, [I do not feel Blacks are treated differently], but I know some Blacks who do." And a few women overtly evoked the language of "color blindness," saying, "We try to be color-blind," or "I forget that Ethel is Black."

Another interesting variant on the color-blind perspective is reflected in the responses of some women who claimed that people in their workplaces hold prejudicial attitudes, but do not discriminate on the basis of race. These women tended also to implicate both Black and White people equally in holding prejudicial attitudes. In so doing, they minimized the significance of stereotypical attitudes and power differences across races by highlighting what they saw as a balance of views. Donna Latimer, a manager at a utility company, said: "A good part of the company has an attitude that the majority of Blacks are inferior to Whites and some of the Blacks feel that the Whites are inferior. Yet, policywise, there can be no discrimination." By equating Black and White people, these views have a message of equality. This position is captured in the words of Alice Norwood, a public relations specialist: "In the final analysis, I believe it is very equal and it all comes out the same in the wash, but in the process of hiring and firing, that's [race] always a big topic of conversation."

*White Women and*
*Color Consciousness*

When they were conscious of the existence of racial discrimination, as more than one-fourth of the White women in this sample were, they were often in a unique position to observe the everyday practice of racism. Barbara Worthington, a White 40-year-old college professor, was one of the White women who clearly saw racism in her environment. She discussed the way racially exclusionary practices were carried out in the Science Department at her university:

> First, we have no Blacks in this department. The few that have applied while I've been here have been automatically eliminated from consideration. Part of the reason was that they told in their original application that they were Black. There is a standard equal opportunity form . . . and some people make a big point of saying, "I'm a Black applicant." And this does not confer a special advantage, especially to many of my colleagues it's a disadvantage, because they feel that if this person were adequately trained,

competitive, etc. with similar qualifications, they would not need to declare themselves a Black candidate up front. So they feel that by doing that, they are asking for special consideration. That's a kind of backlash and that's not something you can take to court.

Mary Ellen Madsen, a public school teacher, worked in an integrated setting, where she also noted differential treatment. She said: "On occasion, I've heard remarks made [about a teacher] like 'Well, she's Black, what do you expect?' No, I don't think they're treated fairly. There are some excellent Black teachers in my school and no one will ever know it purely because they're Black." And Toni McKenna, a librarian, mentioned more structural concerns: "So many Blacks in the organization are in the lower levels of the spectrum. So many more clerks are Black than are White. They have lower salaries, they have lower positions and rank, and all that other stuff."

Finally, the comments of the 12 White women who thought Black people received preferential treatment are also revealing. Two of the women indicated that their workplaces gave advantages to Black workers, but they saw the need for these perceived advantages. Nicole Osborne, a legal aid attorney, said:

Legal aid is a different type of law practice. . . . In legal aid we go overboard in trying to provide opportunities because our clients are Black and I think that is important. I think we are sensitive to the needs for minorities to have opportunities in the professions and it has been a good opportunity for many minorities to get a job and get good experience practicing law. But I think there has been some concern that it has worked against Whites who also were sensitive to the needs of legal representation for poor people and want that opportunity too. . . . Sometimes color is a factor.

The remaining 10 White women expressed varying degrees of dissatisfaction with the preferences they observed. Perhaps the most vociferous in her response was Jeannette Wilson, a senior marketing consultant at a radio station:

They [Blacks] are given opportunities that most of them are not . . . maybe I better rephrase that. They are given opportunities . . . people that apply that are White would be better qualified, but because of the fact that there is a Black quota that has to be met, they have to take the inferior persons and that really chaps me!

Nell Jordon, a zone manager for an auto company, stated:

> This is a personal opinion, and I don't even know if it's justified. They put so much emphasis on hiring Blacks, that women are still the second-rate citizens that we've always been. I understand that, and I'm not griping about it, but I think it's about time we got as much attention.

And Katherine Davis, an administrator with a youth agency for girls, said: "There has been some reverse discrimination. There were some opportunities given to Black staff members that were not given to White staff members."

These comments do not necessarily reflect the rantings of crazed White supremacists, but rather the views of middle-class White women who are conscious of race and see Black people as advantaged. They represent about 15% of our sample, a sizable enough group to be a significant force in the workplace, and yet only half the size of the group of White women who clearly perceived racial discrimination. If the views of these two groups signify the bulk of the perceptions of White professional managerial women, antiracist movements would have achieved far more than they have. Instead, the larger obstacle to achieving White women's support for Black people's struggles against racism is the pervasive belief in a "color-blind" ideology and practice. It is a set of beliefs that minimizes the importance of race by not seeing it or by recognizing race while denying power differences among races and thereby treating any observed differences in stereotyped negative attitudes or behaviors as "balancing out," as unimportant.

## PERSONAL EXPERIENCES
## WITH SEXISM AND/OR RACISM

### General Assessment of Discriminatory Treatment

We next asked the women about any personal experiences of unfairness: "Do you feel you have received any unfair treatment at work because you are a [Black] woman?" We used different question wording to approximate as closely as possible the ways that Black and White women think about their own race and gender status (Collins 1990; Frankenberg 1993). We found that 42% ($n = 42$) of the Black women and only 25% ($n = 25$) of the White women felt they had been treated unfairly because of their gender or race/gender status. Further, eight of the White women and only two of the Black women indicated that the unfairness had happened to them on a previous job—not in their current workplace.

When discussing their personal experiences with inequities, both Black and White women most often discussed the subtle, indirect, and informal ways they are treated—racist and sexist jokes, exclusion from networks, subtle put-downs, sexual innuendoes, and so forth. Twelve Black women and only one White woman made specific reference to overt sexual harassment, or used the terms *sex discrimination* or *race discrimination*. Hiring and promotions were also frequently mentioned, although less often than the informal mechanisms mentioned above. These subtle and informal mechanisms of control were captured by Sandra Maxwell, an African American corporate attorney:

> Basically I feel like there are periods where colleagues feel very threatened by you. They feel that you move faster, that your work is better and is noted more by some of the senior people. So things are done to bring you down. They are done to "put you back in your place," so they say. And I have run into that more than a number of times. And you feel—maybe I should wait until my time—*or* you come to the feeling that I want to fight it all the way.

Joan Harden, a Black associate news producer at a television station, described the treatment she experienced: "They tell a lot of racial jokes. They're always categorizing people differently, especially Blacks. They seem to be quite prejudiced." Margaret Ford, a private attorney, described pay and the job ceiling: "Well, the initial compensation that I received [was low], and the fact that there's no partnership track or any real interest in making me a partner."

White women's comments on discrimination were not only less frequent than among the Black women, but they were even more likely to focus on the subtle and indirect nature of the inequality. Julie Townsend, an elementary school principal, said:

> I think I receive subtle sexual harassment. For example, yesterday I was meeting with a male professor, who used to meet with the assistant director and me and she couldn't be there, so he said, "Well, at least I get to meet with one good-looking dame." The stuff that is totally inappropriate because it has nothing to do with what you are doing.

Barbara Worthington, the college science professor, was atypical of the White women in that she described in great detail the overt sex discrimination that was pervasive in her department. Recall that she was also quite aware of the way racism operated to exclude African American candidates from her department. As her comments indicate, a lawsuit surely heightened her awareness:

> I don't think that I have received the same amount of opportunities as men—the same amount of research support which is monetary support, travel money to attend professional meetings, for professional advancement. . . . I was hired here primarily because they saw this as a woman's job. They had a sex discrimination suit in this department which the department lost, and when the lawyer called on me to testify, I asked not to because I needed the job and I was not willing to perjure myself to keep the job and he said he understood. . . . I hope the experience will make me a little more sensitive to people's feelings about professional status, promotion, pay, etc.

Far fewer women, both Black and White, said they personally experienced unfair treatment than identified global racism, sexism, or both, in their workplaces. Faye Crosby (1993) has noted that denial of personal disadvantage, even when people recognize broad patterns of discrimination, is quite common, and that is likely the case with some of these women. These people feel they are generally treated fairly in a system they recognize as unfair.

The comments of Darlene Hooks, a Black woman librarian, are instructive. Darlene recognized that the sexism in the system constitutes a glass ceiling for all women: "Women are not given the same employment opportunities. The men hold the top management levels in my business and the women are all the subordinates. So there is no way women have the same opportunities, because men hold all the top levels and the women will hold the second-level positions." When asked about personally being treated unfairly, Darlene said she had not been so treated, because "there are not many Black librarians in the field, so people seek me out." Yet in reality there is still a glass ceiling that Darlene knows she will not shatter.

The issue of age and job tenure can also be a factor in shaping women's likelihood of experiencing treatment that they consider discriminatory. For women at early career stages, the denial of promotions and the impact of informal differential treatment may not yet be felt.

## CONCLUSION

The women in this study have much in common. They are full-time professionals and managers who display strong commitment to their careers. They share similarities in their workplaces, occupations, credentials, experiences, ages, industrial locations, and even class backgrounds. These many similarities form a backdrop against which we can clearly assess their perceptions of racism and sexism in their respective work experiences.

The majority of White women (56%) and a much greater proportion of Black women (74%) believed that women are subject to differential treatment in their workplaces. When asked about the treatment of Black people, a large majority of Black women perceived differential treatment, whereas fewer White women perceived discriminatory treatment by race in the workplace. The vast majority of White women perceived no race discrimination, in a stance that affirms the pervasive extent of color-blind ideology, and a significant minority (about 15%) felt that Black people were advantaged and Whites disadvantaged in their workplaces. Only about 30% of White women saw Black people as disadvantaged in their workplaces. The range of perceptions of racism among White women indicates both potential obstacles for their Black coworkers and the potential for White women to work in coalitions with Black colleagues against racial injustice in the workplace. It is only in comparative studies that document the meaning of race to White and Black women that we can begin to assess the foundation for such coalitions.

Both Black and White women were far more likely to identify group than personal disadvantage, affirming Crosby's (1984) contention that people deny personal disadvantage even when they know it affects their group. Still, 42% of the Black and 25% of the White women identified personal experiences of discriminatory treatment in the workplace. When speaking of the types of discrimination they faced, whether group or individual, the women repeated common themes. Lack of promotional opportunities, treatment based on stereotypes, and having to work harder to "prove" themselves were most often cited; salary differentials were less often mentioned.

Overall, the workplace continues to be problematic for many professional and managerial women. However, few workplaces provide opportunities for dialogue about the nature of those problems. Simply noting the structural similarities in Black and White women's positions relative to White men will not in itself overcome the different ways these barriers are experienced and interpreted by Black and White women. Collective actions on the part of women in the workplace may be essential to implementing system changes, particularly changes that modify the work environment for people after they have been hired and when they are seeking advancement within the agency or firm. Thus the "color-blind" ideology of most White women may represent a significant deterrent to those actions. Our data suggest that effective coalition building may require increased awareness of the different perceptions of racism and sexism in the workplace, particularly greater awareness on the part of White women of the racial discrimination Black women face in these settings.

## REFERENCES

Baca Zinn, Maxine, Lynn Weber Cannon, Elizabeth Higginbotham, and Bonnie Thornton Dill. 1986. "The Costs of Exclusionary Practices in Women's Studies." *Signs: Journal of Women in Culture and Society* 11:290-303.

Bell, Ella Louise. 1990. "The Bicultural Life Experiences of Career-Oriented Black Women." *Journal of Organizational Behavior* 11:459-77.

Bell, Ella Louise, Toni C. Denton, and Stella M. Nkomo. 1993. "Women of Color in Management: Toward an Inclusive Analysis." Pp. 105-30 in *Women in Management: Trends, Issues, and Challenges in Managerial Diversity,* edited by E. A. Fagenson. Newbury Park, CA: Sage.

Braverman, Harry. 1974. *Labor and Monopoly Capital.* New York: Monthly Review Press.

Carter, Stephen L. 1991. *Reflections of an Affirmative Action Baby.* New York: Basic Books.

Collins, Patricia Hill. 1990. *Black Feminist Thought: Knowledge, Consciousness, and the Politics of Empowerment.* New York: Routledge, Chapman & Hall.

Crosby, Faye J. 1984. "The Denial of Personal Discrimination." *American Behavioral Scientist* 27:371-86.

———. 1993. "Affirmative Action Is Worth It." *Chronicle of Higher Education,* December 15, sec. 2, pp. B1-B2.

Davis, George and Glegg Watson. 1982. *Black Life in Corporate America.* Garden City, NY: Anchor/Doubleday.

Denton, Toni C. 1990. "Bonding and Supportive Relationships among Black Professional Women: Rituals of Restoration." *Journal of Organizational Behavior* 11:447-57.

Ehrenreich, Barbara and John Ehrenreich. 1979. "The Professional-Managerial Class." Pp. 5-45 in *Between Labor and Capital,* edited by P. Walker. Boston: South End.

Feagin, Joe R. and Melvin P. Sikes. 1994. *Living with Racism: The Black Middle-Class Experience*. Boston: Beacon.

Frankenberg, Ruth. 1993. *White Women, Race Matters: The Social Construction of Whiteness*. Minneapolis: University of Minnesota Press.

Fulbright, Karen. 1986. "The Myth of the Double-Advantage: Black Female Managers." Pp. 33-45 in *Slipping through the Cracks: The Status of Black Women*, edited by M. Simms and J. Malveaux. New Brunswick, NJ: Transaction.

Higginbotham, Elizabeth. 1987. "Employment for Professional Black Women in the Twentieth Century." Pp. 73-91 in *Ingredients for Women's Employment Policy*, edited by C. Bose and G. Spitze. Albany: State University of New York Press.

————. 1994. "Black Professional Women: Job Ceiling and Employment Sectors." Pp. 113-31 in *Women of Color in U.S. Society*, edited by M. Baca Zinn and B. T. Dill. Philadelphia: Temple University Press.

Hochschild, Jennifer L. 1993. "Middle-Class Blacks and the Ambiguities of Success." Pp. 148-72 in *Prejudice, Politics, and the American Dilemma*, edited by P. M. Sniderman, P. E. Tetlock, and E. G. Carmines. Stanford, CA: Stanford University Press.

McGuire, Gail M. and Barbara Reskin. 1993. "Authority Hierarchies at Work: The Impact of Race and Sex." *Gender & Society* 7:487-506.

Morrison, Ann M. and Mary Ann Von Glinow. 1990. "Women and Minorities in Management." *American Psychologist* 45:200-208.

Nelson, Jill. 1993. *Volunteer Slavery: My Authentic Negro Experience*. Chicago: Noble.

Nkomo, Stella M. 1988. "Race and Sex: The Forgotten Case of the Black Female Manager." Pp. 133-50 in *Women's Career: Pathways and Pitfalls*, edited by S. Rose and L. Larwood. New York: Praeger.

Northcraft, Gregory B. and Barbara Gutek. 1993. "Point-Counterpoint: Discrimination against Women in Management—Going, Going, Gone or Going But Never Gone?" Pp. 219-45 in *Women in Management: Trends, Issues, and Challenges in Managerial Diversity*, edited by E. A. Fagenson. Newbury Park, CA: Sage.

Omi, Michael and Howard Winant. 1994. *Racial Formation in the United States: 1960-1990*, 2nd ed. New York: Routledge.

Phelan, Jo. 1994. "The Paradox of the Contented Female Worker: An Assessment of Alternative Explanations." *Social Psychology Quarterly* 57:95-107.

Reskin, Barbara F. and Patricia A. Roos, eds. 1990. *Job Queues, Gender Queues: Explaining Women's Inroads into Male Occupations*. Philadelphia: Temple University Press.

Roberts, Sam. 1994. "Black Women Graduates Outpace Male Counterparts." *New York Times*, October 31, pp. A8, A12.

Sokoloff, Natalie. 1992. *Black Women and White Women in the Professions*. New York: Routledge.

Spelman, Elizabeth V. 1988. *Inessential Woman: Problems of Exclusion in Feminist Thought*. Boston: Beacon.

Tickamyer, Ann, Susan Scollay, Janet Bokemeier, and Teresa Wood. 1989. "Administrators' Perceptions of Affirmative Action in Higher Education." Pp. 125-38 in *Affirmative Action in Perspective*, edited by F. Blanchard and F. Crosby. New York: Springer-Verlag.

U.S. Bureau of the Census. 1983. "Detailed Population Characteristics: Tennessee." In *U.S. Census of the Population 1980.* Washington, DC: Government Printing Office.

Vanneman, Reeve and Lynn Weber Cannon. 1987. *The American Perception of Class.* Philadelphia: Temple University Press.

Weber Cannon, Lynn, Elizabeth Higginbotham, and Marianne Leung. 1988. "Race and Class Bias in Qualitative Research on Women." *Gender & Society* 2:449-62.

Williams, Patricia. 1991. *The Alchemy of Race and Rights.* Cambridge, MA: Harvard University Press.

Woody, Bette. 1992. *Black Women in the Workplace: Impact of Structural Changes in the Economy.* New York: Greenwood.

# 8

# Korean Immigrant Wives' Labor Force Participation, Marital Power, and Status

## PYONG GAP MIN

This chapter examines the extent to which the increase in Korean immigrant women's labor participation in family businesses increases their marital power and status. Telephone interviews with 298 married Korean women in New York City constitute a major data source for this chapter. A large majority of immigrant Korean wives, 70%, participate in the labor force, and an overwhelming majority of them work excessively long hours. This migration of Korean women to the United States implies a radical increase in their labor participation. However, their economic contribution has not significantly increased their marital power and status. This lack of change is partly because a large proportion of Korean working women work for family businesses as unpaid family workers and partly because Koreans' concentration in small businesses hinders both husbands and wives in altering the traditional gender role ideology brought from Korea.

AUTHOR'S NOTE: An earlier version of this chapter was presented as a paper at the annual meeting of the American Sociological Association, Washington, D.C., August 12, 1990. I would like to acknowledge that the work reported here was supported by the Professional Staff Congress of City University of New York Research Award, 1988.

Resource theory (Blood and Wolfe 1960; Centers, Raven, and Rodriguez 1971) posits that a wife's employment increases her marital power because it enables her to bring economic and other resources to the marriage. However, how much a wife's employment increases her marital power depends on the particular cultural context that prescribes marital relations (Rodman 1967). The distribution of marital power is usually more flexible in the United States and other Western countries than in more patriarchal Asian and Latin American countries. Thus wives' employment is expected to increase their marital power to a greater extent in Western countries than in Third World countries.

The vast majority of post-1965 immigrants to the United States have come from Third World countries, especially from Asia and Latin America. Many of these new immigrant groups show high female labor force participation rates (Foner 1986; Perez 1986; Pressar 1987; Stier 1989), although married women in these Third World countries usually do not work outside of the home. Researchers have shown that the participation of these immigrant women in the labor force has not resulted in significant modifications of their conjugal power or other aspects of gender role attitudes and behavior (Ferree 1979; Foner 1986; Kim and Hurh 1988; Liu, Lamanna, and Murata 1979; Min 1995; Sluzuki 1979). They have indicated that most immigrant wives suffer from overwork inside and outside the home, but that their increased labor force participation has not liberated them from the chains of traditional patriarchy.

Korean immigrant women, like other immigrant women from Third World countries, usually did not work outside the home in Korea. However, in the United States they play an active role in the family economy, particularly in the operation of family businesses (Kim and Hurh 1988; Min 1988b). In this chapter, I examine the extent to which Korean immigrant wives' increased labor force participation has increased their bargaining power in their marriages and their status in the Korean immigrant community, based on a sample of married women in the New York City Korean community. Previous studies have shown that Asian and Latino immigrant women's employment role has not significantly improved their marital power and status, mainly because of the traditional patriarchal ideology and social structures brought from their native countries. In this chapter, I look at Korean immigrant women's involvement in family businesses and their employment in ethnic businesses as additional variables interacting with patriarchy to reduce the positive effects of employment on Korean women's marital power and status.

## DATA SOURCES

The major data source for this study consists of telephone interviews with 298 married Korean women in New York City. The Kim sample technique was utilized for sampling Korean households in New York City.[1] The 1988 New York City telephone directories for the five boroughs listed 3,313 Kim households. Of these, 650 were randomly selected. Only Korean women who were married immigrants were asked to be interviewed. Of the selected households, 125 were not married households and thus were not eligible for the interview. Only one married woman from each household was interviewed. In cases where two or more married couples resided in one household, the wife of the household head was interviewed. A total of 298 Korean women from the 525 households eligible for the interview (56.8%) were successfully interviewed by telephone. Of the 227 households not interviewed, only 42 (8%) rejected the interview; the others were otherwise unavailable.

The interview schedule included 54 items on socioeconomic background and gender role attitudes and behaviors. The average interview was completed in 20 minutes. The interviews were conducted by two bilingual Korean students between August and November 1988.

The following three items were used to measure gender role attitudes:

1. In a normal family the husband works outside the home and the wife works inside.
2. The husband should make decisions on important family affairs.
3. The husband should be able to have dinner outside the home with his friends without asking his wife, if the situation dictates.[2]

Each item had five response options with 1 = *strongly agree* and 5 = *strongly disagree*. Scores on the above three items were summed to form a scale in which a low score indicates traditional gender role attitudes.

A revised version of Blood and Wolfe's (1960) instrument was used to measure marital power. This instrument consists of several items concerning family decision making, an important dimension of marital power (McDonald 1980). Respondents were asked to indicate whose opinions are more important in making decisions in the following areas:

1. wife's employment
2. buying or renting a house or apartment
3. purchasing health/life insurance
4. buying a car
5. discipline of children
6. the number of children to have

They were asked to choose one of five responses, where 1 = *the husband's opinions are far more important than the wife's* and 5 = *the wife's opinions are far more important than the husband's*. A scale of marital power was created by adding the scores on the six items. Only 134 women responded to all the items included in this scale, because only women with at least one school-age child were in a position to answer the question on children's discipline.

Finally, I conducted interviews with leaders of Korean trade associations in New York during the last 3 months of 1989. The data from these interviews (presented in Table 8.5, later in the chapter) show Korean women's severe underrepresentation in major Korean trade associations.

## CHARACTERISTICS OF RESPONDENTS AND THEIR FAMILIES

Table 8.1 provides background information about the respondents, their spouses, and their families. The average age of the respondents was 38. Their average number of years of education was 13, with 48% having completed 4 years of college. Substantially more of their husbands had higher education, with three-fourths having completed 4 years of college. The higher rate for men is not surprising given that in Korea, education is considered more important for men than for women. The respondents and their husbands had completed most of their education in Korea. Only 10% of the respondents and 14% of their husbands received 1 or more years of education in the United States.

All the respondents were born in Korea; they had an average of 7 years' residence in the United States. More than 90% of the respondents came to the United States in 1974 or after. These findings are not surprising, given that the New York City area Korean community is largely the by-product of the Immigration Act of 1965. Although Koreans have been immigrating to the United States for 90 years, an over-

**TABLE 8.1** Respondents' Personal and Family Characteristics

| | |
|---|---|
| Mean age | 37.9 |
| Mean years of education | 13.4 |
| Husbands' mean years of education | 15.3 |
| Percentage who completed 4 years of college | 48.0 |
| Percentage with husbands who completed 4 years of college | 74.0 |
| Mean years of residence in United States | 7.4 |
| Percentage who immigrated to United States in 1974 and after | 90.0 |
| Percentage who married in Korea | 80.0 |
| Mean number of family members | 3.8 |
| Mean number of children living with respondent | 1.6 |

whelming majority of the earlier Korean immigrants settled on the West Coast, particularly in Hawaii and California. The New York-New Jersey metropolitan area, home to 140,000 Koreans and currently the second-largest Korean center after Los Angeles, is primarily a community of more recent immigrants.

The vast majority of the respondents, 80%, married in Korea and subsequently immigrated to the United States as a family unit. The respondents' average number of family members was 3.8, and only 14% were two-member (the respondent and her spouse) families. Some 85% of the respondents reported that they had 1 or more children living with them, with an average of 1.6 children.

## CONCENTRATION IN SMALL BUSINESSES AND WIVES' INCREASED LABOR FORCE PARTICIPATION

Under the influence of Confucianism, traditional Korean society maintained a rigid form of patriarchy. The husband exercised enormous power and authority over his wife and children, with clear role differentiation between spouses. Although industrialization and urbanization have significantly altered the traditional family system in South Korea during recent years, they have not significantly altered the traditional patriarchal system associated with Confucianism (Min 1988a).[3] In South Korea, the wife is expected to stay home as a full-time homemaker, and the husband's main role is to provide financial support for the family (Choe 1985). Both traditional gender role expectations and employment/wage discrimination discourage married women from participating in the labor market. Many girls work as wage earners, but once they marry they usually stop working outside the home. Thus only a small proportion of married women in South Korea participate in the labor market. The 1980 Korean census indicates that 30% of Korean women 14 years old and older living in cities were in the labor force, and only 19% of married women living in cities worked outside of the home (Korean National Bureau of Statistics 1983).[4]

Of the study respondents, 42% reported that they had worked outside the home in Korea at one time or another, but most of them worked before they married. Of those women who were married in Korea ($n = 239$), only 23% said that they worked in Korea after marriage. Some respondents might have immigrated to the United States as soon as they had wedding ceremonies in Korea, and thus they did not have an opportunity to work in Korea. Even if this scenario is considered, still less than one-third of the respondents who had been married in Korea long enough to find jobs were likely to have been economically active.

The immigration of Koreans to the United States has led to many changes in the traditional Korean family system. Among the most significant is the radical increase in women's paid employment. The New York City sample shows that the labor force participation rate of Korean immigrant women is exceptionally high. A total of 70% of the respondents were found to participate in the labor market, with the majority (56%) working full-time; 86% reported that they had worked outside the home in the United States at one time or another.

Table 8.2 shows the labor market distribution of married Korean women and their husbands in New York City. Nearly 50% of the working women are self-employed, and another 36% are employed in Korean firms. Thus 85% of the female Korean workforce in New York City is in the ethnic subeconomy, either engaged in family businesses or employed in other Korean firms. A still higher proportion of their husbands (61.4%) are self-employed, with only 14% employed in the general labor market. Most Korean immigrant women easily find jobs in Korean-owned businesses located in the New York Korean community. A variety of Korean-owned retail stores (selling grocery, produce, and Korean-imported fashion items), restaurants, manicure shops, dry cleaning shops, and garment factories provide jobs for many Korean immigrant women. The prevalence of family businesses in the Korean community also contributes to the high labor force participation rate of Korean immigrant women. Although most are severely limited in their

**TABLE 8.2** New York City Korean Wives' and Husbands' Labor Market Distribution

| Labor Market | Wives | | Husbands | | Total | |
|---|---|---|---|---|---|---|
| | N | % | N | % | N | % |
| Self-employed | 102 | 48.8 | 172 | 61.4 | 274 | 56.0 |
| Employed in Korean firms | 76 | 36.4 | 69 | 24.6 | 145 | 29.7 |
| Employed in non-Korean firms | 31 | 14.8 | 39 | 13.9 | 70 | 14.3 |
| Total | 209 | 100.0 | 280 | 100.0 | 489 | 100.0 |

ability to speak English, they have no difficulty finding work in their own family businesses or coethnic businesses.

The fact that nearly half of Korean working women are self-employed suggests that small business families constitute a significant proportion of Korean immigrant families. Table 8.3 shows the different types of work coordination between husbands and wives in dual-earner couples. In 38% of dual-earner families, the husband and wife are engaged in the same business; in 9% of these families, the spouses work for separate businesses. Some 65% of dual-earner families are involved in small businesses, with at least one partner self-employed.

This pattern is reminiscent of a large proportion of the Chinese American families who engaged in small businesses during the period 1920-43. Glenn (1985) characterizes the Chinese American family in this historical period as the "small producer family," indicating that one of its distinctive characteristics was no clear demarcation between family and work life. The term aptly characterizes the Korean business family. For many Korean immigrant couples, work in the family business is an extension of family life. In the store, partners speak the Korean language and maintain Korean customs, including traditional male and female gender roles. Because both partners spend long hours in the store, many couples prepare Korean food in a separate office (in New York City, usually in a basement). As is usually the case at home, the wife cooks for and serves the husband. The only major difference between the Chinese small producer family and the current Korean small producer family seems to be that children were involved in the earlier Chinese business, whereas they are usually not involved in the Korean family business. The Korean family business is largely operated by the husband and wife; children are expected to concentrate on schoolwork.

**TABLE 8.3** New York City Korean Dual-Earner Couples' Work Coordination

| Category | n | % |
|---|---|---|
| Husband and wife work for same business | 76 | 38.6 |
| Husband and wife work for separate businesses | 18 | 9.1 |
| Husband self-employed and wife employed | 28 | 14.2 |
| Husband employed and wife self-employed | 6 | 3.0 |
| Husband and wife employed | 69 | 35.0 |
| Total | 197 | 100.0 |

## LABOR-INTENSIVE SMALL BUSINESSES AND LONG HOURS OF WORK

Popular Korean businesses in New York City include produce and grocery retail businesses. Approximately one-fourth of the respondents and their husbands who are self-employed operate a fruit and vegetable grocery or liquor business. Wholesale and retail businesses dealing in manufactured goods—such as wigs, hats, jewelry, and clothing imported from Korea and other Asian countries—constitute the second-largest category of Korean businesses in New York. Retail fish, dry cleaning, and manicure services are among the other Korean businesses. These are labor-intensive small businesses, and thus both husbands and wives work long hours outside the home.

Table 8.4 presents the mean number of weekly work hours by sex and the type of labor market (self-employed, employed in ethnic firms, and employed in nonethnic firms). There is a significant gender differential in weekly work hours in the labor force, with husbands working an average of 57 hours per week and wives 51. However, what is more significant is the differential in weekly work hours among the three groups of workers for both men and women. Although self-employed Korean immigrants work substantially longer hours than other employed Korean immigrants, Koreans employed in Korean businesses work longer hours than those employed in non-Korean firms. Because the majority of Korean immigrants are self-employed and another significant proportion are employed in Korean firms, the vast majority of Korean immigrants, both males and females, work extremely long hours, much longer than the general U.S. population. More than 50% of the husbands and 40% of the wives were found to work 60 or more hours per week; 67% of the husbands and 59% of the wives work 6 or 7 days a week.

**TABLE 8.4** New York City Korean Wives' and Husbands' Weekly Work
Hours by Type of Labor Market

|  | Self-Employed | | Employed in Ethnic Firms | | Employed in Nonethnic Firms | | Total | |
|---|---|---|---|---|---|---|---|---|
|  | N | X̄ | N | X̄ | N | X̄ | N | X̄ |
| Husbands | 168 | 61.3 | 66 | 52.8 | 37 | 43.7 | 271 | 56.9 |
| Wives | 100 | 55.9 | 76 | 49.2 | 31 | 37.6 | 207 | 50.7 |

Korean immigrant women make a very important income contribution to their families' finances, perhaps equal to that of their husbands, although this is very difficult to measure accurately. This is especially true of Korean immigrant wives who engage in family businesses or who operate their own businesses. When two partners operate the same business, the wife is usually in charge of the cash register and the husband takes care of the total management of the store. The reduction of cash and merchandise shortages through the control of the cash register by the wife is one of the central factors that make Korean small businesses successful (Min 1988a). Many Korean businessmen in New York, especially those who are successful in business, spend a significant amount of time participating in community activities. They also play golf, gamble, visit Korea, and spend time participating in other recreational and social activities. During their time away from their businesses, their wives tend the stores, shops, or offices.

The 1980 U.S. Census indicates that Korean American women employed full-time had earnings that were only 59% of the earnings of their male counterparts in 1979 (U.S. Bureau of the Census 1983), which is similar to the gender gap in wages for the general population. These kinds of official data seem to underestimate greatly the extent to which Korean immigrant wives contribute to family income. Many Korean immigrant wives who worked for family businesses in 1979 seem to have reported in the 1980 census that they did not participate in the labor force or that they worked as unpaid workers for the family business. Therefore, their contribution to family income was not reflected in the census income data. Survey studies conducted by Korean scholars may reflect the economic role of Korean immigrant wives more accurately than government data (see, for example, Kim and Hurh 1988; Min 1989). Yet self-reported income in these independent survey studies also appears to underestimate the contribution of self-employed Korean women to family income, because in most Korean self-employed families, the husband's earnings are practically inseparable from the wife's. Furthermore, self-employed Korean respondents tend to report that the husband is mainly responsible for the income from the family business. Accordingly, in order to assess effectively the economic contribution of Korean immigrant wives engaged in family businesses, one needs to examine the roles they play in these businesses, rather than use self-reported income data.

## BUSINESS SUCCESS AND ENHANCEMENT OF HUSBANDS' POWER AND STATUS

As mentioned previously, married women's participation in the labor force generally enhances their power and influence relative to their husbands'. Particularly, those married Korean women who run their own businesses (12% of working wives in the case of the New York Korean community) seem to enjoy a level of independence and autonomy unimaginable in South Korea.

However, those Korean women who assist their husbands in the family store do not seem to enjoy the economic and psychological independence that most other employed U.S. wives seem to enjoy. The survey data do not include information about who was the legal owner of the family business, but my casual observations of Korean immigrant businesses suggest that in most cases the husband is the legal owner. Korean immigrants, both husbands and wives, may believe that who is the legal owner of the family business is not of economic importance. Yet it has practical implications; when the husband is the legal owner, the social security tax for the self-employed family is deposited for the husband only. Some Korean women realize that they have lost their social security taxes as self-employed persons only when they consider divorce after severe marital conflicts.

In addition, the Korean immigrant husband usually controls the money and personnel management of the family business, which gives him power in terms of making decisions in the operation of the business. Although the wife takes care of the cash register, the husband usually deposits money in the bank and orders merchandise. Moreover, it is usually the husband who hires and fires employees and decides whether the business should be expanded. Non-Korean employed U.S. women may increase their bargaining power by bringing home separate, visible paychecks. Korean immigrant wives who work for family businesses do not have this independent source of income, although they too make significant contributions to the family economy.

The status of a Korean immigrant woman as a "helper" in the family business rather than as the owner or co-owner of a business also diminishes her social status and influence in the Korean immigrant community. Korean entrepreneurs establish associations based on business lines, and major business associations exercise powerful influence on community politics in the entrepreneurial Korean community. Self-employed men, rather than their female partners, represent their businesses by joining specialized business associations and engaging in organizational activities. Even if the wife plays the dominant role in managing the family business and the husband plays the role of helper, Koreans usually consider the husband the owner. As a personal example, although I helped my wife in our store only irregularly, I rather than she was invited to participate in business association meetings. Hence, whereas business associations in the Korean immigrant community consist almost exclusively of male members, many Korean women are as active as or even more active than their husbands in actual business operations. Table 8.5 shows the number of total affiliated members and the number of female members for each of the five major business associations in the New York Korean community. Only 21 Korean businesswomen are affiliated with one or another of the five major Korean business associations, accounting for less than 1% of total affiliated members.

Successful male Korean entrepreneurs exercise powerful influence on community politics through their leadership positions, not only in trade associations, but also through other nonbusiness ethnic associations. By virtue of their financial ability, many successful Korean businessmen are invited to become staff and board members of important nonbusiness ethnic associations as well. Those Korean businessmen with key positions in major business and nonbusiness ethnic associations spend a lot of time and money on their ethnic organizations. While they spend time and money on these public activities, their wives are responsible for the business operation. Although most self-employed Korean immigrants work long hours for moderate levels of income, some achieve a high level of economic success. When small family businesses turn into lucrative enterprises, both Korean husbands and wives enjoy economic benefits. However, business success often gives social status and position only to Korean husbands.

**TABLE 8.5** Proportion of Korean Female Entrepreneurs Affiliated with Major Korean Business Associations in New York

| Business Association | Number of Members | Female Members | |
|---|---|---|---|
| | | N | % |
| Korean Importers Association | 102 | 1 | 0.2 |
| Korean Green Grocers Association | 1,050 | 8 | 0.8 |
| Korean Fish Retailers Association | 675 | 7 | 1.3 |
| Korean Garment Contractors Association | 190 | 5 | 1.7 |
| Korean Dry Cleaners Association | 195 | 0 | 0.0 |
| Total | 2,212 | 21 | 0.9 |

## ETHNIC ECONOMY AND
## MAINTENANCE OF PATRIARCHY

I have noted above that Korean immigrant wives' contribution to the family income does not help them increase their marital power and status, partly because their engagement in family businesses, unlike paid employment from other businesses, does not give them economic independence from their husbands. There are no separate and specific paychecks. Another reason Korean immigrant women's labor force participation does not lead to a significant increase in their power and status may have something to do with the maintenance of the traditional Korean gender role ideology. As previously emphasized, male chauvinism is stronger in South Korea, with its Confucian cultural tradition, than in the United States. Immigration to the United States does not mean that this traditional ideology is abandoned.

Exposure to the U.S. work environment is likely to help Korean immigrants to change the Korean traditional gender role orientation, although the process may be very slow. However, as previously noted, a large majority of Korean immigrants are involved in a Korean sub-economy, either as business owners or as employees of ethnic businesses. Survey studies conducted in New York City and Los Angeles indicate that the vast majority of the employees of Korean-owned stores are either Korean or Hispanic immigrants (Min 1989, 1996). Because Hispanic immigrants hired by Korean stores also have a severe language barrier, they often communicate with Korean owners and employees using a limited number of Korean words. It is also noteworthy that Hispanic immigrants hired by Korean stores usually hold a conservative gender role ideology similar to that of Korean immigrants. Although

**TABLE 8.6** New York City Korean Women's Gender Role Attitudes and
Marital Decision Making by Employment Status

| | N | $\overline{X}$ | SD | Significance at the 0.05 Level |
|---|---|---|---|---|
| **Gender role attitudes[a]** | | | | |
| (1) Housewives | 86 | 7.69 | 2.66 | (1) – (2) = no |
| (2) Working wives in the ethnic market | 178 | 8.15 | 3.01 | (1) – (3) = yes |
| (3) Working wives in the general labor market | 31 | 9.23 | 2.87 | (2) – (3) = no |
| **Marital decision making[b]** | | | | |
| (1) Housewives | 35 | 15.31 | 3.66 | (1) – (2) = no |
| (2) Working wives in the ethnic market | 83 | 15.39 | 3.85 | (1) – (3) = yes |
| (3) Working wives in the general labor market | 16 | 18.50 | 2.34 | (2) – (3) = yes |

a. A higher score indicates more disagreement with a traditional gender role stereotype and thus a more egalitarian gender role orientation.
b. A higher score indicates wife's greater influence in decision making.

Korean-owned businesses usually serve native-born White and African American customers, their communications with customers for the most part are minimal. For these reasons, Korean immigrants concentrated in the Korean ethnic economy have little opportunity to learn U.S. customs, including the more egalitarian gender role orientation accepted by the majority of those in the United States.

In order to examine the effects of a Korean subeconomy on the maintenance of traditional Korean gender role orientation, I compared three groups of the respondents—full-time housewives, working wives in the Korean ethnic market (those self-employed or employed in Korean-owned firms), and wives employed in nonethnic firms—on gender role attitudes and marital power. As the data presented in Table 8.6 demonstrate, the respondents in the general labor market had more egalitarian gender role attitudes than those in the Korean ethnic market, who in turn had more egalitarian attitudes than housewives. Although the difference between married women who worked in the Korean ethnic market and homemakers is not statistically significant, the difference between married women employed outside the Korean ethnic market and homemakers is significant. With a larger subsample of women employed in the general labor market, a significant difference might possibly be found between those employed inside and outside the

Korean ethnic market. Consistently, Korean women employed in the general labor market maintain more egalitarian relations with their husbands in terms of family decision making than either of the other two groups.

Those respondents employed in non-Korean firms have generally received a higher level of education and have been in the United States longer than the other respondents. Thus their more egalitarian gender role attitudes and more egalitarian relations with their husbands may be due partly to those factors. However, it is likely that their contacts with U.S. workers in their workplaces have also contributed to their more egalitarian gender role attitudes and behavior. Unfortunately, with the data gathered in this survey, it is not possible to measure the effects of the labor market context on gender role attitudes and behavior independent of the respondents' background characteristics.


## CONCLUSION


Although industrialization has brought about many changes in the traditional Korean family system, a strict gender division of labor is still maintained in South Korea. Most married women in South Korea stay at home as full-time housewives; a very small proportion participate in the labor force. The immigration of Korean women to the United States has radically increased their labor force participation rate. The data used in this study, based on interviews with Korean married women in New York City, show that the vast majority of them not only participate in the labor force, but work exceptionally long hours.

A wife's labor force participation allows her to bring more resources to her marriage, and should usually increase her power and status relative to her husband's. Thus, in principle, Korean immigrant women's increased labor participation should significantly increase their marital power and status. Unfortunately, however, Korean wives' role as "helpers" in family businesses or as employees in other businesses in the Korean ethnic market does little to increase their marital power and status. A large proportion of Korean working women engage in family businesses in which their husbands, as the legal owners, control the overall management. More important, Korean women engaged in family businesses do not receive the separate paychecks that give other employed U.S. women bargaining power.

Not only does Korean women's heavy involvement in family businesses provide a structural source for their disadvantage in marital
power and status, Korean immigrants' concentration in small ethnic
businesses—either as business owners or as employees—provides a
cultural source for their disadvantage. Korean immigrants' social segregation, partly caused by their workplace segregation, helps to perpetu-
ate traditional Korean customs, including the practice of a rigid form of
patriarchy.[5] Thus structural and cultural factors interact to reduce any
positive effects of Korean immigrant women's labor force participation
on their marital power and status.

## NOTES

1. Approximately 22% of Koreans have the surname Kim (Korean National Bureau
of Statistics 1977), and the telephone subscription rates of Korean immigrants are very
high (Shin and Yu 1984). Kim is a uniquely Korean surname, and Kims socioeconomically
represent the Korean general population (Min 1989; Shin and Yu 1984). Therefore, a
relatively unbiased sample of Korean households may be obtained through a sampling of
Kims from local telephone directories.
2. This item was included because the practice of the husband's eating dinner outside
the home without asking his wife is considered a good indication of male supremacy in
South Korea.
3. The North Korean communist government, like other communist governments,
legislated a number of measures to abolish feudalistic customs that restricted women's
rights and to increase women's employment. Therefore, women enjoy higher status and
more power in North Korea than in South Korea.
4. Most Korean women living in rural areas participate in family farming.
5. The cultural homogeneity of Korean society also contributes to Korean immigrants'
social segregation.

## REFERENCES

Blood, Robert O. and Donald M. Wolfe. 1960. *Husbands and Wives: The Dynamics of
    Married Living.* New York: Free Press.
Centers, Richard, Bertram H. Raven, and Aroldo Rodriguez. 1971. "Conjugal Power
    Structure: A Reexamination." *American Sociological Review* 36:254-78.
Choe, Jae Suk. 1985. *Studies of Contemporary Korean Families,* 2nd ed. (in Korean).
    Seoul: Illjisa.
Ferree, Myra Marx. 1979. "Employment without Liberation: Cuban Women in the United
    States." *Social Science Quarterly* 60:35-50.

Foner, Nancy. 1986. "Sex Roles and Sensibilities: Jamaican Women in New York and London." Pp. 133-51 in *International Migration: The Female Experience,* edited by R. Simon and C. Brettell. Totowa, NJ: Rowman & Allanheld.

Glenn, Evelyn Nakano. 1985. "Racial Ethnic Women's Labor: The Intersection of Race, Gender, and Class Oppression." *Review of Radical Political Economics* 17:86-108.

Kim, Kwang Chung and Won Moo Hurh. 1988. "The Burden of Double Roles: Korean Wives in the U.S.A." *Ethnic and Racial Studies* 11:151-67.

Korean National Bureau of Statistics. 1977. *Population Composition by Surnames: A Report on the Data from the 1970 Korean Census of Population.* Seoul: Korean Economic Planning Board.

―――. 1983. *1980 Population and Housing Census,* Vol. 2, *15 Percent Sample.* Seoul: Korean Economic Planning Board.

Liu, William T., Maryanne Lamanna, and Alicia Murata. 1979. *Transition to Nowhere: Vietnamese Refugees in America.* Nashville, TN: Charter House.

McDonald, G. W. 1980. "Family Power: The Assessment of a Decade of Theory and Research." *Journal of Marriage and the Family* 42:841-54.

Min, Pyong Gap. 1988a. *Ethnic Business Enterprise: Korean Small Business in America.* Staten Island, NY: Center for Migration Studies.

―――. 1988b. "The Korean American Family." Pp. 199-230 in *Ethnic Families in America: Patterns and Variations,* edited by C. Mindel, R. Habenstein, and R. Wright, Jr New York: Elsevier.

―――. 1989. "Some Positive Functions of Ethnic Business for an Immigrant Community: Koreans in Los Angeles." Report submitted to the National Science Foundation.

―――. 1996. *Caught in the Middle: Korean Communities in New York and Los Angeles.* Berkeley: University of California Press.

Perez, Lisandro. 1986. "Immigrants' Economic Adjustment and Family Organization: The Cuban Success Reexamined." *International Migration Review* 20:4-20.

Pressar, Patricia R. 1987. "The Dominicans: Women in the Household and the Garment Industry." Pp. 103-29 in *New Immigrants in New York,* edited by N. Foner. New York: Columbia University Press.

Rodman, Hyman. 1967. "Marital Power in France, Greece, Yugoslavia, and the United States: A Cross-National Discussion." *Journal of Marriage and the Family* 29:320-24.

Shin, Eui-Hang and Eui-Young Yu. 1984. "Use of Surname in Ethnic Research: The Case of Kim in the Korean American Population." *Demography* 21:347-59.

Sluzuki, L. E. 1979. "Migration and Family Conflict." *Family Process* 18:381-94.

Stier, Haya. 1989. "Immigrant Women Go to Work: An Analysis of Immigrant Wives Labor Supply for Six Asian Groups." Paper presented at the annual meeting of the American Sociological Association, Washington, DC.

U.S. Bureau of the Census. 1983. *1980 Census of Population* PC80-1-C1, Washington, DC: Government Printing Office.

# PART IV

# Working for a Better Community: Dilemmas in Building Solidarity

Gradually, social scientists have begun to recognize that the unpaid labor in which women engage contributes to community maintenance and development. However, such reproductive labor has usually been discussed within the framework of social welfare or political activism. The inclusion of community activity within the framework of "women's work" is relatively new. We thus conclude our discussion of ethnicity, race, and class issues among working women by exploring the unpaid labor that they contribute to building better communities. The two studies presented in this section highlight similarities and differences in the circumstances under which women engage in unpaid labor in their neighborhoods. In the past, most of the attention paid to the activity referred to as *voluntarism* has focused on the middle and upper classes. When poor and working-class women have engaged in the same type of unpaid labor aimed at social reform, it has typically been classified as *political activism*. Still, such activities should hardly be subjected to the same analysis when the women involved in them do not share similar living conditions or have access to the same public and private resources, services, and facilities. Although women engaged in volunteer work aimed at benefiting children and families that are not their own frequently must shape their activities around the cultural biases of the White middle class, advocating for paved streets, libraries, and public parks takes on different meanings when women from different race, class, and

ethnic backgrounds contribute unpaid labor to issues affecting their communities. Women directly affected by these conditions experience different
material circumstances, and their perspectives are shaped by their class,
racial, ethnic, and immigrant status in society. Consequently, these women
may not share the same definitions of the problems or the solutions as women
who volunteer.

In the following chapters, Mary Pardo and Lynda Dickson offer important
new studies on women's unpaid labor in community work. Each of these
sociologists points to how social, economic, and political factors shape the
kinds of work these women engage in, the obstacles they encounter, and the
skills they develop from the work. In Chapter 9, Mary Pardo notes how the
word *voluntarism* glosses over complex power relationships between women
and the social institutions in which they work. Her study helps us understand
that these women experience such work as mandatory—work that has to be
done—rather than optional, as the term *voluntarism* would suggest. In
Chapter 10, Lynda Dickson similarly builds on this difference by referring
to Black women's club activity as the "third shift"—that is, the one following the first shift, employment, and the second shift, family. The historical
moments caught in each of these studies demonstrate how community
participation becomes essential activity rather than simply a reflection of
individual choice. These findings pose questions and challenges to the way
we frame discussions about community service, social activism, and grassroots political activity.

Madres del Este de Los Angeles, Santa Isabel (MELASI) is the focus of
Mary Pardo's research. The women belonging to MELASI began this grassroots organization in East Los Angeles through unpaid labor as parishioners
and as the parents of children attending the parochial school attached to the
church. Mandated participation in fund-raisers for churches and schools
calls into the question the "volunteer" nature of this unpaid labor. Furthermore, the importance of collective responsibility is stressed over highly
rewarded individual responsibility. Pardo reports on some highly publicized
cases that took place in the late 1980s, when Latina mothers in Los Angeles
challenged the state's use of the Eastside as a dumping ground for projects
unwanted by "better" neighborhoods, specifically, a prison and a toxic waste
incinerator. This ethnographic study demonstrates how women engaged in
unpaid labor challenged the institutional constraints that the Catholic Church
imposed on their working conditions. The women sought to change the
church from a religious institution to a community-based social institution,
and to eliminate its patriarchal organizational structure. Through their unpaid labor, these Latinas not only improved opportunities for their children,

but indirectly provided leadership training for participation in broader-based community activism, resulting in the creation of much-needed community resources.

Lynda Dickson's chapter is based on historic and ethnographic research on four Black women's clubs in Denver, Colorado, from 1900 to 1925: Pond Lily Art and Service; Taka Art and Literary; Carnation Art, Literary and Charity; and Self-Improvement and Social Service. Data collected from interviews and club documents do not depict full-time homemakers engaged in social reform outside their communities, as might have been the case for middle-class White women. Rather, the data reveal the realities of racial segregation. During this period, Black middle-class families were confined to live side by side with poorer Black families, and Black professionals were limited to clients in their own community. Nor did status differences among the classes resemble those in the White community. Instead, skilled and educated workers in the Black community were frequently relegated to low-level service occupations, thus middle-class status depended upon other criteria, including individual characteristics, lifestyle, and community participation. Thus, unlike the profile of White clubwomen during the same era, these women were typically full-time employees who maintained their own households. The unpaid labor contributed to club activities thus became a "third shift," whereas the emphasis on self-help and racial solidarity was focused on the betterment of living conditions in their own community and collective efforts against racism.

# 9

# Working-Class Mexican American Women and "Voluntarism": "We Have to Do It!"

## MARY PARDO

Using "unpaid labor" rather than "voluntarism" to conceptualize women's community work clarifies its significance for urban communities of different economic class composition. Middle- and upper-class women also provide unpaid labor in the interests of their communities; however, they are more able than working-class women to purchase or find adequate basic services available in their neighborhoods. This chapter shows how women's unpaid labor in a Catholic parish school and neighborhood compensated for inadequate public facilities and services. The women perceived their unpaid work as a collective effort necessary to the welfare and safety of their families. While doing unpaid work, the women developed invaluable skills and social networks that allowed them to address larger community issues successfully. In some instances, the women challenged the institutions where their unpaid work originated.

AUTHOR'S NOTE: I want to thank particularly Mary Romero for her assistance, as well as Elizabeth Higginbotham, the series editors, and reviewers for their invaluable assistance, which helped me clarify the themes in this essay.

*Pardo:* I've interviewed women in the nearby middle-class community and they do volunteer work but not nearly as much as the women in Eastside Los Angeles. Why do you think this is so?
*Robles* [laughing]: They don't have to do it because the community is not so bad off. . . . We have to do it!

Erlinda Robles, a lifetime resident of Eastside Los Angeles, responded to my question and challenged two commonly held notions about women's voluntarism and its meaning in community settings. First, her answer invites us to reconsider the label "volunteer work," a label that conjures images of freely offered activity embraced during leisure hours.[1] Like household labor, women's voluntarism has often been distinguished from real work because it is a "labor of love," natural, thereby unskilled, and done within the context of women's roles as mothers. As such, women's voluntarism is often taken for granted and devalued in much the same way as other work defined as "women's work." The significance of "women's work" in the reproduction of communities and class becomes invisible (Romero 1992). Second, Erlinda's answer challenges the notion of a universal category of "women's voluntarism," undifferentiated by ethnicity, race, and class. Unlike the charity work in which upper-class women engage, working-class women's unpaid work is rarely considered "charity" because their families and community frequently reap direct benefits. Unable to purchase the same privileges as upper-middle- and upper-class women, working-class women are frequently drawn into unpaid labor in order to obtain services unavailable or unaffordable in their own communities, such as private education, safe neighborhoods, and cultural activities.

The term *voluntarism* not only hides the contribution of unpaid work to the reproduction of class, it also glosses over the gender-based power relations present in most local social institutions. These institutions, such as schools and churches, provide places for women to carry out unpaid labor in a collective manner. Although the social institutions through which women "volunteer" may differ, all social institutions attempt to shape the way women carry out their work. In the process of doing unpaid work, women may challenge, resist, or negotiate around patriarchal structures within the social institutions to which they belong. It is at this point that we can further understand the agency of women and the resourceful and creative ways they contribute to the reproduction of their families and social class.

In this essay, I consider the volunteer activities of women as "unpaid labor." Treating these efforts as unpaid labor moves us closer to understanding what is occurring from the women's perspectives, as expressed in Erlinda Robles's remarks. Using an ethnographic case study, I look at the unpaid labor of working-class Mexican American women in East Los Angeles. The women belong to a grassroots organization, Madres del Este de Los Angeles, Santa Isabel (MELASI). The case of MELASI provides an ideal opportunity for exploring the relationship between unpaid community work and unpaid reproductive labor that women do as mothers. The case study highlights the kinds of unpaid labor, the structure of the activity, and the meaning that voluntarism has for Mexican American working-class women. It also illustrates the ways in which women negotiate the terms and conditions of their work and how they empower themselves to identify their own problems and solutions.

The purpose of this essay is not to review the history of women's volunteer work, but rather to explore the themes that capture these Mexican American women's perceptions of unpaid work as a negotiated process shaped by women and local social institutions. However, as the case study of MELASI demonstrates, conceptualizations in historical examples are useful in analyzing the unpaid labor of Mexican American women in East Los Angeles. Below, I selectively review social science accounts of women's unpaid labor, attending to the ways it has been conceptualized and how it is differentiated by race and class.

## CONCEPTUALIZING WOMEN'S
## UNPAID COMMUNITY WORK

Historical examples illustrate the ways women's unpaid work has been conceptualized, labeled, and, in the end, mystified in order to reconcile opposing views of "women's proper role." Feminist scholars argue that women's unpaid labor contributes to the survival of working-class families (Sacks 1989) as well as to the maintenance of the status of privileged classes (Daniels 1988; Enloe 1989). Although women may do this work on a regular basis, it comes to light only during periods of urban conflict. Many accounts focus on periods of social reform, for example, the Progressive Era (1860-1920). During the Progressive Era, middle-class White women's volunteer work and social activism were labeled in terms that reconciled women's community activism with the traditional role of motherhood. By the 1910s, the notion of "municipal housekeeping" emerged and promoted women's voluntary organizations. Jane Addams explained that the community was merely an extension of the home, and women should contribute to safe, clean communities (McCarthy 1990). Under the label of "social or municipal housekeeping," women applied domestic skills to the community at large as they promoted civic reform around the turn of the century. Clubwomen sponsored civic projects, creating libraries and beautifying streets and parks. As one city official stated, "Women by natural instinct as well as by long training have become the housekeepers of the world, so it is only natural that they should in time become effective municipal housekeepers as well" (quoted in Schackel 1992, p. 7). Because women's unpaid work takes place in the home and in the community, it appears to occur "naturally" and is labeled in that way.

Labeling women's community activism "public motherhood" also reconciled political action with traditional roles. As Gittell and Shtob (1980) argue, women enlarged their sphere of homelike duties to encompass the community. Manipulating labels smoothed the way for the acceptance of the changing content of women's activities, but it also accomplished something else: It echoed the justifications patriarchal ideology made to cheapen and devalue women's unpaid work. Alluding to the natural traits of women's community involvement not only depoliticized and mystified its political and public nature but also cloaked its contribution to class reproduction. Labeling women's unpaid community work "social housekeeping" or "philanthropy" aligns these efforts with traditional roles.

Differentiated by class and ethnicity, unpaid work or voluntarism inspired and trained women for political activism. During the Progressive Era, women's voluntary activities led to the development of new careers and professions for middle-class women, the promotion of reform initiatives, and the development of social institutions (McCarthy 1990). Although much of White middle- and upper-class women's volunteer work advocated reforms that generally benefited the welfare of all children, it reflected the cultural biases of the middle class (Ladd-Taylor 1991). Working-class women were at odds with some of the reforms. According to Ladd-Taylor (1991), the child labor laws conflicted with working-class women's practice of sending children to work. This example illustrates how perceptions and family survival strategies differed between working-class and middle-class women.

Once we take seriously women's "voluntarism" as unpaid work in the home and in the community, we begin to appreciate the complexity of the social relations from which it originates. Part of the complexity of the social relationships includes the class as well as the ethnic/racial composition of a community that organizes and structures women's unpaid work. Most working-class African American, Mexican American, and White women have based their volunteer work on the immediate needs of their own communities.[2] Ethnicity and class often converge with the stratification of place found in almost all major U.S. cities. Thus neighborhoods reflect as well as help to structure and organize responses to inequality (Logan 1978) and shape women's voluntarism.

African American women's unpaid work within church-based organizations provides insight as to the way women of color carved out autonomy within local congregations led by male pastors. In a study of the Sanctified Church (1892-1942), Gilkes (1988) found that the fundraising power of women limited direct male domination of the women's activities. African American women reminded men, "if it wasn't for women, you wouldn't have a church" (p. 237). As Gilkes argues, even though women may have become frustrated by male domination in church-based organizations, they avoided open rebellion. Women reconciled their frustrations regarding sexism because they felt that the virulence of racial oppression warranted unity and cooperation between Black men and women.

As was true at the turn of the century, race, as well as class, continues to shape the unpaid labor of women. African American women's voluntarism, originating in church settings and women's clubs, later contributed to the grassroots foundation of the civil rights movement (Gilkes 1988; Harley 1988; Jones 1992; Barnett 1995). African American women perceived the community as united, as well as threatened, by racism. Similar themes may be identified in the widespread involvement of working-class women in neighborhood organizations that characterized the 1960s and 1970s. Across the nation, working-class African American, Mexican American, and White women addressed civil rights and welfare rights, and participated in the development of Model Cities programs (Fincher and McQuillen 1989; Naples 1991). Rather than volunteering to help the less fortunate, working-class women worked to make possible decent schooling, safe streets, and at least minimal health conditions for their own families and communities, as state services lagged behind community needs.

In sum, feminist insights have begun to address women's unpaid work with attention to the dynamics of gender, race, and class. Until a rupture occurs in everyday social life, the work is often taken for granted. When it is recognized, women's unpaid work is often misrepresented. Calling women's unpaid community work voluntarism misrepresents its central importance to the reproduction of class. Labels can shape our perceptions of these activities as well as constrain women's activities. In the process of carrying out unpaid community work, women often must negotiate with or challenge the institutions within which they work. When we observe how women identify and then strategize to meet the material needs of their communities, we see how women's unpaid work is specified by class, ethnicity, and race.

In the context of the current national economic recession, high levels of unemployment, and cutbacks in public services, women's unpaid community work continues to be significant, and particularly crucial, for low-income communities. The case study presented below of the origins and development of a grassroots community group of Mexican American women illustrates how these women's unpaid work directly improved opportunities for their children, indirectly provided leadership training for participation in broader-based community activism, and resulted in the creation of much-needed community resources. A small local success, MELASI is a case of women's unpaid community work that glows in comparison to the gloom and doom of the national protracted recession and federal disinvestment.

## AN ETHNOGRAPHIC CASE STUDY:
## MADRES DEL ESTE DE LOS ANGELES, SANTA ISABEL

### The Community Context

Boyle Heights, a Latino working-class neighborhood on the Eastside of Los Angeles, has an estimated population of 89,000, twice the density of the rest of the city of Los Angeles. Half of the population is under 25 years of age, and residents are primarily low-income, blue-collar workers. About half of the population is foreign born. Most are renters rather than homeowners; however, there is a significant percentage of long-term residents who give stability to the neighborhood. The median family income, based on what the 1980 U.S. Census designated as Spanish-origin for the Boyle Heights area, is $12,000, with 25% of the residents earning incomes below the poverty level. The job distribution for women is concentrated in the operator/laborer category (36%) and in service (18.8%), with the smallest proportion of women working as managers and professionals (6%). More than 43% participate in the labor force, and women head 19.5% of the households. Of course, the census data do not capture what may be a significant number of women who work in the informal economy in Los Angeles (Lopez-Garza 1989).

Two general observations about the relationship between the Catholic Church and the Mexican American community are appropriate at this point. First, the local parish pastor decides on his own degree of community involvement. Some priests choose to focus their efforts on the immediate responsibilities of administering sacraments and monitoring church groups rather than addressing community issues; others may choose to lend support to neighborhood advocacy groups. Second, for Mexican American women, the Catholic parish has long served as the site for schooling, youth activities, family counseling, and links with other social institutions (Grebler, Moore, and Guzman 1979; Williams 1989; Ruiz 1993). The parish boundaries define one of the spaces where community identity develops and associations flourish. Thus the Catholic Church in working-class Mexican American neighborhoods holds great potential as a base for collective work and community advocacy. However, the pastor's interpretation of his responsibilities and the working relationship between pastor and parishioners greatly determine whether the church encourages community action. The decision to address community issues varies from parish to parish and is not predetermined.

## Methods

I used ethnographic research methods to develop a case study of the origins and development of MELASI. In 1988, I began participant observation, in-depth interviews, and a selected review of newspaper articles for the period 1985-1994.[3] I used an open-ended interview guide that included questions on each respondent's biography, first community experiences, perceptions about community issues, current activism, and the relationship between her household work and community work. Interview questions were translated into Spanish, but only one non-English interview was conducted. All the other women I interviewed were bilingual and English dominant. Half of the women's answers included

Spanish phrases, reflecting the bilingual nature of their daily communication in the Eastside community.

This essay draws on interviews with 12 women, 8 of whom were between 50 and 60 years of age and 4 of whom were between 40 and 50. None worked for wages at the time of the study. The women entered the labor force only at particular points in their family lives when the need was great, particularly when their children entered the local Catholic high school and tuition fees escalated beyond what one wage could cover. Most of the women stated that they preferred to care for their children rather than seek employment and send their children to day care. As their husbands had stable employment and salaries sufficient to support their families, they chose to stay home after they married. The women's husbands worked in a variety of predominantly unionized blue-collar jobs: Among the husbands were a baker, a construction worker, a machinist, and one who had been in the armed services and then worked in plant maintenance. The four women between 40 and 50 years of age had worked for wages. For these women, increasing inflation eliminated the option of remaining home to raise their children; the current cost of living required two salaries.

## Women's Unpaid Work
## and the Origins of MELASI

The women who founded and organized MELASI began their unpaid labor as parishioners in the Catholic parish. Fulfilling the traditional women's role in de facto sex-segregated organizations, the women pursued their class and cultural interests. As the women experienced tension within one Catholic parish, they sought affiliation with another parish and developed a nonprofit community-based component directed by their concerns. Below, I first present the experiences of women during the 1960s and 1970s, when women began volunteering at the parish school in order to offset tuition fees. I then offer an account of the mass community mobilization that occurred in the 1980s, and finally provide an overview of MELASI's incorporation in the 1990s.

During the 1950s, the Catholic Church began building parochial schools attached to the parishes in East Los Angeles. According to the local pastors, parents became attracted to parishes with schools and parent groups. Pastors called it a "drawing card via the 'Mothers club' " (McNamara 1975). Erlinda Robles, a Mexican American woman who still lives on the street where she was born and raised, participated throughout the 1960s in the "mothers' club." She recalls fund-raising activities such as the Sunday sales of Mexican food. Most of the women interviewed had contributed more than 30 years of unpaid work to raise funds to support the school and other parish activities. Women and men volunteered to help with the building of the church by holding bazaars to raise building funds. Evelina Banuelos explained, "We helped for 40 years to get the funds to build the church. Jamaica [charity bazaar] after jamaica . . . not just one jamaica, not two jamaicas, it was about three or four per year."

Whereas men volunteered skills and labor on weekends, women's unpaid work became a daily activity used to maintain and sustain the Catholic school. The tedious and often physical maintenance work sometimes saved the church a lot of money. Erlinda Robles recalled:

> One day, the Parents Guild noticed how dirty the walls in the school were and it was decided that they needed painting. The men volunteered to paint, but they could only do it on the weekends because they worked all week. Before they were going to paint, the walls had to be washed. So, during the week, we started washing the walls. We didn't even have ladders, so we stacked tables on top of each other and scrubbed those walls. The nun would look in and get worried; she would bring us sandwiches. By the time we finished and they came and looked at the walls, they said that they were so clean that they didn't have to paint after all! We saved them several hundred dollars!

Erlinda noted also that a small group of women usually carried out the work that benefited many.

By the late 1970s, the financial need of the parochial school increased and the church mandated parent participation in fund-raisers. A decrease in the rate of women's participation in church fund-raisers coincided with the increase of Mexican American women's labor force participation. The Parents Guild president confronted increasing difficulty in rounding up the volunteer labor needed to carry out weekly fund-raising breakfasts. As president of the Parents Guild, Rosa Villaseñor spoke of how she had to demand participation of a single mother at one of the meetings:

> She said she could not afford to pay or participate because she was a single parent going to night school and working. I told her that it was not fair for her to get away with having all the other mothers doing her work. She was doing things to better herself and that was fine for her. I told her either she

paid or she should come on Sunday mornings at least for the *desayunos* [breakfasts]. I couldn't let her get away with it because then the other women would say, "Well, why should I do it?" She wasn't too happy about it, but she started helping on Monday mornings.

When Rosa told me this story, I reacted with sympathy toward the single working mother who was seeking higher education. From an individualistic point of view, the single mother could have used the free time to study. But from Rosa's position of responsibility for the collective, the woman's release from group efforts would work to the detriment of a system of "volunteer" labor. It would sabotage group cohesiveness and commitment; quite literally, Rosa could not "let her get away with it."

Further tensions resulted from an incident involving the women who volunteered in the parish school and also participated in running a community recreation center. These women established driver's training classes at the center after a four-month struggle that involved a series of hearings, meetings, and demonstrations. To celebrate the victory, the women wanted to host a dinner, and they asked the priest if they could use the church kitchen facilities to prepare the food. He initially refused the request because the victory and the issue were not church related. The women argued that if he wanted to see them around doing all the usual unpaid work, he should carefully reconsider their request. They combined the two spheres of social and church activity when they demanded the use of the church facilities to prepare a celebration of a success not directly church based.

## Community Conflicts Make
## Women's Unpaid Work Visible

The women's daily unpaid community work occurred with little recognition and certainly no media attention until two major community controversies brought the women into the public eye. In March 1985, the state made public a bid it had made on an expensive parcel of industrially zoned land. Then Governor George Deukmejian had resolved to place a 1,700-inmate penal institution in East Los Angeles, within a mile of the long-established Boyle Heights community and within two miles of 34 schools. The state bid violated convention by failing to provide a public community hearing or to compile an environmental impact report.

The state's complete disregard for both legal procedures and the public's need for information meant that the only way to stop the process was to disrupt it. A broad-based coalition emerged, representing community interests with different resources: moral authority and legitimation from the church, invaluable research skills and political contacts from a few middle-class professionals, financial support from neighborhood merchants, and human power from a mass of committed parishioners. The women who later formed MELASI participated in the coalition, which mobilized broad opposition to the prison, transforming the issue into a symbol of the legacy of "dumping" unwanted projects on the Eastside.

In conjunction with weekly demonstrations in East Los Angeles, more than 200 women gathered under the name Mothers of East L.A. (MELA). They covered their heads with symbolic white scarves and traveled on chartered buses to demonstrate on the steps of the California state capitol. Until the proposed prison's defeat in 1992, the women continued to demonstrate against it, even as they gradually took on other issues and developed a larger collective identity. Despite some fear of having spread themselves too thin, the women decided to fight the proposed placement of a toxic waste incinerator in the city of Vernon, a small industrial city immediately adjacent to Boyle Heights (Pardo 1990). The women defeated the waste incinerator and also went on to challenge a chemical waste treatment plant and an oil pipeline.

Whereas the fight against the prison engaged only the Latino community, when the women took up the fight against the toxic waste incinerator, they began linking up with other ethnic communities. Greenpeace, an environmental activist group, joined some of the meetings, provided testimony at the hearings, and then invited MELA to Greenpeace-supported demonstrations organized in other working-class communities. In November 1988, the women traveled to the small town of Casmalia, 150 miles north of Los Angeles, to join in a demonstration for the closing of a toxic dump site (Russell 1989). Grassroots groups from other small California cities with large minority populations, such as Kettleman City, McFarland, and Richmond, as well as Casmalia, joined the march led by MELA. As a result of these pressures, Assembly Bill 58 (Roybal-Allard), which provides all Californians with the minimum protection of an environmental impact report before the construction of hazardous waste incinerators, was signed into law.

## The Establishment of MELASI

After establishing considerable community presence and a reputation for championing community causes, MELA split into two separate groups, generally along parish lines. The separation of the groups occurred when the women, and some men, began raising questions about the group decision-making process (Acuña 1992, p. 80). Questions of concern included the following: Which community issues would be addressed? Who was entitled to use the name? What would be the relationship of the pastor to the group? Who was to act as spokesperson for the group? One group continued to work with Resurrection Parish and the pastor who had named and worked with the group. Because the split generated some confusion and tension, Juana Gutiérrez, a leader and core member of the first group who later established MELASI, wrote an open letter that was published in a local newspaper:

La señora Gutiérrez es una activista comunitaria de tiempo atrás y sum membresía con el grupo comunitario Mothers of East Los Angeles es relativa únicamente al grupo Mothers of East Los Angeles que se reúne en la Parroquia de Santa Isabel. Este grupo no tiene presidente, pero sí un concilio de gobierno. Otros miembros de este concilio son Erlinda Robles de la Parroquia de Talpa, Lucilla Mendoza de la Parroquia de Dolores Mission, y Lucía Mendívil y Rosa Villaseñor también de la Parroquia Santa Isabel. . . .

Los grupos Mothers of East Los Angeles de Santa Isabel y de la iglesia de la Resurrección, aunque tienen luchas en común, operan independientemente uno del otro. (Gutiérrez 1990, p. 1)

[Mrs. Gutiérrez is a former community activist and her membership in the community group Mothers of East Los Angeles is only related to the group of Mothers of East Lost Angeles that meets at the Parish of Santa Isabel. This group does not have a president, but it has a governing council. Other members belonging to this council are Erlinda Robles, from the Parish of Talpa; Lucilla Mendoza, from the Parish of Dolores Mission; Lucía Mendívil and Rosa Villaseñor also from the Parish of Santa Isabel. . . .

Even though the groups Mothers of East Los Angeles of Santa Isabel and of the Church of the Resurrection have common struggles, they operate independently of one another.] (my translation)

This letter made the groups' separate identities public knowledge, yet both groups continued to address quality-of-life issues in East Los Angeles. At Resurrection Parish, the group of predominantly women worked closely with Frank Villalobos, an urban planner, and Pastor John Moretta.

After 1990, the newly formed MELASI continued to attend community hearings on urban development issues that affected the Eastside community. MELASI developed a relationship with the pastor that differed from that of the group at Resurrection Parish. The women in MELASI kept the pastor informed of their activities, but he supported rather than directed their programs. Juana Gutiérrez continued to act as the spokesperson for MELASI. In 1992, she along with the other members developed the collaborative Water Conservation Program with the Metropolitan Water District, the Department of Water and Power, and Corporate Technologies Service International (CTSI). The joint effort allowed MELASI to generate funding to develop several community betterment programs.

Meanwhile, a budget crisis in Los Angeles led to drastic cutbacks in funding for clinics offering infant immunization and basic health care. Well aware of the likely repercussions of budget cutbacks and the fact that 75% of Eastside residents are uninsured, MELASI decided to target children up to two years old and created the Child Immunization Project in conjunction with nearby White Memorial Hospital. MELASI coordinated a project that involved high school student volunteers going door to door to inform Eastside residents about the importance and availability of vaccinations and tuberculosis testing and also to offer free transportation to the hospital.

The new partnership between MELASI and the large corporations was celebrated with a dinner and dance featuring a mariachi band and a Mexican *quebradita* dance band in the church meeting hall. The program for the event explained the objectives and accomplishments of the group:

> In just one year, the Water Conservation Project has been the impetus for the creation of 27 employment opportunities, with medical coverage and salaries well beyond the poverty level of many inner city employment projects. Of the jobs created, 20 are filled by heads of households. And not only were these jobs created during a national and more specific state economic crisis, they were created without the influx of any additional taxpayer foundation or government monies.

MELASI's partnership with the Water Conservation Project made possible the creation of new jobs, the infant immunization project, and a number of community service programs, including both a graffiti cleanup project run entirely by inner-city youth and a college scholarship program.

## Discussion

This case shows how the class composition of a community shapes both women's perceptions of what needs to be done and the women's relationships to local institutions. For these working-class Mexican American women, the site of unpaid work began in the Catholic parish. For analytic purposes, we can consider the Catholic parish church a community-based social institution and differentiate it from the Catholic Church as a religious institution. As such, it offers a space not dominated by the state or church hierachies. Furthermore, in terms of traditional family gender relations, it is a legitimate space for women to gather that is also trusted by new immigrants.

The term *voluntarism* obscures the way working-class women use unpaid labor to compensate for inadequate wages. Initially, their children's educational needs led almost all the women into community work. Part of a mother's traditional responsibility includes overseeing her child's progress in school, interacting with school staff, and supporting school activities. While meeting these responsibilities, the women met other mothers and developed a network of acquaintanceships and friendships based on mutual concern for the welfare of their children. From this base, the women addressed broader community issues.

Although upper- and middle-class women may provide unpaid volunteer labor, they do not confront unsafe neighborhoods as directly as do working-class women. Middle- and upper-class women are more readily able to pay for such advantages as parochial school tuition. They do not necessarily rely on the Catholic Church to provide services that the state is not providing for them. In this Eastside community, the Catholic Church accepts "volunteer work" in lieu of full tuition fees, thus part of the women's labor was exchanged for lower fees. This arrangement offered the women who regularly carried out extensive unpaid work to set their own agenda rather than simply rely on the church agenda.

Many activist groups in Mexican American communities have developed from the Catholic Church base. However, working relationships between pastor and community members must be negotiated. Women and other community members must resolve questions regarding who will direct the decision-making process. In the case of Madres del Este de Los Angeles, Santa Isabel, the women took the lead and devised a space that created paid work for community members, resources for youth, and health services for infants.

Much like the resources provided through the "voluntarism" of middle- and working-class women during the Progressive Era, these resources are necessary, not superfluous. However, there is a crucial distinction between some of the historical examples and the activities of the women in this case study: Middle-class professionals do not guide the activities of these working-class women as they did during the Progressive Era. The women themselves or community members define issues and direct activities.

The history of MELASI illustrates the process by which hundreds of working-class Mexican American women became politically informed and activated. In the case of MELASI, the women became public figures through conflict with the state. Through in-depth interviews, I found that the work these women carried out for political mobilization was quite embedded in the unpaid work they did as mothers and as members of the parish.

These women became core activists and mobilized the social networks they had established through many years of living and volunteering in the community. This mobilization, as I have noted, capitalized on references to the traditional gender role of motherhood, which became partially transformed in order to legitimate opposition to a state prison project. By the time MELASI emerged, the women began to work with environmental groups around the state. Now several of the women are sought after to voice a variety of community concerns.

## CONCLUSION

The findings of the case study presented here have methodological and conceptual implications. First, this study illustrates that methods of gathering information and theories about social relations are intimately intertwined. As Smith (1987) argues, making this relationship visible sharpens our methods and theories. Feminist scholarship that places women of color at the center, as this study does, helps us to see the social relations of class, gender, and ethnicity in grounded settings (Soldatenko 1991; Zavella 1991). It also contributes to what Sacks (1989) calls "a unified theory of class, race, and gender." Through the words of the women participants themselves, we can construct a more unified picture of how women's unpaid labor contributes to social and community betterment.

Second, this study challenges the commonsense notion of voluntarism as well as social science references to voluntarism, which inadequately capture the significance of women's unpaid work to community safety and welfare. Some community members explain, and in essence make trivial, women's volunteer work by saying, "They do it because they have the time." One social scientist has speculated, "Personal lifestyles of women . . . are conducive to community work" (Dabrowski 1983, p. 430). These simplistic explanations miss the world of activities in which women may elect to spend their time. They also miss the complex process by which women negotiate with male-dominated social institutions in order to meet community needs. Most important, the class and ethnic composition of a community structures its needs; unlike middle-class communities, working-class communities lack basic services that they may not be able to purchase.

Third, in working-class Mexican American and other Latino communities, the Catholic Church as a local institution has tremendous potential for advocating community betterment. Mexican American women have demonstrated leadership in several church-based community organizations, such as Communities Organized for Political Service in Texas, the United Neighborhood Organization in Los Angeles, and the East Valley Organization in a Los Angeles suburb. All of these are based on the Chicago "Back of the Yards" community empowerment model crafted by Saul Alinsky. Women continue to be active members and leaders in all these groups. The pattern suggests that the church parish is a strategic place for the development of Mexican American women's leadership skills.

Even though the extent of Mexican American working-class women's unpaid work in Los Angeles is seldom recognized, this work helps to sustain a decent quality of community life in the face of economic recession, falling real wages, and current anti-immigrant sentiments. As in urban centers across national boundaries, from Mexico City to Los Angeles, women often spend more time in their neighborhoods than do men, and thus develop a keener sense of community needs and often take the lead in community betterment projects (Velazquez 1990; Garland 1988). Gender is a central category of social organization in regard to unpaid labor in community settings. Working-class women who carry out extensive unpaid labor often feel compelled to do so, by the church, peer pressure, or familial need. Thus the notion of voluntarism fails to

capture the great efforts of women who attend to the taken-for-granted
unpaid work that helps a working-class community survive. Quite the
contrary—as Erlinda Robles emphatically stated, "We have to do it!"

## NOTES

1. This essay departs from a larger comparative study of women's grassroots activism
in a working-class and middle-class community. See my earlier essay "Mexican American
Grassroots Community Activists" (Pardo 1990) for a brief discussion of the ways women
become activists; see my "Creating Community" (Pardo 1991) for a detailed discussion
of how Mexican American women's volunteer work creates community.

2. Firor (1991) argues that 19th-century White middle-class women did more than
simply reproduce class relations; they also challenged the conditions that generated
inequality and poverty.

3. Rodolfo Acuña, a Chicano historian and much-respected friend, wrote a series of
op-ed pieces about the prison and incinerator issues for the *Los Angeles Herald Examiner*
and the *Los Angeles Times*. These essays provided invaluable syntheses of the political
participants, coalitions, and conflicts between Mexican American elected representatives
and the community.

## REFERENCES

Acuña, Rodolfo. 1992. *Forming the Debate: The Present Interprets the Past*. Renato
    Rosaldo Lecture Series Monograph 8, Series 1990-91. Tucson: University of Arizona,
    Mexican American Studies and Research Center.
Barnett, Bernice McNair. 1995. Black Women's Collectivist Movement Organizations:
    Their Struggles during the Doldrums." Pp. 199-219 in *Feminist Organizations: Harvest of the New Women's Movement*, edited by Myra Marx Ferree and Patricia Yancy
    Martin. Philadelphia: Temple University Press.
Dabrowski, Irene. 1983. "Working-Class Women and Civic Action: A Case Study of an
    Innovative Community Role." *Policy Studies Journal* 11:427-35.
Daniels, Arlene Kaplan. 1988. *Invisible Careers: Civic Women Leaders from the Volunteer
    World*. Chicago: University of Chicago Press.
Enloe, Cynthia. 1989. *Bananas, Beaches, and Bases: Making Feminist Sense of International Politics*. Berkeley: University of California Press.
Fincher, Ruth and Jacinta McQuillen. 1989. "Women in Urban Social Movements." *Urban
    Geography* 10:604-13.
Firor, Anne Scott. 1991. *Natural Allies: Women's Associations in American History*.
    Chicago: University of Illinois Press.
Garland, Anne Witte. 1988. *Women Activists: Challenging the Abuse of Power*. New York:
    Feminist Press.

Gilkes, Cheryl Townsend. 1988. "Together and in Harness: Women's Traditions in the Sanctified Church." Pp. 223-44 in *Black Women in America*, edited by Michelene R. Malson, Elisabeth Mudimbe-Boyi, Jean F. O'Barr, and Mary Wyer. Chicago: University of Chicago Press.

Gittell, Marilyn and T. Shtob. 1980. "Changing Women's Roles in Political Volunteerism and Reform in the City." Pp. 64-75 in *Women and the American City*, edited by C. R. Stimpson, E. Dixler, M. J. Nelson, and K. B. Yatrakis. Chicago: University of Chicago Press.

Grebler, Leo, Joan W. Moore, and Ralph C. Guzman. 1979. *The Mexican American People*. New York: Free Press.

Gutiérrez, Juana. 1990. [Letter to the editor]. *Eastside Journal*, February 7, p. 1.

Harley, Sharon. 1988. "For the Good of Family and Race: Gender, Work, and Domestic Roles in the Black Community 1880-1930." Pp. 159-72 in *Black Women in America*, edited by Michelene R. Malson, Elisabeth Mudimbe-Boyi, Jean F. O'Barr, and Mary Wyer. Chicago: University of Chicago Press.

Jones, Beverly W. 1992. "The Political Implications of Black and White Women's Work in the South, 1890-1965." Pp. 108-29 in *Women, Politics, and Change*, edited by Louise A. Tilly and Patricia Gurin. New York: Russell Sage Foundation.

Ladd-Taylor, Molly. 1991. "Hull House Goes to Washington: Women and the Children's Bureau." Pp. 110-26 in *Gender, Class, Race, and Reform in the Progressive Era*, edited by Noralee Frankel and Nancy S. Dye. Lexington: University Press of Kentucky.

Logan, John. 1978. "Growth, Politics, and the Stratification of Places." *American Journal of Sociology* 84:404-14.

Lopez-Garza, Marta. Summer 1989. Immigration and Economic Restructuring: The Metamorphisis of Southern California. *California Sociologists* 12(2): entire issue.

McCarthy, Kathleen. 1990. "Parallel Power Structures: Women and the Voluntary Sphere." In *Lady Bountiful Revisited: Women, Philanthropy, and Power*, edited by Kathleen McCarthy. New Brunswick, NJ: Rutgers University Press.

McNamara, Patrick H. 1975. "Mexican Americans in Los Angeles County: A Study in Acculturation." Unpublished manuscript, St. Louis University, St. Louis, MO.

Naples, Nancy. 1991. "Contradictions in the Gender Subtext of the War on Poverty: The Community Work and Resistance of Women from Low-Income Communities." *Social Problems* 38:316-32.

Pardo, Mary. 1990. "Mexican American Grassroots Community Activists: Mothers of East Los Angeles." *Frontiers* 11:1-7.

————. 1991. "Creating Community: Mexican American Women in Eastside Los Angeles." *Aztlan: Journal of Chicano Studies Research* 20:39-72.

Romero, Mary. 1992. *Maid in the U.S.A.* New York: Routledge.

Ruiz, Vicki L. 1993. "Star Struck: Acculturation, Adolescence and the Mexican American Woman, 1920-1950." Pp. 109-29 in *Building with Our Hands, New Directions in Chicana Studies*, edited by A. del La Torre and B. M. Pesquera. Berkeley: University of California Press.

Russell, Dick. 1989. "Environmental Racism: Minority Communities and Their Battle against Toxics." *Amicus Journal* 11:22-32.

Sacks, Karen. 1989. "Toward a Unified Theory of Class, Race, and Gender." *American Ethnologist* 16:534-50.

Schackel, Sandra. 1992. *Social Housekeepers: Women Shaping Public Policy in New Mexico 1920-1940*. Albuquerque: University of New Mexico Press.

Smith, Dorothy. 1987. *The Everyday World as Problematic: A Feminist Sociology.* Boston: Northeastern University Press.

Soldatenko, Maria Angelina. 1991. "Organizing Latina Garment Workers in Los Angeles." *Aztlan: Journal of Chicano Studies Research* 20:73-96.

Velazquez, Daniel Rodriguez. 1990. "From Neighborhood to Nation." *North American Congress on Latin America* 18:22-29.

Williams, Norma. 1989. *The Mexican American Family: Tradition and Change.* New York: General Hall.

Zavella, Patricia. 1991. "Mujeres in Factories: Race and Class Perspectives on Women, Work, and Family." Pp. 312-36 in *Gender at the Crossroads of Knowledge: Feminist Anthropology in the Postmodern Era,* edited by Micaela di Leonardo. Berkeley: University of California Press.

# 10

# The Third Shift:
# Black Women's Club Activities
# in Denver, 1900-1925

## LYNDA F. DICKSON

One salient example of unpaid work among African American women in the late 19th and early 20th centuries is found in the activities of federated women's clubs in Denver, Colorado. There is evidence that the members of these clubs were for the most part middle class, using "respectability" as the major criterion for membership; married with children; and employed outside of the home. Their club work created a third work shift, contributing to racial uplift efforts within their communities. The African American federated women's clubs (i.e., those affiliated with the National Association of Colored Women's Clubs) embraced the then prevailing defensive philosophy of self-help, self-improvement, and racial unity. This is apparent in the major manifestations of their unpaid work during this period: (a) self-improvement efforts; (b) helping the poor and needy within the community in both individual cases and through more formalized giving, such as contributing to the Red Cross; (c) working with children and young adults; (d) fund-raising; and (e) cooperative efforts among clubs.

One of the clearest historical examples of women's unpaid work is found in the activities of the African American women's clubs that

AUTHOR'S NOTE: This essay is adapted from my dissertation, "The Early Club Movement among Black Women in Denver, 1890-1925," Department of Sociology, University of Colorado, Boulder, 1982.

flourished in urban settings during the late 19th and early 20th centuries. Secular women's clubs, which, according to W. E. B. Du Bois ([1898] 1969), represented "distinctly the efforts of the better classes of Negroes to rescue and uplift the unfortunate and vicious" (quoted in Lerner 1973, p. 37), emerged specifically in those areas having sizable Black populations, educated Black women with "leisure" time, and unmet needs of the Black poor.

By 1890, the city of Denver met these three characteristics, and thus had its share of Black women's clubs. There were 22 federated clubs organized in Denver between 1900 and 1925, but only four still exist today. The activities of these remaining clubs are the focus of this chapter. I contacted presidents and historians from each of the clubs, and carefully examined all available club materials, including scrapbooks, minute books, ledgers, notices of events sponsored by the clubs, and correspondence with other clubs (both locally and with the National Organization of Colored Women's Clubs). In addition, in 1980 and 1981, I interviewed the eldest living members of the clubs. From these primary and numerous secondary sources, an interesting picture of Denver's early Black clubwomen emerges.

The names of the clubs, Pond Lily Art and Service Club (founded in 1902), Taka Art and Literary Club (1903), Carnation Art, Literary and Charity Club (1903), and Self-Improvement and Social Service Club (1906), reflect an interest in self-improvement, but the clubs were equally concerned with helping the less fortunate and fostering overall community improvement. In addition, these clubs formed an association that established a day nursery in 1916. It appears that the maintenance of this nursery is a major factor in explaining why these particular clubs managed to survive for more than 90 years.

Although the activities and achievements of all early clubwomen, regardless of race, represent clear examples of women's unpaid work, there is evidence, discussed below, that African American clubwomen were more likely than their White counterparts to also be employed outside the home. Thus, whereas White clubwomen may have used club work to fill their ample "leisure time," Black clubwomen used what little "leisure time" remained before, in between, and after they fulfilled work and family obligations for such civic activities. In this sense, their club work represented a "third shift." It is in this context that this chapter expands on my earlier works on the activities of late-19th-century Black women's clubs in Denver. More specifically, those earlier works were devoted to documenting the very existence of the clubs, describing what they did, and the local context (the Denver setting) in which these activities occurred (Dickson 1982). Here the focus shifts to a consideration of the *personal* (i.e., work and family) context in which this unpaid work (club work) occurred. To portray the characteristics of these early clubwomen adequately, I need to provide first a brief description of Denver's Black community during the late 1800s.

## DENVER'S BLACK COMMUNITY

During the last two decades of the 19th century, Denver experienced rapid growth, and increasing numbers of African Americans, along with other racial groups, came to the city in the hope of benefiting from this expansion. Prior to 1870, the few Black residents in Colorado (46 in 1860, 450 in 1870) were primarily miners or trappers; a few were slaves. The increase in Colorado's Black population after 1870 appears to correspond with the Black exodus from the South to northern and western states. The largest increase occurred between 1880 and 1890 (from 2,435 to 6,215), with Denver having the greatest concentration of Colorado's Black population (Hill 1946). An important feature of the Black migration was the inclusion of a fair share of women. In fact, by 1900, females outnumbered males within the Black community. The larger number of females encouraged greater stability within the community, and families tended to be the rule rather than the exception (Dorsett 1977).

Denver's growing Black community followed many of the same patterns found in the northern cities of the Midwest and East, such as Chicago, Boston, Philadelphia, and New York. The early migrants to each of these urban Black communities were mostly southern, largely upwardly mobile, often skilled and educated workers. Within these cities, the Black population was small; in Denver it was never more than 4% prior to 1930. In terms of treatment by the broader community, there was tolerance while the numbers remained small, but intolerance became the rule as the numbers of Black residents increased. Residential segregation was pronounced, often relegating the Black community to the worst areas of the city. And due to greater opportunities for domestic employment in urban areas, the initial population was predominantly female. The Black population increased around World War II, with an influx of southern migrants. Intolerance among White citizens increased, and established Black residents attributed the increased racism to the greater number of "backward" Negroes from the rural South. This attitude, along with socioeconomic factors, supported the establishment of a class system within the Black community that Neilson (1977) describes as a "distorted facsimile" of that found in the broader community.

## CHARACTERISTICS OF
## EARLY CLUBWOMEN

Just as class variations are important in contemporary U.S. society, that was also the case in the late 19th and early 20th centuries. Further, the class issue then (and to a large extent today) was complicated by the intervening variable of race. Thus to say that the Black clubwomen were "middle-class" suggests something different from the middle-class status of White women's club members, historically and currently. As Neilson (1977) points out in his work on northern urban Black communities, the development of a class structure within Black communities, although made possible through and perhaps modeled after the class structure in the larger society, was nevertheless altered to conform to the realities within the Black setting. Limited employment opportunities and the resulting concentration of Black people in the lowest levels of the service sector resulted in a stronger distinction between *what* an individual did and *who* he or she was. This point has been made by Harley (1988), who quotes a former domestic worker: "One very important difference between white people and black people is that white people think that you *are* your work. . . . Now, a black person . . . knows that what I am doing doesn't have anything to do with what I want to do or what I do when I am doing for myself [or for others]" (p. 168). As Denver's Black women's clubs were a product of the middle-class segment of the community, it is necessary to pursue this point a bit further.

Prior to 1900, Denver's Black population was widely dispersed residentially, with Black people living in close proximity to their White employers. As the number of Black residents increased and transportation improved, White employers moved further away from the central city. A centralized community, known as Five Points, became the established Black community. This separation from White residents, combined with continued association through employment, had the effect of helping to define what "community" meant in Black terms.

According to Neilson (1977), "Community did not depend so much on numbers, but became a social construct in the minds of the city's residents" (p. 50). Although many White residents tended to lump all of those in the Black community into a single category, in fact, the segments of the Black community were quite distinct. Criteria such as occupation, education, and income were in some cases important, but they did not carry the same class connotations in the Black world as in the White. A social worker could qualify as a "society" leader just as easily as a minister or businessman, but so might a domestic worker. This lack of the use of occupation as a stringent marker of class was evident in the Black community even into the 1920s. For example, Mrs. Ida DePriest, who formed the Colored Women's Republican Club in the early 1890s, received much positive publicity in White newspapers. In fact, a 1901 *Denver Times* article referred to her club as one that "had accomplished more telling work . . . than any other colored organization in the state," attributing this largely to the "very capable" Mrs. DePriest (March 28, 1901, p. 4). Judging from the continual coverage of the DePriest family in Black newspapers, they were also considered respected in this sphere. Yet the 1918 *Denver City Directory* lists Mrs. DePriest as a maid for the Denver Dry (a department store) and her husband as a janitor.

If occupation was not the major criterion, what determined middle-class status for Black Americans prior to the turn of the century? Clearly the status of employers was a major source of distinctions among workers. Then, as now, workers often "borrowed" the respect and prestige associated with given employers. This "status borrowing" no doubt took on special significance during a period when few occupations were open to Black men and women.

Of at least equal and related importance as an indicator of social class was "respectability," which meant earning a living in an acceptable and more or less steady manner, accompanied by appropriate lifestyle and public conduct. Further, respectability for the early clubwomen meant having "willing hands," a "desire to help others," and a desire to "do something for the race, especially the children," but perhaps most important, "high moral character." This last criterion, as we will see shortly, represented a response to the prevailing negative perceptions about Black women.

But middle-class status, by any criteria, should not lead to the assumption that these early clubwomen were women of leisure, as was often the case of White clubwomen during this period. One of the oldest "federated women" in Denver, Mrs. Florence Moore, joined Carnation Art, Literary and Charity Club in 1917 at the age of 26. She was not employed when she joined, but after her husband died in 1927, she worked in various capacities (primarily domestic work) until 1962. She noted that whereas some of the members were homemakers, most were day workers (domestics who did not live in their employers' households). The majority of the members were also married, and their educational levels ranged from eight years of school to college degrees. Another interviewee, Mrs. Ora Harvey, moved to Denver in 1920 and became a member of Pond Lily in 1925 (personal communication, January 1982). Mrs. Harvey recalled that most of the members of her club were married, and about half had children. Soon after moving to Denver, she was employed by a "very rich White woman" as a live-in housekeeper and earned what was then the very high salary of $100 per month. She noted that most of the other members were also employed. Many were domestics, but some were also hairdressers or seamstresses, and one was a schoolteacher. Sources other than my interviews provide more contradictory information on the issue of whether *all* or merely *most* early clubwomen were employed, but one major indication that a large number did work is the fact that meetings for all the clubs were held on weekdays, as domestics and laundresses rarely had Saturdays off. As members of the Coterie Club were quick to point out, they had the only club that always held meetings on Saturdays, clearly implying that there were no domestics or laundresses in the club (Samira Mathes, member of the Coterie Club, personal communication, November 1981).

Thus, as we shall see, the activities of African American federated clubwomen in Denver not only serve as an excellent historical example of women's unpaid work, but for many of the clubwomen this unpaid work occurred in addition to both paid employment and household work. Harley (1988), in fact, argues that it was precisely *because of* paid employment that clubwomen were able to provide whatever financial assistance they could to organizations within the Black community.

The existence of a sizable Black population, a pool of middle-class women, and unmet needs of the Black poor are the necessary, but not sufficient, preconditions to club development among Black women at local levels in Denver by the late 19th century. These preconditions may not have led to a club movement had there not been a further impetus at both national and local levels—specifically, a prevailing negative image of Black people generally, and Black women particularly. Virtually all the activities of Black clubwomen reflect not merely awareness of this image, but reaction to it. According to this image, Black women, regardless of class, were lazy, immoral, and lacking in the qualities of "noble womanhood" (Giddings 1984; Hine 1990). Black women were poor mothers, as evidenced by their unwillingness to encourage chastity in their daughters (Gutman 1976). Relatedly, the "rampant" sexual promiscuity of Black women not only was said to have undermined the institution of marriage within the Black community, but was used to explain the supposed attraction of Black men toward White women. This attraction, according to one observer in 1889, occurred because of the "wantonness of the women of his own race" (cited in Morton 1991, p. 28). As Giddings (1984) notes, during the early 20th century the very idea of a "moral Black woman" was incredible; she quotes from a commentator for *The Independent* in 1902: "I sometimes hear of a virtuous Negro woman, but the idea is absolutely inconceivable to me. . . . I cannot imagine such a creature as a virtuous Negro woman" (p. 82). Those middle-class women who led the movement were particularly incensed by this image, and they realized that in order to dispel it, they must work toward uplifting their lower-class sisters. Although they had a vested interest in working toward the improvement of all Black women, the leaders of the movement at both national and local levels clearly made a distinction between themselves and the masses, as indicated by the national motto, "Lifting as we climb."

## CLUB ACTIVITIES

Examination of available materials from the four still-existing clubs reveals that they participated in many activities that do not fit into neat categories or recurrent patterns. Providing assistance to the "sammies" (soldiers) during World War I, for example, and protesting the 1915 showing of *Birth of a Nation* were important, yet isolated events. More frequent are indications of activities that fall into the following categories: (a) self-improvement, which included activities contributing to members' arts and crafts, music, literary, and intellectual development; (b) help to the poor and needy, in both individual cases and through more formalized giving, such as contributing to the Red Cross; (c) work with children and young adults to encourage higher health and educational standards; (d) fund-raising activities; and (e) cooperative efforts among clubs. Each of these major areas is detailed below.

## Self-Improvement

It is interesting to note that many clubs formed after 1900 included the words *art* and *literary* in their names and cited as their major goal the development of artistic and literary skills in their members. The structure of the meetings was generally such that three of four monthly meetings were devoted to art activities and the fourth was "literary day."

Teachers were invited to club meetings to teach specific skills, such as needlepoint. Prizes were awarded for the best work, and the "best pieces" were put on display during art exhibits as well as at city, state, and national meetings. Members looked forward to the awarding of these prizes, for it was an honor to receive such recognition. That the clubs took their artwork seriously is indicated in Taka Art and Literary Club's minutes for 1920. The president spoke of the club's art display during the 1919 State Association meetings in Boulder, saying that she was "ashamed of their work" and hoped the members would take more interest in their creations for the next convention (Taka minutes, June 30, 1920). Prior to 1916, the clubs evidently used White judges to assess their work, for in that year, the City Federation sponsored the motion that "colored judges be found to judge our art work" (Taka minutes, June 7, 1916).

Other indications of interest in self-improvement are found in the programs presented on the clubs' literary days. These programs focused on current literature, plays, and prominent musical figures among the race. Members were expected to be prepared for these programs. The clubs encouraged members to develop their skills in speaking before groups by requiring 3- to 5-minute oral presentations on various topics, such as "How Can I Make Club Work More Interesting?" "What Am I Thankful For?" and "Pleasant Features of My Summer Vacation." On this point, Mrs. Ora B. Harvey, a member of Pond Lily Art and Service from 1925 until her death in 1988, recalled that she had always been afraid to speak in front of a group before joining, but Corinne Lowry (then president of the club) cured her of this fear. Mrs. Lowry simply told her to keep something in her hands during a talk, and, according to Mrs. Harvey, it worked every time. Members of the clubs also put on debates on various issues, with several members taking opposite sides.

Nonparticipants would then vote on which side had made the most convincing argument.

It is important to point out that these activities were not mere exercises; club bylaws clearly specified the number of pieces of artwork expected of each member as well as other requirements, including the wearing of club regalia, the amount of dues to be paid, how often members were expected to act as hostesses for meetings, and how members were to conduct themselves within and outside club meetings. Also specified were the fines to be imposed for failure to fulfill these requirements. Judging from the number of fines imposed, ranging from 2 cents for not being prepared with a quotation during roll call to 25 cents for not attending a City Federation meeting, to a dollar for not having a finished piece of artwork for the State Association conference, these bylaws were rigidly followed.

Earlier researchers of voluntary associations within Black communities, including Black women's clubs, interpreted the apparent emphasis on ritual, formalized meetings, and strict adherence to parliamentary procedure as "pathological" in that these elements represented attempts to mimic upper-class White groups of earlier generations (Myrdal 1944; Drake and Cayton 1945). Although there is clear evidence that Denver's Black women's clubs were equally formal, I suggest that this must be viewed in the context of the broader goal of self-improvement. Club members derived personal satisfaction from developing artistic skills, the ability to speak before a group, leadership skills, and expertise in raising funds. Further, we should consider that these clubwomen were responding to the public perception of Black women as loud, immoral, and uncouth. Through rigid adherence to rules governing their own behavior, clubwomen hoped to demonstrate to themselves and others within the Black community that Black women could behave in a manner worthy of respect.

Giddings (1984) reminds us that those organizations with *literary* or *improvement* attached to their names did more than pursue self-improvement or cultural activities. We must recall that the limited formal public and human service agencies that existed during this period manifested little concern about helping minorities. In early-20th-century Denver, White charities did little for the Black community (Dorsett 1977). The absence of broader social services for poor Black residents made it all the more important that self-help efforts extend to Denver's Black community whenever possible. Black women's clubs clearly did their share of community "self-help."

## Assistance to the Poor and Needy

It was of primary importance for all of the clubs to provide assistance in individual cases of charity brought to the clubs' attention. An individual member would hear of a case and then report it to the group, and the club would decide whether to provide outright assistance, refer the case to a benevolent charity or rescue committee for investigation, or, in a few instances, forgo providing help.

The Taka Art and Literary Club's minutes provide specific examples of assistance. In 1915, the records show, "Aldine Allen given a pair of shoes," and "Lydia Hall given a ton of coal." Together, these items cost the club $6.20. Other entries show "Mrs. Clay's little boy needs shoes" and $2.00 allocated; also, "Mrs. Jackson needs assistance"—her rent was paid for the month, and she was given a sack of flour. In 1916, the minutes show $1.00 allotted for a prescription for a sick woman, $5.00 donated toward the purchase of artificial limbs for a Mr. Palmer, $1.50 donated toward helping a woman secure a railroad ticket, and $2.00 sent to a destitute family at 2528 California Street. In 1919, the minutes include references to Taka's relief committee visiting the sick and needy, and the donation of one dozen eggs and two quarts of milk to a sick man.

In many instances, clothing or perhaps a bottle of cod liver oil was the only help needed. In others, money was required to help individuals in prison, as in 1920, when $5.00 was given to a Mrs. Mary Collins toward securing her freedom. Also during that year, the Taka Art and Literary Club received a letter from a mother in Colorado Springs whose son had recently been sentenced to Canon City Prison. The club members gave $10.00 to assist in his appeal (Taka minutes, March 12 and October 20, 1920).

In spite of the above examples, it appears that the Taka Art and Literary Club did not give blindly. In fact, Mrs. Contee suggested in 1919 that the members should spend more time determining whether the unfortunate "really needed help" before giving it. Occasional references appear in the minutes to the Relief Committee's visiting a sick individual or family and reporting that "no help was needed in this case." Factors other than need appear to have influenced a 1921 decision when Mrs. Gatewood presented the case of a woman with two children who was about to be evicted from her parents' home; the motion to pay part of the rent for an apartment for the woman was denied.

Examples of more formalized giving are indicated by the group's regular contributions to the YWCA, in the form of money (e.g., a $20.00

donation) or other items. For example, Mrs. Bondurant made a report to the Taka Art and Literary Club on the needs of the "Y," and six bed sheets, costing $13.00, were donated. The minutes indicate that the club made regular contributions to the Red Cross and to Federated Charities; in 1921 the members raised $303.43 for this latter organization. After the Community Chest was established in 1922, the club made regular pledges, paid off in weekly installments. Carnation Art, Literary and Charity Club also made regular contributions to both the YMCA and the YWCA; the Colored Blind Home; the Community Chest; the Lincoln Orphanage in Pueblo, Colorado; and Shorter, Zion, and Central Baptist churches.

As the above examples illustrate, Black women's clubs played a major role in both formal and informal giving. Yet they also serve to reinforce Hine's (1990) reminder that Black charitable giving more often occurred on a small-scale, personalized level; clubwomen often knew the individuals and families they were assisting.

**Work with Children and Young Adults**

The clubs maintained an ongoing interest in the welfare of children, especially in their educational attainment, physical health, and social development. Although most efforts in these areas were expressed through work with the nursery and dormitory established by the Negro Women's Club Home Association, other projects were carried out within individual clubs. In 1919, for example, the Taka Art and Literary Club took an active interest in the Twenty-Fourth Street School, sending a representative to visit the facility in order to "see what could be done towards encouraging our children to improve their appearance" (Taka minutes, November 19, 1919). Plans were drawn up for getting the children to take an active interest in their own health and appearance. To encourage them in this effort, the club gave a party for the children, serving ice cream cones. Apparently this effort continued, for in the 1920 minutes, reference is made to the "very encouraging" report of the Twenty-Fourth Street School Health Crusade.

Clubs expressed their specific concern with young women of the race by sponsoring junior clubs. Pond Lily, in fact, was responsible for initiating the idea for a State Association of Colored Girls in 1928, and it also sponsored the Pond Lily Rose Buds. The Carnation Art, Literary and Charity Club established the Carnation Buds in 1943 (Carnation Summary, 1950). The Taka minutes refer to members working with "our girls club," the Eureka Club, as early as 1913. This club evidently disbanded, for in 1919, some discussion ensued on the issue of organizing a girls' club, and later in the year the Junior Takas was formed (Taka minutes, June 18, 1919).

## Fund-Raising Activities

As is no doubt apparent at this point, in order for the clubs to carry out many of the above activities, they required a considerable amount of money. Further, we must recall that these women were "middle class" based more on their respectability than on their pocketbooks. Thus it is not surprising that much time and effort was devoted to fund-raising activities. These ranged from club sponsorship of card parties, bake sales, rummage sales, and home-cooked dinners to putting on concerts, poetry readings, and plays. Fund-raising efforts were usually carried out under the auspices of a club's ways and means committee, but in many instances members were asked to make out-of-pocket donations. The more creative, or less financially able, would hold their own entertainments, including box suppers or card parties, and turn the proceeds over to the club. In 1918, Mrs. Contee gave an entertainment benefit that realized $30.45. The Taka Art and Literary Club members were so pleased that a motion prevailed to "see that this [information] gets into the Denver Star" (Taka minutes, September 1, 1918). Other fund-raisers included a "guessing contest," a Japanese entertainment, a "Martha Washington tea party," "clown dances," chitterlings dinners, and an "Uncle Sambo and Aunt Dinah" entertainment. In order to encourage attendance at these events, the clubs would often give small prizes to the first person at the door or the person bringing the most guests.

It is interesting to note the tremendous amount of cooperation that fund-raising required of club members. This was the case for most of the club endeavors, but it is particularly in looking at fund-raising activities that one gains a sense of the members working as a team, with each giving according to her abilities. When a club's minutes indicate that the group sponsored a bake sale, a contemporary scenario might come to mind in which each member contributed a cake, pie, or some other baked item. However, at this time, it was much more likely that each member donated an ingredient for baked goods. Thus, although occasionally one finds notes in the minutes such as "Mrs. Gatewood donated a cake," more frequent references are "Cannon [donated] sugar," "Caldwell [donated] six eggs," "Waldon [donated] one pound of butter." If a member had nothing to contribute, she would volunteer to collect the ingredients and do the actual baking.

Thus, in examining the clubs' records, it becomes apparent that "club work" was precisely that: individual effort and group cooperation. Although there were individual members who were able to give more than others in terms of time, effort, and materials, the successful functioning of the clubs called for considerable teamwork. This deep sense of cooperation is an aspect of women's unpaid labor that either goes unrecognized in the U.S. philosophy of individualism or, because it is unpaid, is disparaged as women's "busywork." What is more remarkable yet is that this teamwork extended beyond individual clubs, as we shall see as we turn to cooperative efforts among clubs.

### Cooperative Efforts among Clubs

Being a "federated woman" meant more than actively participating in one's own club; there were definite expectations that club members also provide assistance to other clubs. There are numerous indications that the clubs cooperated with one another on both formal and informal levels. The available books of minutes refer often to communications received from other clubs, in the form of notices of events, invitations, solicitations, and simple greetings. In many instances only passing reference is made to a "communication" received from another club, but even these unspecified correspondences are valuable, for they not only serve to indicate that the clubs kept in touch with each other, they provide a sense of the number of different clubs that existed during a given time period, as well as some clue as to which clubs were the most active.

The Taka minutes for the period between 1916 and 1920, for example, provide numerous references to communications received from Carnation Art, Self-Improvement, Pond Lily, and Twentieth Century clubs, the last of these being referred to no less than 20 times, suggesting that it was extremely active in intergroup cooperation during this period. But there was also correspondence from the Golden West Club, Progressive Art, Martha Washington Study, Dumas Reading and Literary, Searchlight Club (of Cheyenne), Garden Study Club, the Emerald Club, and the Sojourner Truth Club. Some of these clubs lasted longer than others, but none of them exists today.

Although cooperative effort among clubs is indicated in reciprocal attendance at entertainments (as evidenced by numerous reminders to the secretaries of clubs to send thank-you notes to clubs that had supported various functions), a more formal indication of such cooperation was the establishment of the Denver Federation of Colored Women. Mrs. Alice Webb organized the federation in 1903. Mrs. Webb had visualized a nonprofit organization whose primary purpose would be to raise the cultural standards of colored girls and women. Believing this goal could best be accomplished through the combined efforts of many clubs, she asked the Pond Lily, Taka Art and Literary, Carnation Art, and Self-Improvement clubs to join her. In 1908 this organization changed its name to the City Federation of Colored Women's Clubs, and the four charter clubs were joined by the Woman's League, Margaret Murray Washington Art, Sojourner Truth, Twentieth Century, and Sunshine clubs. The City Federation then became affiliated with the State and National Associations.

The City Federation focused on issues and activities of a broader scope than did the individual clubs. In 1914, for example, a proposition for a sanitarium was discussed. Each club was asked to contribute $5.00 per month to benefit the facility. Another undertaking of this organization was a drive to benefit the poor and needy in the South. Individual clubs were asked to bring clothing and other items, as well as to contribute money for the cause.

Another significant project sponsored by the City Federation was the establishment of the Mother, Home, and Child Committee, which consisted of a representative from each club, who met once a month with the City Federation "chairman." The committee's motto was "We keep our ears open for needs, our hands ready to help." The committee would hear about a case, investigate it, and proceed from there. In one case, a young girl had come to Denver after running away from home because she was pregnant. The baby was born at Denver General Hospital, "without a diaper." Committee members went to the hospital with essential baby items, saw that the girl got to her room, packed her clothes, and contacted her parents. In another instance, it was brought to the committee's attention that on Sundays, small children were being left in the movie theater all day. Parents would not see them from 11:00 a.m. until 9:00 p.m. These children would often be crying, hungry, and tired. The committee organized and members took turns going to the theater, checking for children who stayed beyond the usual time and helping them to get home.[1]

By far the most salient example of cooperative efforts among clubs was the establishment and maintenance of the Negro Woman's Club Home, a dormitory for "deserving" girls (i.e., young, single working women with "high moral character") and a day nursery for children. The home, which opened its doors on December 16, 1916, represented the combined efforts of seven clubs that formed the Negro Women's Club Home Association in March 1916. These clubs raised all of the funds for the home by either purchasing shares of stock or soliciting sustaining members. They also contributed whatever the home needed, ranging from dishes and utensils, milk, bread, and clothing for the children in the nursery to the buying of sheeting for the exterior of the building, screens for the windows, and rakes for the yard. Yet perhaps more important than any of the financial contributions was the amount of time club members spent working at the home. Mrs. Ora B. Harvey of the Pond Lily Art and Service Club recalled that she "changed many a diaper" and "cooked many a meal" for the home. Other members recall working toward keeping the facility clean and run smoothly. Judging from the interviews with clubwomen from the still-existing clubs, work for and in the Club Home was by far the most time-consuming, yet rewarding, experience for them. Both the nursery and dormitory continued to prove successful, and in 1921 the association's report to the State Board of Charities and Corrections indicated that the home had four paid officers. The nursery cared for 30 children and the dormitory housed 9 girls (*Annual Report, 1922*).

These cooperative efforts required additional funds from members, of course. For example, the Negro Women's Club Home Association (NWCHA), consisting of seven clubs, itself became a federated club, and joined the City, State, and National Associations of Colored Women's Clubs. Thus, members in the individual clubs paid weekly club dues; the club in turn paid city, state, and national dues because the club was part of the NWCHA. When the dues are added to the numerous collections taken up during meetings for one purpose or another regarding the Club Home, combined with the collections made for charity cases, contributions to the YWCA, and other organizations, it is little wonder one irate member of Carnation Art suggested, "Why not raise the club dues rather than nickel- and dime-ing us to death?" (Carnation Art minutes, 1919). This question focuses our attention on another important aspect of "third shift" work for early Black clubwomen: In addition to time and effort, invariably additional money was required.

## SUMMARY AND CONCLUSIONS

In this chapter I have described the activities and achievements of Black clubwomen in late-19th- and early-20th-century Denver. Their activities—including those devoted to self-improvement, helping the poor and needy, working with children and young adults, working cooperatively with other clubs, and perpetual fund-raising—provide excellent examples of unpaid work that benefited both club members and the broader community. Club members' "middle-class" status, as well as their affiliation with the National Association of Colored Women's Clubs, required, or perhaps demanded, conformity to the dominant ideology espoused by African Americans during the late 19th and early 20th centuries: The progress of the race could be achieved only through the united efforts of the race itself. The emphasis on self-help and racial solidarity as defense reactions to White hostility and exclusion was manifest in all areas within Black communities. It was this reaction that in part fueled the efforts of Black clubwomen to use what remaining time and energy they had, after fulfilling their paid work requirements and caring for their own homes and families, to focus on club work.

What lessons may be learned from this historical example of unpaid work among African American women? Is it possible that conditions in late-20th-century U.S. society in general, and in African American communities in particular, are too different to allow for any meaningful comparisons? Certainly the strategies available for participation in community improvement efforts have become more sophisticated, which may appear to reduce the need for more grassroots efforts. Further, the problems within Black communities have become so complex that broader-scale efforts are demanded. In fact, Jewell (1988) argues that it is precisely because of the shifting emphasis toward structural problems within the Black community, and the resulting growth of social welfare policies, that the earlier self-help institutions have declined.

Further, the increasing class divisions among African Americans that have been made possible through expanded economic and residential opportunities must be addressed. In the Black community, the "wavy" class boundaries of the past are being replaced by the more rigid ones that apply to all members of society. These more rigid class boundaries may affect participation in Black communities in at least two respects: access to broader opportunities and the willingness to work with the now more clearly defined "lower-class" members of the Black community. On the first point, 19th-century African American women had few other options than to be community workers and activists in these clubs; now Black women who are ambitious and highly motivated have a wider range of opportunities for broader community service through both unpaid (volunteer) and paid work. In the latter instance, a cursory examination of employment patterns of college-educated Black women reveals that they are concentrated in the public sector, disproportionately in "helping" professions (e.g., social work, nursing, education, and counseling). It could be argued that today's granddaughters of early clubwomen are engaging in activities similar to those their grandmothers took part in, but now they are doing so as paid workers.

In terms of the second area, the willingness to work with the less fortunate, recall that early clubwomen had a vested interest in improving the lot of their lower-class sisters; they knew that the then-prevailing negative images of Black womanhood were applied to *all* Black women, regardless of class. Possibly today's middle-class Black women, believing that class is now more significant than race, do not have the same vested interest in working with their less fortunate sisters.

Although there are many distinct differences between the social structure and work opportunities of early-20th-century Denver and the greater United States today, history does find a way of repeating itself. And here, the role of ideology in shaping behavior becomes paramount. The 1980s witnessed dramatic reductions in social welfare spending, with accompanying calls for local support, including more community-based or self-help efforts. The plight of inner-city communities in particular has led to increased discussion within African American communities about possible community-based solutions. The activities of organizations such as the National Council of Negro Women and the Coalition of 100 Black Women and of Black sororities and women's auxiliaries in Black churches suggest that the search for solutions is clearly an agenda item for Black middle-class women in the 1990s. It is possible that we are witnessing the emergence of a 1990s version of the self-help ideology.

Perhaps, as Dorothy Height (1989) argues, the history of self-help among Black people, as exemplified by African American clubwomen, will serve as a model that may be helpful in the search for innovative approaches to the problems facing us in the 1990s. At the very least, this history may remind us that a third shift, or community participation, is perhaps essential. Combining work and family obligations with community participation is a possible method for personal and community survival.

## NOTE

1. Another plausible explanation for these children's presence in the movie theater, suggested by an early clubwoman who was interviewed for this study, is that mothers who were domestics used the theater as a baby-sitting service. Thus the children could not go home.

## REFERENCES

*Annual Report to the State Board of Corrections for the Negro Women's Club Home, year ending June 20, 1921.* 1922. (In possession of Mrs. Dorothy Reaves, Denver, CO)

Carnation Art, Literary and Charity Club Constitution and Bylaws; Summary of Past Contributions. 1950.

*Denver City Directory, 1900-1915.* 1918. (In possession of Colorado State Historical Society, Denver, CO)

Dickson, Lynda F. 1982. "The Early Club Movement among Black Women in Denver, 1890-1925." Ph.D. dissertation, University of Colorado, Boulder.

Dorsett, Lyle. 1977. *The Queen City: A History of Denver.* Boulder, CO: Pruett.

Drake, St. Clair and Horace R. Cayton. 1945. *Black Metropolis: A Study of Negro Life in a Northern City.* New York: Harcourt, Brace.

Du Bois, W. E. B. [1898] 1969. *Some Efforts of American Negroes for Their Own Social Betterment.* New York: Arno/New York Times.

Giddings, Paula. 1984. *When and Where I Enter: The Impact of Black Women on Race and Sex in America.* New York: William Morrow.

Gutman, Herbert. 1976. *The Black Family in Slavery and Freedom, 1750-1925.* New York: Pantheon.

Harley, Sharon. 1988. "For the Good of Family and Race: Gender, Work, and Domestic Roles in the Black Community 1880-1930." Pp. 159-72 in *Black Women in America,* edited by Michelene R. Malson, Elisabeth Mudimbe-Boyi, Jean F. O'Barr, and Mary Wyer. Chicago: University of Chicago Press.

Height, Dorothy. 1989. "Self-Help: A Black Tradition." Pp. 106-8 in *Annual Editions: Race and Ethnic Relations 91-92,* edited by John Kromkowski. Guilford, CT: Dushkin.

Hill, Daniel. 1946. "The Negro in the Early History of the West." *Iliff Review* 3(Fall).

Hine, Darlene Clark. 1990. "We Specialize in the Wholly Impossible: The Philanthropic Work of Black Women." Pp. 70-93 in *Lady Bountiful Revisited: Women, Philanthropy, and Power,* edited by Kathleen McCarthy. New Brunswick, NJ: Rutgers University Press.

Jewell, K. Sue. 1988. *Survival of the Black Family.* New York: Praeger.

Lerner, Gerda. 1973. *Black Women in White America.* New York: Random House.

Morton, Patricia. 1991 *Disfigured Images: The Historical Assault on Afro-American Women.* New York: Praeger.

Myrdal, Gunnar, with Sterner, R., & Rose, A. (1944). *An American Dilemma: The Negro Problem and Modern Democracy.* New York: Harper & Row.

Neilson, David Gordon. 1977. *Black Ethos.* Westport, CT: Greenwood.

Taka Art and Literary Club Constitution, Minute Books. Various years. (In possession of Mrs. Dorothy Reaves, Denver, CO)

# Epilogue

## MARY ROMERO

Although calls for racial, class, and ethnic diversity may at times appear to have taken on the religious tone of the invocation of a "holy trinity," a surprisingly large number of studies still continue to be funded and published that ignore the existence of women of color and issues of social class or culture. This volume has brought together works by researchers engaged in the study of race, class, and ethnicity as it relates to women's work. Undoubtedly, interest in this work is a response to ongoing concerns among feminists regarding the development of research agendas that are inclusive of *all* women's experiences. Unfortunately, Sojourner Truth's most commonly quoted question, "Aren't I a woman?" is still an appropriate response when research is mired in assumptions that all woman are White, ethnically homogeneous, and partaking in a universal gender experience.

When gender and race are separated or treated simply as variables, the unique historical and social experiences of Mexican American,

235

Vietnamese, Salvadoran, Panamanian, Dominican, and other women of color are submerged in abstract categories: woman or minority. A similarly misguided approach has been the continued use of a binary paradigm of race in the United States. Classifying groups as either White or Black further serves to erase the variety of ethnicities/races among women in the United States (e.g., West 1993; Hacker 1992). By asking our contributing authors to center their analyses on race, class, and ethnicity, we sought to shift the focus in this volume away from a general category of "women" and work to highlight new understandings of this experience.

The studies presented in the preceding pages are representative of recent feminist research on women and work in multicultural contexts. The chapters link gender and race in the actual historical and social spaces where they converge—in one work site or in different sites, at specific time periods or under different social, economic, and political conditions. Taken together, the work thereby emphasizes the study of social interaction between genders, along and across economic, political, and class boundaries. Rather than limiting the analyses to gender-specific comparisons that assume similarities among women, the investigations illuminate the range of distinction, difference, and diversity. Similarly, our intention, as editors, was to include important areas of the work experience in the lives of women of color in order to challenge continuing perceptions of women's unpaid labor. In this epilogue, I will describe certain intriguing issues that emerge from centering the analysis of work and women on race, class, and ethnicity. I want to guide the reader's attention to further directions for inquiry stimulated by this analysis, and to suggest additional research on women and work that is inclusive of race, class, and ethnicity.

## CONCEPTUALIZING WOMEN'S WORK EXPERIENCES

Recognizing that a woman cannot be a woman without race, ethnicity, and social class allows us to begin examining both the range of diversity and the kinds of commonalities that make up the gendered work experience. For example, as an important step toward bringing a more inclusive perspective to women's work, we may examine the experiences of working- and middle-class women as they encounter racial/ethnic power differentials in the workplace. Similarly, an inclusive approach requires researchers to move beyond the limited focus of class tensions between White working- and middle-class women to explore how race and ethnicity shape their social interactions. A few researchers have begun to dissect the meanings attached to the social construction of the categories "White women" and "Euro-American women" (Frankenberg 1993). Others continue to normalize Whiteness in the construction of female gender by treating these notions unproblematically, as static categories, thereby avoiding questions about the social construction of Whiteness. Comprehending the racial formation of Whiteness among the wide range of groups collapsed into "European Americans" is essential to an understanding of how gender has been racialized and class based.

Analyses of women's work that place questions about race, class, and ethnicity alongside gender have furthered the development of conceptual frameworks that capture the complexities of women's daily lives. Feminist research in the area of labor studies has expanded the conceptualization of work beyond the two-dimensional perspectives of public/ private and productive/reproductive dichotomies. That oversimplification obscures women's work to the point of invisibility. The separation of work and family no longer dominates research, academic training, or public policy. We now recognize that separate spheres do not exist and understand that there are significant and inescapable interrelationships between production and reproduction. Relationships between women's traditional family roles and roles prescribed in the labor market (i.e., the job descriptions and expectations embedded in employment considered "women's work") have seriously challenged the myth of "separate worlds" and "public" occupational structures (Pleck 1976; Hall 1982; Davidoff 1979). Yet the labor force retains evidence of "a man's world" through gendered institutions that emphasize the masculine work norm as the generic standard with which to measure women's work (Cockburn 1983, 1985; Game and Pringle 1983; Acker 1992).

Opening gender analysis to issues of race, class, and ethnicity draws attention to additional challenges to the myth of "separate worlds." Alongside masculine work norms are embedded a host of racial, ethnic, and class biases. For instance, in research on professionalism, institutional definitions of professionalism and professional roles do not exist in generic form; rather, norms and values have been fashioned to fit the White, middle-class male group dominating given professions (Bell 1990; Bell, Denton, and Nkomo 1993; Carter, Pearson, and Shavlik 1987-88; Foster 1991; James and Farmer 1993; Tokarczyk and Fay

1993; Romero 1997). Consequently, most professions are shaped and supported by a "commitment to the norms and values of the dominant (white middle class) society" (Gilkes 1982, p. 290). Research on the work experiences of African American, Jamaican, Puerto Rican, Japanese American, and Chicana women directs our attention to the ways in which gender norms are racialized and pose different obstacles for these women in gaining employment opportunities and promotions, and in meeting demands in the home and in the community.

Specific studies of the work experiences of women who are not identified as White or Euro-American offer critical insights into the complexities of race and ethnicity. Furthermore, comparisons of the interethnic experiences of immigrant and domestic women of color help identify social factors that explain the manifold ways that women experience race, ethnicity, and social class. Thus Joyce Chinen's case study of the manufacture of "alohawear" in Hawaii, presented in Chapter 3 of this volume, draws attention to the importance of distinguishing between the history of colonialism that shaped the economic roles of Native Hawaiian women and the different experiences of domination and subjugation felt by workers who are immigrant women and second-generation women of color. Although many groups have immigrated to the United States, the social meaning attached to immigration status continues to be determined by the political and economic factors that were present in specific historical periods. Stephen Steinberg's critique of sociology's mainstream paradigms of ethnic relations, presented in his book *The Ethnic Myth,* is still applicable to studies that implicitly or explicitly hold White ethnics as the comparative group and thus lose important distinctions among persons of color. Steinberg (1989) identifies two major ways in which the myth of ethnic success is constructed:

In the first place, the problem is stated falsely when it is assumed that all immigrant groups started out on the bottom. In point of fact, ethnic groups in the United States come out of very different historical and material circumstances, and therefore different outcomes may only reflect different beginnings. Secondly, depending on the time of their arrival and the patterns of settlement, immigrant groups encountered different opportunities, as well as different external obstacles of their economic advancement. The experiences of the immigrant generation, furthermore, tended to establish a foundation that placed next generations at greater or lesser advantage. (p. 83)

Consequently, the "gains" made by domestic women of color who were tracked into state supported vocational-technical education at community colleges and state universities to pursue lower-level managerial and semiprofessional positions do not reflect gender or ethnic "progress" so much as change in occupational structure and economy.

## EXPANDING NOTIONS OF WORK: FAMILY AND COMMUNITY

Keeping race, class, and ethnicity at the center of a gendered analysis of women's work opens new possibilities for our understanding of relationships between productive and reproductive labor. Women's employment in the underground economy suggests the limitations posed by the "separate sphere" approach to the sociology of work. Discussions of employment opportunities and networks frequently have assumed worker characteristics outside of family and community. However, limited access to professional (and other middle-class) networks makes critical the family and community resources not usually recognized. Thus, in her study of Japanese American women employed as private household workers, Evelyn Nakano Glenn (1986) identifies the functions of community networks in locating employment opportunities in domestic service. Glenn shows how workers' communities can operate as important employment resources, particularly in cases where workers are relegated to jobs available only in the underground economy. Family and community members share information about potential employers and assist in making contacts for women seeking paid employment. In addition, as Glenn observes, at the same time community networks operate as an important means to employment, the networks existing in poor and working-class communities and families remain quite limited and thus also function to confine women to traditional types of employment.

Pierrette Hondagneu-Sotelo's study of Latinas employed in domestic service, presented in Chapter 5 of this volume, expands our understanding of the means an ethnic community may use to structure opportunities within specific political conditions. Hondagneu-Sotelo shows how resources in the community are not limited to potential job leads; they also disseminate information and help individuals to establish apprenticeships. Work arrangements between older immigrants and recent arrivals constitute structures, created within the community, that regulate the entry of workers into domestic service and address employment status shaped by current immigration legislation (Hondagneu-Sotelo 1994a, 1994b; Repack 1995). Here, regulation functions to establish pay, working standards, and practices for coping with questions of citizenship when one is employed in the underground economy. In Chapter 2 of this volume, Sharon Harley also notes numerous examples of research on Black women that illustrate the significance of such "neighborhood networks" in organizing workers and establishing expectations for their roles during strikes. In these extended examples we see how, in addition to the family, communities influence the entry of workers into particular sectors of the economy, function as a source of resistance, and constrain individual choices.

Previous studies of women's unpaid work have typically examined women's work in the home. However, recent research on race, class, and ethnicity suggests different understandings of how paid and unpaid labor outside the household shapes our lives, communities, and the larger society. Here, too, a class-based analysis of race and ethnicity reveals the ways that White middle-class working women's experiences have become incorporated as the norm in the conceptualization of the relationship between work and family, particularly in assumptions about the paid and unpaid nature of household labor (Glenn 1992; Romero 1992). Additionally, discussions of unpaid labor that have led to the development of such concepts as the "double day" and the "second shift" serve to limit our understanding of community work. The very concepts whereby unpaid labor became visible have been largely shaped around the circumstances of middle-class women's forms of reproductive labor: thus community work fell into the category of "voluntarism." Activism became the term when unpaid community labor involved poor and working-class women. A class analysis of this work not only exposes the bias of our analytic categories, which distinguish one as political activism and the other as social welfare work, but also highlights how women are positioned differently in community work.

Bringing racial/ethnic, immigrant, and working-class women's community work into the discussion of unpaid labor highlights the class-based inequalities that women experience in fulfilling their prescribed roles as mothers. Mary Pardo (see Chapter 9 of this volume) and Lynda Dickson (see Chapter 10) contribute to a new area in the field of "women and work" that acknowledges the unpaid labor involved in community maintenance and development. Madres del Este de Los Angeles, Santa Isabel, and the members of turn-of-the-century Black women's clubs engaged in unpaid labor to compensate for inadequate public services in their communities. Because poor and working-class women do not have the same political and economic means that middle-class women do, their reproductive labor frequently extends outside the boundaries of the nuclear family into the larger community. In order to provide for their children's safety, education, and basic food and shelter needs, these women engage in what Lynda Dickson terms a "third shift." When unpaid community labor is exchanged directly for goods and services that higher-class families are able to pay for, such as school tuition, the disguise of "volunteer" work is stripped away, and we come to understand the mandatory nature of unpaid community labor in poor and low-income neighborhoods. The limited purchasing power of poor and working-class women emphasizes important differences among working women. Investigation of the actual skills poor and working-class women must utilize to complete their unpaid labor emphasizes the necessity of a class- and race-informed framework for understanding the relationship between the worker and the value attributed to her labor.

Recognizing the unpaid work in family and community pushes our analysis into areas of women's resistance to exploitation, inequality, and perceived injustice. Several researchers have shown how community ties among women workers can play an important role in union organizing (Lamphere 1987; Sacks 1988; Zavella 1987; Westwood 1984). Poor, working-class, immigrant, and racial/ethnic minority women have labored to exert political influence and engaged in forms of resistance to social injustice, even while they have been characterized by union organizers as difficult groups to unionize. Characteristics attributed to their gender roles, including lack of commitment to work roles outside the home and the additional demands of family life on their time, have frequently been cited as reasons for women's low participation in unions. However, Louise Lamphere and Patricia Zavella found these characteristics to be less significant in predicting the level of workers' resistance than the managerial structure and labor process of the work setting (see Chapter 4, this volume). Some attribute the difficulty in organizing to their class location, citing their position on the lowest rung of the occupational ladder, participation in the underground economy, and immigration and citizenship status. On the contrary, however, historical research has ample documentation of labor struggles and active resistance engaged in by Black women workers (see Harley, Chapter 2, this volume). Recent research similarly challenges the belief that undocumented workers fear apprehension and deportation, and thus accept "low wages, abusive treatment by supervisors, and otherwise poor working conditions, that citizen workers in the same industries refuse to tolerate" (Delgado 1993, pp. 9-10). In her study of Los Angeles garment workers, Maria Soldatenko (1991) debunks common myths about Latinas' lack of union participation being a result of their cultural traits, including lack of English skills and knowledge of U.S. social institutions, absence of union experience in their countries of origin, and the tradition of machismo. Soldatenko demonstrates that White male union leaders have failed to organize this population because they have ignored the specific needs associated with these women's gendered immigrant status.

## DIRECTIONS FOR CONTINUED RESEARCH

Recent attacks on affirmative action and attempts to roll back civil rights legislation have popularized notions that gender, racial, and ethnic discrimination is a thing of the past, or even that discrimination is "caused" or exacerbated by attempts to remedy it. These claims are often supported by data suggesting that working conditions and opportunities have improved for women workers. However, these myths ignore old and new areas of discrimination as well as the ways that women of color experience both gender and ethnic discrimination. We still lack a theory that begins by placing the "other" at the center of the analysis. Labor theory has fallen short of explaining how racism shapes the work experiences of people of color and Whites in relation to class and gender: On the one hand, micro-level theories, relying heavily on sociopsychological approaches to race relations, fail to make the connection to the global economy and state policies. On the other hand, macro-level theories are limited by their use of an "add-on" approach to the incorporation of racial/ethnic minorities and immigrants in their analyses. The consequence of simply adding gender or race to existing theories is that once again White women and men of color are constituted as analytic categories that do not explain the labor market experiences of women of color. A prime example is the classification of small, labor-intensive industries as peripheral to the economy, a practice that relegates the garment industry (an important employer of Latina and Asian immigrant women) to the periphery. Research is necessary to connect and modify micro and macro approaches by demonstrating the relationship between the ideologies of racism and sexism and the economy. In the wake of recent "scandals" such as the one brought to light at Texaco (in which tape recordings of managers revealed how they sought to shred files and subvert civil rights investigations, even while using a peculiar language of "diversity" taught by professional social psychologists) and the hundreds of allegations of sexual harassment and rape emerging out of the U.S. Army, we need an unflinching sociology to shine a bright beam on modern managerial theories and strategies, their effects on workers of color, and their relationship to White workers. Only thus can we approach the connection of political economy with the everyday culture of the workplace as shaped by management. In the following paragraphs, I identify some research inquiries that direct our attention to ethnic discrimination and citizenship issues that are frequently ignored in discussions of work and women. I conclude with a call for a gender perspective that includes both men and women, an approach that moves us closer to understanding the racial, ethnic, and class experiences of working women.

Recent research on everyday racism needs to be incorporated into the conceptualization of women and work if we are to further our understanding of ethnic discrimination and the various forms it takes in the work women do (Essed 1991; Das Gupta 1996). Ethnic employees are subject to harassment in the form of racial slurs, stereotyping, and shunning by supervisors and fellow employees. They are frequently evaluated more harshly by superiors, given more assignments, and suffer patterns of intimidation. Issues arising from a worker's cultural background may also influence her opportunities in the labor market. For instance, several studies on the nursing profession direct our attention to everyday racism in the workplace, including nurse-patient relationships (Diamond 1992; Das Gupta 1996; Hine 1989). Nurses of color are subject to harassment via allegations of abuse and incompetence from patients who want to be treated only by White nurses. Nurses of color are particularly vulnerable to scapegoating and belittling, and they are targeted for differential treatment in workplaces where they are marginalized and isolated from other Black nurses. Tania Das Gupta's (1996) research on Black nurses in Ontario, Canada, demonstrates how management practices based on unconscious stereotypes serve to divide workers and reduce worker solidarity. The discretionary application of workplace guidelines and rules also functions as a source of everyday racism. Das Gupta describes how interracial relationships between nurses and nursing management were affected by the restructuring and downsizing occurring in a particular health care system. In the professions, a high degree of subjectivity and discretion in management behavior creates a climate in which it is difficult or impossible to create anti-harassment policies and complaint procedures that address racism.

In recent years, regulations surrounding language use in the workplace have become a popular mode of ethnic discrimination. Issues surrounding language rights and language skills have received media attention in the area of education, but these issues are equally important in other workplaces, where forms of discrimination include harassment, denial of promotions, and firing. English-only legislation has resulted in bilingual employees' being told that they cannot speak any language other than English anywhere on the work site; workers have been reprimanded for speaking Spanish at any time (Rodriquez 1994). Curiously, such linguistic harassment is practiced simultaneous with the need to force bilingual employees to use their language skills on the job. Despite the English-only movement, both business and service sectors are faced with the fact that bilingual employees are most competent to serve bilingual or non-English-speaking clientele. Bilingual employees are frequently pulled away from their regular jobs to translate conversations between monolingual English-speaking employees and non-English-speaking clients/customers. Yet the English-speaking employees' need for assistance does not lead to questions about their ability to do their jobs, and the bilingual abilities of racial/ethnic minority women are rarely considered criteria for higher salary or promotion. Generally, the need for bilingual skills is ignored as a job criterion. The deficiencies of monolingual employees are simply covered up by the availability of bilingual employees to translate. In such cases, bilingual employees are not reprimanded for speaking Spanish, but neither are they compensated for their bilingual skills. Employers have refused to recognize language as a marketable skill and have refused to provide wage differentials to compensate for the skill. Instead, bilingual employees find themselves in a double bind: They must take on the additional work of translators, yet they are evaluated poorly because they cannot accomplish as much of their regular work as expected because they are constantly called away to serve as translators. Several lawsuits are currently pending that hinge on the adverse affects of these exploitative practices on the careers of bilingual employees. Other lawsuits are challenging English-only regulations, arguing that such harassment is discrimination based on national origin.

Researchers have gradually begun to recognize the issue of citizenship among working women, particularly in terms of the privileges the status holds and its impact on gender, race, culture, and class. As Pierrette Hondagneu-Sotelo notes in Chapter 5 of this volume, a worker's citizenship status may be altered during her life, resulting in changes in her opportunities in the labor market. Citizenship status carries significant privileges in the labor force, and this status may take precedence over an individual's education, previous employment record, and marketable skills. In the past, researchers as well as politicians have glossed over nationality differences existing within communities of color. For instance, within the Black community, distinctions between African Americans and Caribbean immigrants have often been ignored by researchers, yet these differences have real consequences in education and the labor market. Feminist scholars have similarly directed attention to important gender concerns shaping the immigration experience (Hondagneu-Sotelo 1994a; Repack 1995; Moro-Torn 1995). For instance, Grace Chang's (1994) research on the implications of the 1986 Immigration Reform and Control Act for undocumented Latinas outlines how women in this group have become the new "employable mothers" and are denied access to the primary labor force.

I want to conclude my discussion of directions for future research in the field of women and work by advocating for new conceptual frameworks in the study of working women to move toward an analysis of gender and away from a focus on "women." Previously, exclusive attention to the experiences of women workers, particularly in comparisons of working-class and middle-class women as well as White women and women of color, has had the unintended consequence of establishing a one-gender history, analysis, and perspective. Instead of eliminating the concept of "separate spheres," researchers have re-created a separation of spheres inhabited by family-identified women and invisible men. This feminist practice obscures gender inequalities and suggests that role conflict is an exclusively feminine dilemma, whereas men's work and family relations remain unproblematic (Kobayashi 1994). The inclusion of both genders is essential to our understanding of the relationships among work, family, and community life. Studies of married working mothers remain incomplete without reference to the thoughts and actions of working-class men. Comparisons between married White women and women of other racial/ethnic groups is incomplete without an understanding of the dual-wage structure and differentially high rates of unemployment that men of color face in the local economy. For instance, in their study of married Cuban women's labor force participation, Maria Patricia Fernandez-Kelly and Anna

Garcia (1992) argue that "for poor men and women the issue is not so much the presence of the sexual division of labor or the persistence of patriarchal ideologies but the difficulties of upholding either" (p. 148). Maxine Baca Zinn (1987) makes the same point in her discussion of minority families:

> Conditions associated with female-headed families among racial-ethnics are different and should be interpreted differently. Because white families headed by women have much higher average incomes than minority families in the same situation, we must not confuse as overall improvement what is in fact an improvement for women in certain social categories, while other women are left at the bottom in even worse conditions. (p. 167)

Ignoring the gender of men obscures White male privilege and the privilege attributed to heterosexuality, both of which shape community resources. Furthermore, comparisons between White women and women of color suggest that racial equality is achieved only when gender differences are identified. Research that does not recognize that each worker has a gender and a race cannot advance our understanding of the work experiences of women of color, nor can it help us begin to understand how work is gendered, ethnicized, racialized, and class based.

## REFERENCES

Acker, Joan. 1992 "Gendered Institution." *Contemporary Sociology* 21:565-95.

Baca Zinn, Maxine. 1987. "Structural Transformations and Minority Families." In *Women, Households, and the Economy,* edited by Lourdes Beneria and Catharine Stimpson. New Brunswick NJ: Rutgers University Press.

Bell, Eleanor. 1990. "The Bicultural Life Experience of Career-Oriented Black Women." *Journal of Organizational Behavior* 11:459-77.

Bell, Ella Louise, Toni C. Denton, and Stella M. Nkomo. 1993. "Women of Color in Management: Toward an Inclusive Analysis." Pp. 105-30 in *Women in Management: Trends, Issues and Challenges in Managerial Diversity,* edited by Ellen A. Fagenson. Newbury Park, CA: Sage.

Carter, Deborah, Carol Pearson, and Donna Shavlik. 1987-88. "Double Jeopardy: Women of Color in Higher Education." *Educational Record* 68-69(Fall-Winter):98-103.

Chang, Grace. 1994. "Undocumented Latinas: The New 'Employable Mothers.' " Pp. 259-86 in *Mothering: Ideology, Experience, and Agency,* edited by Evelyn Nakano Glenn, Grace Chang, and Linda Rennie Forcey. New York: Routledge.

Cockburn, Cynthia. 1983. *Brothers: Male Dominance and Technological Change.* London: Pluto.

————. 1985. *Machinery of Dominance*. London: Pluto.

Das Gupta, Tania. 1996. *Racism and Paid Work*. Toronto: Garamond.

Davidoff, Leanore. 1979. "The Separation of Work and Home? Landladies and Lodgers in Nineteenth- and Twentieth-Century England." Pp. 64-97 in *Fit Work for Women*, edited by Sandra Burman. London: Croom Helm.

Delgado, Hector L. 1993. *New Immigrants, Old Unions Organizing Undocumented Workers in Los Angeles*. Philadelphia: Temple University Press.

Diamond, Timothy. 1992. *Making Gray Gold: Narratives of Nursing Home Care*. Chicago: University of Chicago Press.

Essed, Philomena. 1991. *Understanding Everyday Racism: An Interdisciplinary Theory*. Newbury Park, CA: Sage.

Fernandez-Kelly, Maria Patricia and Anna M. Garcia. 1992. "Power Surrendered, Power Restored: The Politics of Work and Family among Hispanic Garment Workers in California and Florida." Pp. 130-49 in *Women, Politics, and Change*, edited by Louise A. Tilly and Patricia Gurin. New York: Russell Sage Foundation.

Foster, M. 1991. "Constancy, Connectedness, and Constraints in the Lives of African American Teachers." *NWSA Journal* 3:233-61.

Frankenberg, Ruth. 1993. *White Women, Race Matters: The Social Construction of Whiteness*. Minneapolis: University of Minnesota Press.

Game, Ann and Rosemary Pringle. 1983. *Gender at Work*. London: Allen & Unwin.

Gilkes, Cheryl Townsend. 1982. "Successful Rebellious Professions: The Black Woman's Professional Identity and Community Commitment." *Psychology of Woman Quarterly* 6:289-311.

Glenn, Evelyn Nakano. 1986. *Issei, Nisei, War Bride: Three Generations of Japanese American Women in Domestic Service*. Philadelphia: Temple University Press.

————. 1992. "From Servitude to Service Work: Historical Continuities in the Racial Division of Paid Reproductive Labor." *Signs: Journal of Women in Culture and Society* 18:1-43.

Hacker, Andrew. 1992. *Two Nations: Black and White, Separate, Hostile, Unequal* New York: Ballantine.

Hall, Catherine. 1982. "The Butcher, the Baker, the Candlestick Maker: The Shop and the Family in the Industrial Revolution." Pp. 2-16 in *The Changing Experience of Women*, edited by Elizabeth Whitelegg et al. Oxford: Martin Robertson.

Hine, Darlene Clark. 1989. *Black Women in White: Racial Conflict and Cooperation in the Nursing Profession, 1890-1950*. Bloomington: Indiana University Press.

Hondagneu-Sotelo, Pierrette. 1994a. *Gendered Transitions: Mexican Experiences of Immigration*. Berkeley: University of California Press.

————. 1994b. "Regulating the Unregulated? Domestic Workers' Social Networks." *Social Problems* 41(1):50-64.

James, Joy and Ruth Farmer, eds. 1993. *Spirit, Space and Survival: African American Women in (White) Academe*. New York: Routledge.

Kobayashi, Audrey, ed. 1994. *Women, Work, and Place*. Montreal/Kingston: McGill/Queen's University Press.

Lamphere, Louise. 1987. *From Working Daughters to Working Mothers: Immigrant Women in a New England Industrial Community*. Ithaca, NY: Cornell University Press.

Moro-Torn, Maura. 1995. "Gender, Class, Family, and Migration: Puerto Rican Women in Chicago." *Gender & Society* 9:712-26.

Pleck, Elizabeth. 1976. "Two Worlds in One: Work and Family." *Journal of Social History* 10(2):178-95.

Repack, Terry A. 1995. *Waiting on Washington: Central American Workers in the Nation's Capital.* Philadelphia: Temple University Press.

Rodriquez, Rey M. 1994. "The Misplaced Application of English-Only Rules in the Workplace." *Chicano-Latino Law Review* 14:67-80.

Romero, Mary. 1992. *Maid in the U.S.A.* New York: Routledge.

———. 1997. "Class-Based, Gendered and Racialized Institutions of Higher Education: Everyday Life of Academia from the View of Chicana Faculty." *Race, Gender & Class: Latino American Voices* 4(2): 151-173.

Rothblum, D. Esther. 1988. "Leaving the Ivory Tower: Factors Contributing to Women's Voluntary Resignation from Academia." *Frontiers* 10(2):14-17.

Sacks, Karen Brodkin. 1988. *Caring by the Hour: Women, Work, and Organizing at Duke Medical Center.* Urbana: University of Illinois Press.

Soldatenko, Maria Angelina. 1991. "Organizing Latina Garment Workers in Los Angeles." *Aztlan: Journal of Chicano Studies Research* 20:73-96.

Steinberg, Stephen. 1989. *The Ethnic Myth: Race, Ethnicity, and Class in America.* Boston: Beacon.

Tokarczyk, M. M. and E. A. Fay. 1993. *Working-Class Women in the Academy: Laborers in the Knowledge Factory.* Amherst: University of Massachusetts Press.

West, Cornel. 1993. *Race Matters.* Boston: Beacon.

Westwood, Sally. 1984. *All Day, Every Day: Factory and Family in the Making of Women's Lives.* Urbana: University of Illinois Press.

Zavella, Patricia. 1987. *Women's Work and Chicano Families: Cannery Workers of the Santa Clara Valley.* Ithaca, NY: Cornell University Press.

# Author Index

Acker, J., 237
Acuña, R., 208
Addams, J., 200
Amott, T. L., 59
Anzaldúa, G., 132

Baca Zinn, M., 47, 154, 246
Bach, R. L., 106
Baird, Z., 122
Bakan, A. B., 104
Barnett, B. M., 201
Barnett, E. B., 45
Beechert, E. D., 62
Bell, E. L., 156, 157, 237
Benson, S. P., 80-81
Bill, T., 58
Billingsley, A., 39
Blascoer, F., 64
Blood, R. O., 177, 178
Bokemeier, J., 157
Bonacich, E., 59, 68
Bookman, A., 133

Braverman, H., 159
Brill, H., 62, 106
Broughton, C., 40
Brown, E. B., 34, 44, 47, 132
Brown, J. C., 46
Burawoy, M., 81
Burroughs, N. H., 41-42, 45

Carroll-Seguin, R., 58, 62, 63
Carter, D., 237
Carter, S. L., 156
Cayton, H. R., 224
Centers, R., 177
Chang, G., 245
Chapkis, W., 59
Chautevert, M., 44
Cheng, L., 59, 68
Chinchilla, N., 59, 68
Chinen, J. N., 54-55, 57-73, 238
Choe, J. S., 180
Clark-Lewis, E., 44, 47-48, 109
Cockburn, C., 237

Colen, S., 102, 111
Collins, P. H., 3, 58, 59, 103, 132, 157, 169
Costello, C. B., 82
Coyle, L., 82
Crosby, F. J., 171, 172

Dabrowski, I., 212
Daniels, A. K., 199
Das Gupta, T., 243-244
Davidoff, L., 237
Davidson, S., 59
Davis, A., 132
Davis, D. W., 35
Davis, G., 156
Daws, G., 62
De Ley, M. C., 102
Delgado, H. L., 242
Denton, T. C., 156, 157, 237
Deukmejian, G., 206
Diamond, T., 243
Dickson, L., 194-195, 216-233, 240, 241
Dill, B. T., 47, 102, 132, 154
Dorsett, L., 218, 224
Dorton (Kameeleihiwa), L., 62
Drake, St. C., 224
Du Bois, W. E. B., 217
Duron, C., 46-47

Edwards, R., 81
Ehrenreich, B., 159
Ehrenreich, J., 159
Enloe, C., 59, 199
Essed, P., 243

Fantasia, R., 132
Farmer, R., 237
Fay, E. A., 237
Feagin, J. R., 156
Fernandez-Kelly, M. P., 102, 245-246
Ferree, M. M., 177
Fincher, R., 201
Foner, N., 177

Foster, M., 237
Foucault, M., 81
Frankenberg, R., 132, 157, 166, 169, 237
Franklin, V. P., 31
Fuchs, L., 62
Fulbright, K., 156
Fundaburk, E. L., 60, 63

Game, A., 237
Garcia, A. M., 102, 245-246
Garland, A. W., 212
Geschwender, J. A., 58, 62, 63
Giddings, P., 41, 43, 222, 224
Gilkes, C. T., 201, 238
Gittell, M., 200
Glass, J., 38
Glenn, E. N., 30, 34, 37, 40, 58, 82, 102, 103, 109, 111, 133, 182, 239, 240
Grebler, L., 203
Grella, C., 132, 148
Grenier, G. J., 80
Grossman Brezin, E. L., 106
Guerin-Gonzales, C., 30
Gutek, B., 157
Gutiérrez, J., 208, 209
Gutman, H., 222
Guzman, R. C., 203
Gwaltney, J. L., 31

Hacker, A., 236
Hall, C., 237
Hamer, F. L., 41, 43
Hamilton, N., 59, 68
Hansen, K., 132
Harley, S., 2-4, 28-49, 201, 219, 221, 240, 241
Height, D., 232
Hershatter, G., 82
Higginbotham, E., 31, 33, 40, 41, 42, 44, 48, 128, 153-173
Hill, D., 218
Hine, D. C., 222, 226, 243
Hochschild, J. L., 157
Hodson, R., 70

Hondagneu-Sotelo, P., 54, 55-56,
    101-124, 239-240, 245
Honig, E., 82
hooks, b., 132
Howard, R., 80
Hull, G., 132
Hunter, T. W., 31, 42, 44, 45, 47
Hurh, W. M., 177, 184
Hurston, Z. N., 33

Jackson, G. B., 35
James, J., 237
Janiewski, D. E., 36-37, 44, 48
Jensen, J. M., 59
Jones, B. W., 201
Jones, J., 32, 34, 43, 44, 47

Kanter, R. M., 70
Kaplan, E. B., 109
Katzman, D. M., 109, 110
Kelley, R. D. G., 31, 44, 47, 48
Kent, N. J., 62
Kessler-Harris, A., 43, 59
Kim, K. C., 177, 184
King, D. K., 103
Kobayashi, A., 245
Kondo, D. K., 81
Kossoudji, S. A., 111
Kuykendall, R., 62

Ladd-Taylor, M., 200
Lamanna, M., 177
Lamphere, L., 54, 55, 59, 76-98, 133, 241
Lawler, E., 79
Lee, P., 46
Lerner, G., 217
Leung, M., 157, 159
Liu, W. T., 177
Logan, J., 201
Lopez-Garza, M., 203
Louie, M. C., 59

Manicas, P., 62

Mann, S. A., 32-33, 35
Marks, C. C., 30, 40, 42
Mathes, S., 221
Matthaei, J. A., 59
Matthews, V. E., 44-45
McCarthy, K., 200
McDonald, G. W., 178
McGuire, G. M., 154, 155, 163
McNamara, P. H., 204
McQuillen, J., 201
Melosh, B., 81
Milkman, R., 82, 133
Miller, J., 70
Miller, K., 38
Mills, C. W., 64
Min, P. G., 129, 176-190
Mohanty, C. T., 103, 104, 132
Moore, J. W., 203
Moretta, J., 209
Morgen, S., 127-128, 131-151
Moro-Torn, M., 245
Morrison, A. M., 155, 157
Morton, P., 222
Moynihan, D. P., 39
Murata, A., 177
Myrdal, G., 224

Naples, N., 201
Neilson, D. G., 219, 220
Nelson, J., 156
Nieva, V., 79
Nkomo, S. M., 157, 237
Nordyke, E. C., 62
Northcraft, G. B., 157

Omi, M., 58, 59, 157, 166
Ong, P., 59, 68
Ouichi, W. G., 80

Palmer, P., 109
Pardo, M., 194-195, 197-213, 240
Parker, M., 80
Pearson, C., 237
Perez, L., 177

Perkins, D. N. T., 79
Pessar, P., 102
Peters, T. J., 80
Phelan, J., 164
Philipson, I., 132
Pleck, E., 237
Pressar, P. R., 177
Pringle, R., 237

Ranney, S. I., 111
Rapp, R., 132
Raven, B. H., 177
Reagon, B. J., 34, 40
Reed, C., 46
Remy, D., 82
Repack, T. A., 240, 245
Reskin, B. F., 154, 155, 163
Roberts, S., 156
Robles, B., 1-2, 5-26
Robles, E., 199, 204-205, 213
Rodman, H., 177
Rodriguez, A., 177
Rodriguez, R. M., 244
Rollins, J., 82, 102, 109, 111, 117, 133
Romero, M., 42, 58, 82, 102, 117, 120,
    198, 235-246
Roos, P. A., 155, 163
Rosen, E. I., 79
Ruiz, V. L., 82, 102, 203
Rushing, A. B., 44

Sacks, K. B., 82, 133, 199, 211, 241
Salzinger, L., 102, 117
Schackel, S., 200
Schmitt, R., 62
Scollay, S., 157
Scott, J. C., 81
Scott, P. B., 132
Shapiro-Perl, N., 81, 82
Shavlik, D., 237
Shimatsu, Y., 46
Shtob, T., 200
Sikes, M. P., 156
Simon, R. J., 102

Sirola, P. S., 102
Slaughter, J., 80
Sluzuki, L. E., 177
Smith, B., 132
Smith, D., 211
Sokoloff, N., 154, 155
Soldatenko, M. A., 102, 211, 242
Solomon, E., 132
Solorzano-Torres, R., 102
Stannard, D. E., 62
Stasiulis, D. K., 104
Steady, F. C., 31
Steedman, C., 132
Steinberg, S., 238
Steinitz, V., 132
Stier, H., 177

Takaki, R., 129
Terborg-Penn, R., 34, 44
Thomas, R. J., 104
Tiano, S., 59
Tickamyer, A., 157
Tienda, M., 38
Tokarczyk, M. M., 237
Trask, H.-K., 62, 63
Trevizo, D., 102

Vanneman, R., 132, 159, 163
Velasquez, D. R., 212
Villalobos, F., 209
Villaseñor, R., 205-206
Von Glinow, M. A., 155, 157

Watson, G., 156
Weber, L., 128, 153-173
Weber Cannon, L., 132, 154, 157, 159,
    163
Webster, M. W., 45
West, C., 236
Westwood, S., 241
White, D. G., 31, 32, 39, 44
Williams, N., 203
Williams, P., 132, 156

Winant, H., 58, 59, 157, 166
Wolfe, D. M., 177, 178
Wood, T., 157
Woody, B., 154, 155
Wrigley, J., 110

Young, G. E., 109

Zavella, P., 43, 54, 55, 76-98, 133, 211, 241

# Subject Index

Affirmative action, 157
African American(s):
  class boundaries and, 231-232
  employment opportunities and, 219
  fertility rates, 10
  gender roles and, 31, 32, 33, 34-35,
    36, 39
  in Hawaii, 61
  labor statistics, 17
  male family roles, 31, 32, 33
  marital status, 9
  matrifocal families, 31
  negative image of, 222
  percent of population, 6, 7
  population growth, 9
  poverty rates, 21
  values, 31, 33
African American females:
  age distribution, 9, 25
  educational attainment, 15, 17, 25
  income statistics, 19
  labor statistics, 17, 24
  single women, 11, 230

  *See also* African American women;
    African American working women
African American feminist thought, 59
African American men:
  family roles, 31, 32, 33
  pay for, 156
African American single mothers, 11
African American single working
  women, 37-39, 230
African American women:
  attempts to dominate sexuality of, 36
  clubs, 195, 201, 216-233
  community work by, 195, 201,
    216-233
  consciousness and, 59
  employment histories, 2-3
  familial roles, 31, 33
  household work, 34, 35-37
  labor force participation, 3, 17, 24, 38
  matriarch stereotype, 39
  negative image of, 222
  oppression of, 48-49
  politics of labor history, 28-49

resistance legacy, 3
African American working women:
collective resistance, 47
community activities, 217
domestic work, 53
factory work, 53
managerial careers, 128, 153-173
pay, 19, 156
perceptions of work preferences for,
168-169
professionals, 128, 153-173
public sector jobs, 232
resistance and, 40, 42-48
sexual harassment and exploitation of,
36
single, 37-39, 230
unemployment and, 42
work/family nexus, 30-41
work/identity consciousness, 3, 41-48
working class, 28-29
African cultural tradition, 39-40
Age distribution, census data on, 8-9, 25
Albuquerque, New Mexico, apparel and
electronics firms in, 55, 76-98
Alohawear industry, in Hawaii, 54-55,
57-73
Asia:
export-processing zones in, 59
immigrants from, 105
Asian American(s):
fertility rates, 10, 11
labor statistics, 17
marital status, 9
percent of population, 6, 7
population growth, 9
poverty rates, 21
Asian American females:
educational attainment, 15, 24
fertility rates, 9, 24-25
garment production in Hawaii by,
54-55, 57-73
income statistics, 19, 24
labor statistics, 24
median age, 9
organizing among, 46
Asian Pacific American women, garment
production in Hawaii by, 54-55,
57-73

Assembly work, Latina immigrant
women and, 102
Autonomy, demands for, 43

Benefits, job:
Hawaiian garment workers, 68
undocumented immigrants and, 107

California, domestic work by Latina
immigrants in, 101-124
Canneries, union recognition in, 82
Capitalism, 45
labor needs of, 54
patriarchal domination and, 32
Caribbean immigrants, 105, 107, 245
Carnation Art, Literary and Charity Club,
217, 221, 226, 228, 230
Catholic Church, Mexican American
community and, 203, 204-205, 210
Census data, 1-2, 5-26
Central and South Americans, 8
Child labor laws, 37
Children's welfare, social networks
working for, 210, 222-223, 226-227
Churches:
community work for, 194, 201
African American women's
involvement with, 40, 44
labor resistance and, 47
Mexican American community and,
203, 204-205, 210
Citizenship status, labor markets and, 55,
101-124, 245
Class:
African American communities and,
231-232
Black women's clubs and, 219,
220-222
community work and, 193, 200-201,
219, 220-222
employment options and, 2
ethnicity and, 201
immigrant legal status and, 103
power and, 128
vocabulary of, 147
voluntarism and, 193, 198

women's health center and, 127-128,
    131-151
Class consciousness, 69, 132, 135, 137
Class experience and conflict, in feminist
    workplace, 131-151
Class identity, 29, 42-48, 132, 147-148
Clothing manufacturing, in Hawaii,
    54-55, 57-73
Coalitions:
    community activism, 207
    multiracial, 154, 157, 172, 173
    working-class and middle-class
        women, 127-128, 131-151
Collective networking, 42-43
Collective resistance, 82
    African American women, 47
    electronics workers, 77, 89
Colonialization, in Hawaii, 54-55, 58, 62
Color-blind ideology, 157, 166-167, 172
Communal ethos, African American, 31,
    33, 34, 40, 47
Community, as social construction, 220
Community activism, 103, 200, 207-208,
    240
Community conflicts, women's unpaid
    work and, 206-207
Community ties:
    undocumented Mexican immigrant
        women, 56, 101, 102, 103
    union organizing and, 241
Community work, 193-195, 240-241
    African American women, 40, 195,
        201, 216-233
    Latina women, 194, 197-213
    Mexican American working-class
        women, 197-213
    middle-class women, 193, 200, 210
    upper-class women, 193, 200, 210
    working-class women, 195, 197-213,
        241
Competition:
    among workers, 86, 87, 95
    foreign, 79
Confucianism, 180
Consciousness:
    African American women, 41-48, 59
    class, 69, 132, 135, 137
    color, 167-169

Hawaiian garment industry, 69
    mixed, 84
    working-class, 29, 42-48
Contracting firms, on U.S.-Mexico
    border, 59
Control, management policies as systems
    of, 80, 81, 83
Cooperation, among Black women's
    clubs, 228-230
Coworkers, relations with, 70
Criminalization of employment,
    citizenship status and, 105, 106,
    107, 118, 119
Cuban American(s), 8
Cuban American females:
    age distribution, 25
    educational attainment, 24
    income statistics, 24
Cuban women, labor force participation
    of, 245-246
Culture:
    African, 39-40
    demographic changes and, 6
    employment opportunities and, 243
    women's health collective, 137
    work, 81, 83, 87, 96


Day work arrangements, domestic
    workers and, 47, 109-110, 117,
    118-122
Demographic changes, projected, 6, 8-9
Demographic data, 1-2, 5-26
Denver, Colorado, Black women's clubs
    in, 195, 216-233
Denver Federation of Colored Women,
    229
Dependence, of undocumented domestic
    workers, 111-112
Discrimination, 243
    language use and, 244
    professional-managerial women's
        perceptions of, 153-173
Divorce rate, 9-10
Domestic workers:
    African American women, 53
    day work arrangements, 47, 109-110,
        117, 118-122

employment opportunities, 239
job work arrangements, 103, 109-110,
    117-122, 123
Latina immigrant, 54, 55-56, 101-124,
    239
leisure time and, 48
live-in, 103, 109, 110-117, 123
Mexican American women, 54
Mexican undocumented immigrant
    women, 55-56, 101-124
organizing, 44-45
professionalizing, 41
sexual harassment of, 48
undocumented Mexican immigrant
    women, 55-56, 101-124
white women, 53, 54
worker identity, 42
Domination, garment industry and, 59

Earnings statistics, 17, 19-21, 24
Economic profile, of women in the
    United States, 5-26
Economy:
    demographic changes and, 6
    ethnic, 188
    political, 243
    underground, 54, 239, 240
Education, African Americans and, 40
Educational standards, Black women's
    clubs working for higher, 222-223
Education statistics, 15-17, 24
Egalitarian workplace, 82
Electronic firms, in New Mexico, 55,
    76-98
Employment, criminalization of, 105,
    106, 107, 118, 119
Employment options:
    African Americans and, 219
    class and, 2
    cultural background and, 243
    domestic workers, 239
    race/ethnicity/social class and, 2
    undocumented Mexican immigrant
        women, 56, 101-124
    women professionals and managers,
        154, 155
English-only legislation, 244

Entrepreneurship, among Korean
    immigrants, 129, 176-190
Ethnic composition of population, 6
Ethnic economy, 188
Ethnic enclaves, of immigrants, 129
Ethnic hierarchies, of factory and
    domestic workers, 53, 54
Ethnicity:
    class and, 132, 201
    population statistics and, 21
    social constructions and, 132
    work options and, 2
Ethnic relations, in garment industry, 59
Ethnic success, myth of, 238
Euro-American women workers,
    meanings of class among, 131-151
Export-processing zones, 59
Extended family, 14

Factory work, 53-56
Fair Labor Standards Act of 1938, 37,
    117
Familial arrangements, changing nature
    of, 14-15
Family businesses, Korean, 129, 176-190
Family households, census definition of,
    14
Family size, 14
Family wage, 37-38
Family/work nexus, see Work/family
    nexus
Female(s):
    age distribution, 8-9, 25
    traditional occupations, 3
    work ethic, 24
Female employment status, census data
    on, 15
Female-headed households, poverty and,
    21, 24
Feminist(s), women's unpaid work and,
    202
Feminist thought, African American, 59
Feminist workplace, class experience and
    conflict in, 131-151
Fertility rates, 10-11, 24-25, 37
Flextime, 82
Foreign competition, 79

Fund-raising activities, Black women's clubs and, 227-228

Garment industry:
in Hawaii, 54-55, 57-73
in New Mexico, 55, 76-98
Gender:
immigrant legal status and, 103
work assignments and responsibilities and, 164-165
work norms and, 237
Gender identity, African American working women, 29
Gender norms, racialized, 238
Gender relations:
garment industry, 59, 69
Korean women's employment and, 129, 176-190
Gender roles:
African Americans and, 31, 32, 33, 34-35, 36, 39
domestic service and, 42
immigrant working wives, 177
Korean working wives, 180-190
White middle-class, 31, 41
Ghettoization, 163
Glass ceiling, 154, 157, 171
Great Depression, 37, 42, 54

Hawaii, alohawear industry in, 54-55, 57-73
Hawaii Garment Manufacturers Guild, 65
Hazardous waste site, community opposition to, 207
Health care, community activism and, 209
Health care center, women's, 127-128, 131-151
Health hazards, in Hawaiian garment industry, 69
Health standards, Black women's clubs working for higher, 222-223
Heavy industry, decline of, 77
Hierarchical management, 83-87, 96-97
Hispanic(s):
components of population, 8
fertility rates, 10
marital status, 9
percent of population, 6, 7
population growth, 9
poverty rates, 21
Hispanic females:
age distribution, 25
educational attainment, 15, 25
fertility rates, 25
income statistics, 19
Home, working at:
garment production in Hawaii, 64, 66
resistance to sexual harassment and, 48
Household, census definition of, 14
Household work, African American women and, 34, 35-37

Immigrants:
Caribbean, 105, 107, 245
deportation of, 105-106
domestic work by, 54, 55-56, 101-124
entrepreneurship by, 129, 176-190
garment industry and, 59, 61, 66, 72
Japanese, 37
Korean, 129, 176-190
from Third World countries, 177
underground economy and, 54
undocumented Mexican women, 55-56, 101-124
Immigration:
to Hawaii, 54
policies, 103
Immigration Act of 1965, 179
Immigration Reform and Control Act of 1986, 56, 106, 107, 108, 117, 245
Immunization, 209
Income:
inequalities in, 1-2
statistics, 17, 19-21, 24
See also Pay
Industrialization:
Korean families and, 189
Sun Belt, 77
Informal sector labor markets, undocumented Latina immigrant women in, 55-56, 101-124

Institution(s), women's relationships to
    local, 207, 208, 210
Institutional settings, jobs in, 103
International Ladies' Garment Workers'
    Union, 46
Issei immigrants, 37

Japanese American working women, 37
Hawaiian garment industry, 64, 65
Japanese management techniques, 77, 79
Job enrichment, 79
Job rotation, 94
Job work arrangements, domestic
    workers and, 103, 109-110,
    117-122, 123

Korean immigrant wives, labor force
    participation by, 129, 176-190
Korean immigrants, entrepreneurship
    among, 129, 176-190

Labor associations, African American
    women's, 44-48
Labor history, politics of African
    American women's, 28-49
Labor market:
    citizenship status and, 55, 101-124,
    245
    informal sector, 55-56, 101-124
    women channeled into sectors of, 155
Labor market elasticity, household labor
    and, 53, 54
Labor migration, African Americans and,
    40-41
Labor outcomes, educational attainment
    and, 15
Labor statistics, 17, 24
Labor unions, see Union(s)
Language, English-only legislation, 244
Latin America:
    export-processing zones in, 59
    immigrants from, 105
Latina women:
    age distribution, 25
    community work by, 194, 197-213

educational attainment, 15, 25
fertility rates, 25
income statistics, 19
Latina working women:
    apparel and electronics firms in New
    Mexico, 55, 76-98
    consciousness developed by, 43
    domestic work by, 54, 107, 239
    labor force participation, 38
    legal status of, 55-56, 101-124
    organizing among, 46-47
    unions and, 242
Legal status, Latina immigrant women,
    55-56, 101-124
Light industry, geographical location of,
    77
Live-in domestic workers, 47, 103, 109,
    110-117, 123
Living arrangements, census data on, 9,
    14-15
Los Angeles:
    Latina women's community work in,
    197-213
    sweatshops in, 59

Madres del Este Los Angeles, Santa
    Isabel, 199-213
Male(s):
    control of wives, 36, 37
    roles in African American families,
    31, 32, 33
Management:
    control in apparel and electronics
    firms, 55, 76
    hierarchical, 83-87, 96-97
    Japanese techniques, 77, 79
    participative, 77, 79-80, 82, 87-95
Managerial women, race and, 128,
    153-173
Manufacturing, 53
    apparel and electronic firms in New
    Mexico, 55, 76-98
    Hawaiian alohawear industry, 54-55,
    57-73
    restructuring of U.S., 77, 79
Maquiladoras (contracting firms), on
    U.S.-Mexico border, 59

Marital power, Korean women's
employment and, 129, 176-190
Marital status:
census data on, 9-10
Korean women's employment and,
129, 176-190
Marriage, African American women and,
38
Masculine work norm, 237
Maternity leave, 78, 79, 84
Matrifocal African American families, 31
Men, see Male(s)
Mentoring, lack of, 156, 157, 158
Mexican American(s), 8
family size, 14
labor statistics, 17
Mexican American working-class
women, community work by,
197-213
Mexican undocumented immigrant
women, domestic work by, 54,
55-56, 101-124
Mexican women, organizing among,
46-47
Mexico-United States border, contracting
firms on, 59
Middle-class occupations, 128-130
Middle-class White gender norms, 31, 41
Middle-class women:
Black women's clubs, 219, 220-222
coalitions with working-class women,
127-128, 131-151
community work by, 193, 200, 210,
219, 220-222
Mothers, African American women's
work as, 40
Multicultural histories, of women's
work, 49
Municipal housekeeping, 200
Mutual aid associations, 44, 47
Mutuality ethos, of African Americans,
31, 33, 47


Nannies, Latina immigrant women as,
102
National Association of Women Wage
Earners, 45

National Sewing Council, 45
Native Americans:
age data, 9
fertility rates, 10
in Hawaii, 61
percent of population, 6, 7
population growth, 9
Negro Woman's Club Home, 229-230
Neighborhood networks, 42-43, 240
New York:
Korean community in, 176-190
sweatshops in, 59
Nisei, 60-61, 65, 72
Nonfamily household, census definition
of, 14
Nuclear family, 14
Nurses of color, harassment of, 243-244


Oppression:
of African American women, 30, 33,
40, 44-49, 59
political wedge between groups, 156
professional-managerial women's
perceptions of, 153-173
Other Hispanics census group, 8


Participative management, 77, 79-80, 82,
87-95
Patriarchal system:
capitalism and, 32
Confucianism and, 180
Korean immigrants and, 180, 187-189
Pay:
African American women, 30, 31, 45
Albuquerque industrial workers, 78
garment industry, 67-68, 71
incentive, 95
Korean immigrant wives, 184-185, 189
participative management and, 79
piece-rate, 84-86, 87
professional and managerial women,
154, 155-156, 164
public sector work, 163-164
undocumented immigrants, 106, 107,
109, 110-111, 114-115, 117
working-class demands, 43

Piece-rate pay, 84-86, 87
Plantations, southern, 34-35
Political activism, 193, 200, 207-208, 240
Political construction, legal working
    status as, 104
Political economy, 243
Politics, of African American women's
    labor history, 28-49
Pond Lily Art and Service Club, 217,
    223, 226, 228, 230
Poor, assistance to, by Black women's
    clubs, 225-226
Poor women, social reform activities
    and, 193-195
Poor women of color, undocumented
    immigrant, 101-124
Population benchmarks, 2, 24
Population characteristics, 6-9
Populations, comparisons of, 2, 24
Poverty, 1-2
    female-headed households, 21, 24
Power:
    African American families, 31, 32
    class relations and, 128, 132, 136-137,
        138-139, 141, 142, 144, 145-146,
        148
    community work and, 194
    management practices and, 80, 81
    marital, 176-190
    participative management and, 80
    undocumented immigrants and,
        103-104, 105, 106, 107, 109
    women's work and, 236
Prison, community opposition to, 206-207
Professional White, middle-class male
    group and, 237-238
Professional women, race and, 128,
    153-173
Proletarianization, of garment workers,
    64
Promotions, professional-managerial
    women's, 155, 158, 163-164
Public motherhood, 200
Public sector work:
    African American women
        concentrated in, 232
    salaries in, 163-164

Puerto Ricans, 8

Quality circles, 79
Quality-of-life issues, community
    activism and, 206-207, 208
Quality of work life, 79, 80

Race:
    census categories, 7
    class identification and, 132
    immigrant legal status and, 101-105
    managerial women and, 128, 153-173
    population statistics and, 6, 21
    professional women and, 128, 153-173
    social constructions and, 132, 237
    work options and, 2
Racial-ethnic composition, of Hawaiian
    garment industry, 64
Racial hierarchies, factory and domestic
    workers and, 53, 54
Racialization:
    garment industry, 58-59, 72
    of gender norms, 238
Racial oppression, 30, 33, 40, 44-49, 59
Racism, 128
    everyday, 243
    professional-managerial women's
        perceptions of, 153-173
Refugees, 66, 105
Reproduction, delayed, 10
Research directions, 242-246
Resistance:
    African American women, 3, 40, 42-48
    apparel and electronics firms in New
        Mexico, 55, 76-98
    continuum of, 82
    electronics industry, 87-95
    Hawaiian garment industry, 55, 69
    Latina workers, 242
    participative management and, 87-95
    strikes and, 42
    undocumented immigrant working
        women, 106
    See also Collective resistance
Resources, class conflict and, 145-146

Respect, demands for, 44
Respectability, African American
    women's, 41
Rewards, nonmonetary, 86-87

Safety hazards, in Hawaiian garment
    industry, 69
San Francisco Bay area:
    sweatshops in, 59
    undocumented Mexican immigrant
        women in, 56, 101-124
Schools:
    Black women's clubs working with,
        226
    community work for, 194, 226
    women's unpaid work and, 210
Self-identity, census surveys and, 7
Self-improvement, Black women's clubs
    and, 223-224
Self-Improvement and Social Service
    Club, 217, 228
Service sector, 3
    African Americans in, 219
Sexism, professional-managerial
    women's perceptions of, 153-
    173
Sexual harassment and exploitation:
    of African American working women,
        36
    of domestic workers, 48, 113
Sharecropping households, 32, 34-35
Shifts, rotating, 89
Single mothers, census data on, 11-12
Single-parent families:
    census data on, 11-12
    growth over time, 14-15
Single working women:
    African American, 37-39, 230
    live-in domestic work, 110-111, 113
    home for, 230
    Korean, 181
Skill differences, class conflict and,
    145-146
Slavery, 31-33
Small businesses, Korean, 180-190
Social class, see Class

Social construction:
    community as, 220
    legal working status as, 104
    race and ethnicity as, 132, 237
    relations in garment industry, 59
Social entitlements, immigrants and,
    106-107
Social hierarchy, in Hawaiian garment
    industry, 72
Social isolation, of undocumented
    domestic workers, 115-116
Social networks:
    children's welfare and, 210, 222-223,
        226-227
    immigrant community, 56, 101, 102,
        103, 117, 118-122, 123
    undocumented Mexican immigrant
        women, 56, 102
Social norms, White middle-class, 31, 41
Social organization of production,
    Hawaiian garment industry and,
    63, 64
Social reform activities, class and, 193
Social services, lack of, 224
Socioeconomic census data, 1-2, 5-26
Socioeconomic changes, 9
South, movement of light industry to, 77
Statistics, benchmarks used to develop,
    2, 24
Strategies, resisting management's
    system of control and, 81-82, 84
Street vendors, Latina immigrant women
    as, 102
Stress, in Hawaiian garment industry,
    69
Strikes, 42
    African American washerwomen,
        45-46
    garment industry, 46, 59
Subcontracting arrangements,
    undocumented domestic workers
    and, 120-122, 239
Subordination, of undocumented
    domestic workers, 108, 109, 111
Sun Belt, women's resistance in, 55,
    76-98
Sweatshops, in garment industry, 59

Tactics, resisting management's system of control and, 81-82, 84
Taka Art and Literary Club, 217, 225-226, 227, 228
Team structures, 79, 80, 90
Technology:
    effect on working women, 37
    garment industry, 58, 59, 65
Texas, domestic work by Latina immigrants in, 101-124
Third shift, 195, 216-233, 241
Third World countries:
    immigrants from, 177
    movement of light industry to, 77, 79
Trade unions, see Unions

Underground economy, 54, 239, 240
Undocumented Mexican immigrant women, domestic work by, 55-56, 101-124
Unemployment, African American women and, 42
Union(s), 45-48
    cannery, 82
    community ties and, 241
    electronics workers and, 77
    exclusionary policies of, 42, 44
    garment industry, 55, 59
    Latina workers, 242
    participative management and, 88, 90, 92-93
Unionlike associations, 44
United States:
    economic profile of women in, 5-26
    Mexican undocumented immigrant women working in, 54, 101-124
    restructuring of manufacturing in, 77, 79
United States-Mexico border, contracting firms on, 59
Unpaid labor, in community maintenance and development, 193-195, 197-213
Upper-class women, community work by, 193, 200, 210

Values, African American, 31, 33
Voluntarism, 194, 198, 210, 240
Voting rights, 33-34

Wages, see Pay
West:
    migration to, 218
    movement of light industry to, 77
White(s):
    family size, 14
    fertility rates, 10
    in Hawaii, 61
    labor statistics, 17
    marital status, 9
    percent of population, 6, 7
    population growth, 9
    poverty rates, 21
White employers, view toward Black women of, 34
White females:
    educational attainment, 15, 17
    income statistics, 19
    median age, 9
White immigrants, 105
White men:
    earnings of, 154, 155, 156
    privilege and, 246
White middle-class gender norms, 31, 41
White Rose Industrial Association, 44-45
White women:
    color consciousness and, 167-169
    single mothers, 11
    social reform activities, 193
White working women:
    alliances of working class and middle class, 131-151
    apparel and electronics firms in New Mexico, 55, 76-98
    domestic work by, 53, 54
    managerial careers, 128, 153-173
    pay, 156
    professionals, 128, 153-173
Women:
    economic profile of, 5-26
    stereotypes of, 161-163, 165
    structural inequalities among, 1-2

Women's clubs, Black, 195, 201, 216-233
Women's collective, cross-class, 131-151
Women's health center, social class and, 127-128, 131-151
Work assignments and responsibilities, differences in, 164-165
Work culture, 81, 83, 87, 96
Work ethics, females and, 24
Work/family nexus, 2-3, 237
    African American working women, 30-41
    Hawaiian garment workers, 71-72
    Korean women's employment and, 129, 176-190
    New Mexico manufacturing workers, 78-79, 84, 88-90, 94-95, 96
Work hours:
    Hawaiian garment workers, 68
    Korean businesses, 183

undocumented domestic workers, 109, 111
Work identity/consciousness, of African American women, 3, 41-48
Working-class consciousness, 29, 42-48
Working class women, 2
    African American women, 28-29
    coalitions with middle-class women, 127-128, 131-151
    community work by, 193, 195, 197-213, 241
    family dependent on wages of, 79
Working conditions:
    African American women, 31
    in garment industry, 67-70
Working women:
    conceptualizing experiences of, 236-239
    families dependent on wages of, 79
    See also specific race, ethnicity
Worldview, African American, 33

# About the Contributors

**Joyce N. Chinen** is Associate Professor of Sociology at the University of Hawaii-West Oahu. In addition to her sociology teaching, she teaches courses in women and work in the Women's Studies Program at the University of Hawaii-Manoa. Her research is centered on the garment industry and women workers in Hawaii. She is also active in many community projects, including the state of Hawaii's Executive Office on Aging's "Women's AGEnda: Money Matters for Women," Hawaii Committee for the Humanities's project on working women and on Okinawans in Hawaii. She serves as coordinator of Hawaii's Sociologists for Women in Society.

**Lynda F. Dickson** is Associate Professor and Chair in the Department of Sociology at the University of Colorado, Colorado Springs. Her research and teaching areas include the sociology of families, poverty, and Black women's clubs. Her recent publications include "African-American Women's Clubs in Denver," in *Essays and Monographs in Colorado History* (1992); "The Colored Women's Club Home Association" and "Black Club Women in Denver," both in *Black Women in America: An Historical Encyclopedia,* edited by Hine, Brown, and

265

Terborg-Penn (1993); "The Future of Family in Black America," in *Journal of Black Studies* (June 1993); and, with Richard Dukes, "The Effects of Gender and Role Context on Perceptions of Parental Effectiveness," in *Free Inquiry in Creative Sociology* (May 1992).

**Sharon Harley** is Director and Associate Professor in the Afro-American Studies Program at the University of Maryland, College Park. After receiving her doctorate in history from Howard University, she became a pioneer in the study of Black women's history. Her research has particularly focused on the history of Black wage-earning women and Black women's organizational activities in the District of Columbia. She is coeditor of *Afro-American Women: Struggles and Images* (1997) and *Women in Africa and the African Diaspora* (1987). Her recent scholarly articles have appeared in *Gender, Class, Race, and Reform in the Progressive Era*, edited by Noralee Frankel and Nancy S. Dye (1991), and *Gender, Families, and Close Relationships: Feminist Research Journeys*, edited by D. Sollie and L. Leslie (1994). She makes major events and personages in Afro-American history available to the public in her recent publication *The Timetables of African American History* (1995).

**Elizabeth Higginbotham** is Research Professor in the Center for Research on Women and Professor of Sociology and Social Work at the University of Memphis. Her publications have appeared in *Gender & Society* and *Women's Studies Quarterly*, as well as in many edited collections. Her chapter in this volume is one of many from the project Social Mobility, Race, and Women's Mental Health. This study, a collaboration with Lynn Weber, is a broad investigation of the role of upward mobility in the educational experiences, work life, family life, well-being, and mental health of 200 Black and White professional and managerial women in the Memphis area.

**Pierrette Hondagneu-Sotelo** is Assistant Professor in the Department of Sociology at the University of Southern California, where she also teaches in the Program for the Study of Women and Men in Society and the Chicano/Latino Studies Program. She is the author of *Gendered Transitions: Mexican Experiences of Immigration* (1994) and has published articles in *Social Problems, Qualitative Sociology, Gender & Society, American Sociologist, Socialist Review*, and *Clinical Sociology Review*.

**Louise Lamphere** received her Ph.D. from Harvard University in 1968 and is currently Professor of Anthropology at the University of New Mexico. She has also taught at the University of Rochester (1967-68) and at Brown University (1968-1975 and 1979-1985). Her research interests include women and work, gender theory, urban anthropology, immigration, kinship and social organization, and Navajo women's roles. She is coeditor of *Woman, Culture and Society,* with the late Michelle Zimbalist Rosaldo (1974), and author of *From Working Daughters to Working Mothers* (1987). As Cochair of the Changing Relations Project, which is concerned with relations between new immigrants and established residents in six U.S. cities, she edited *Structuring Diversity* (1992) and *Newcomers in the Workplace* (1994). Her most recent book on working women is *Sunbelt Working Mothers: Reconciling Family and Factory* (1993), coauthored with Patricia Zavella, Felipe Gonzáles, and Peter Evans. In 1994 she received the Conrad Arensberg Award from the Society for the Anthropology of Work, and in 1995 she received the Society for the Anthropology of North America Prize for the Critical Study of North America. She is currently writing a biography of Eva Price, a Navajo healer and community activist, that will also include narratives from Price's daughter and granddaughter.

**Pyong Gap Min** is Professor of Sociology at Queens College and the Graduate School of the City University of New York. As a Korean immigrant, he has done research mainly on Korean and other Asian immigrants, with a focus on Korean and immigrant entrepreneurship, Asian/Korean Americans' ethnicity, and Korean immigrant women's gender role. His publications include *Ethnic Business Enterprise: Korean Small Business in Atlanta* (1988) and *Caught in the Middle: Korean Communities in New York and Los Angeles* (1996). He is also the editor of *Asian Americans: Contemporary Trends and Issues* (1995). In addition, he has published numerous journal articles and book chapters in both the United States and Korea.

**Sandra Morgen** is Director of the Center for the Study of Women in Society and Associate Professor in the Department of Sociology at the University of Oregon. An anthropologist by training, she has edited two books: *Women and the Politics of Empowerment: Perspectives from the Workplace and the Community* (with Ann Bookman, 1988) and *Gender and Anthropology: Critical Reviews for Research and Teaching* (1989). Her publications on women and work and women's health have appeared in *Social Science and Medicine, Signs: Journal of Women in Culture and Society, Feminist Studies,* and *Human Relations.* After more than 15 years of research on the women's health movement, she is currently writing a book titled *Into Our Own Hands: The Women's Health Movement in the U.S., 1970-1990.*

**Mary Pardo** teaches in the Department of Chicana and Chicano Studies at California State University, Northridge. She has developed and taught courses on the Chicana, on Third World women, and on social science research methods in Chicana/o studies. Her research interests include women of color and political participation, and she is currently completing a book on Mexican American women and grassroots activism in Los Angeles.

**Bárbara J. Robles** currently holds a position at the Joint Committee on Taxation, U.S. Congress, where she is assigned to analyze consumption expenditures for the possible impacts to the economy of switching to a consumption tax system from the current income tax system. She was Assistant Professor in the Department of Economics at the University of Colorado at Boulder when she wrote the chapter that appears in this volume. Her current research interests include child-care cost and quality issues and small business credit accessibility and educational loan burdens for women and members of ethnic/racial minority communities.

**Mary Romero** is Professor at Arizona State University. She is the author of *Maid in the U.S.A.* (1992); coeditor of *Challenging Fronteras: Structuring Latino and Latina Lives in the U.S.* (1997); coeditor of two volumes of the National Association for Chicano Studies Conference Proceedings, titled *Community Empowerment and Chicano Scholarship* and *Estudios Chicanos and the Politics of Community*; and editor of three sets of syllabi and instructional materials for Chicano and Latino studies in sociology for the American Sociological Association Teaching Resource Center. She has also published in *Qualitative Sociology, Sex Roles, Feminist Issues, Language Problems/Language Planning, Humanity and Society, Aztlan, Latino Studies Journal, Journal of Hispanic Policy,* and *Race, Gender and Class.* She serves as a coeditor of the **Gender Lens Series** published by Sage Publications and Pine Forge and is an Associate Editor of *Signs: Journal of Women in Culture and Society.* Over the past 16 years she has held administrative positions at

Yale University, San Francisco State University, and the University of Oregon. She has also taught at the University of Colorado, University of Texas at El Paso, and University of Wisconsin—Parkside.

**Lynn Weber** is Director of Women's Studies and Professor of Sociology at the University of South Carolina. She served as Director of the University of Memphis Center for Research on Women from 1988 to 1994 and as Associate Director of the center from 1982 to 1988. At the University of Memphis, she worked with Elizabeth Higginbotham on a project exploring the process of upward social class mobility among Black and White professional and managerial women. Based on this work, she has coauthored publications with Higginbotham on family and community involvement, race and class bias in research on women, and perceptions of discrimination. She is coauthor, with Reeve Vanneman, of *The American Perception of Class* (1987). She is currently writing a book on the intersections of race, class, gender, and sexuality.

**Patricia Zavella,** an anthropologist, is Professor of Community Studies at the University of California, Santa Cruz. Her analysis of how occupational segregation in the canning labor market is intertwined with the organization of Chicanas' reproductive labor has been published as *Women's Work and Chicano Families: Cannery Workers of the Santa Clara Valley* (1987) and "The Politics of Race and Gender: Organizing Cannery Workers in Northern California," in *Women and the Politics of Empowerment: Perspectives from the Workplace and the Community,* edited by Ann Bookman and Sandra Morgen (1988). In collaboration with Louise Lamphere, Felipe Gonzáles, and Peter Evans, she has analyzed how Sun Belt industrialization has affected Hispana and Anglo women in Albuquerque, examining "participative management" in factories and women's varied economic contributions, which are creating new patterns of dividing reproductive work and finding social support. This research has been published in the book *Sunbelt Working Mothers: Reconciling Family and Factory* (1993). Her current research focuses on poverty in Santa Cruz County. Historicizing racial and gender segregation in an agricultural and service-based economy, she examines how Whites, Chicanos, and Mexican transnational migrants cope with poverty and construct community, diverse households, and "family" based on economics, cultural notions, and sexuality.